Writing
THE PIONEER WOMAN

Writing
THE PIONEER WOMAN

Janet Floyd

UNIVERSITY OF MISSOURI PRESS
COLUMBIA AND LONDON

Copyright © 2002 by
The Curators of the University of Missouri
University of Missouri Press, Columbia, Missouri 65201
Printed and bound in the United States of America
All rights reserved
5 4 3 2 1   04 03 02 01 00

Cataloging-in-Publication data available from the
Library of Congress
ISBN 0-8262-1381-2

∞™ This paper meets the requirements of the
American National Standard for Permanence of Paper
for Printed Library Materials, Z39.48, 1984.

Text designer: Stephanie Foley
Jacket designer: Jennifer Cropp
Typesetter: Bookcomp, Inc.
Printer and binder: Thomson-Shore, Inc.
Typefaces: Caslon Antique, ITC Galliard, and Linotype Zapfino

For June Menzies

Contents

	INTRODUCTION	1
1.	A TRADITION OF PIONEERS	18
2.	PRIVATE ENTERPRISE	
	The Emigrant Autobiographies of Kitturah Belknap and Susanna Moodie	43
3.	RECIPES FOR SUCCESS	
	Catharine Parr Traill's Empire of Woman	76
4.	DOMESTICITY AND DIRT	
	Eliza Farnham's *Life in Prairie Land* and Christiana Tillson's *Reminiscences of Early Life in Illinois*	102
5.	"A SPACE IN WHICH TO BE IMAGINATIVE"	
	Caroline Kirkland's *A New Home, Who'll Follow?*	124
6.	PLOTTING THE GOLDEN WEST	
	Autobiographers of the Mining West	145

7. "To Recover Those Once Lost and
   Now Forgotten"
   Anne Langton's Journal and Memoir   167

   Conclusion
   Writing the Pioneer Woman   187

   Works Cited   193

   Index   217

Acknowledgments

IT IS A PLEASURE to acknowledge those who have helped me to read the writing of pioneer women and to finish this book: in particular, Stephen Fender, my doctoral supervisor at the University of Sussex, who suggested that I study emigrant autobiography in the first place; Rupert Wilkinson and Helen Taylor, who in examining the thesis on which this study is based, prompted me to think afresh; Sue Lewis, who drew me into the investigation of the fields of gardening and needlework; Roger Lowman and Alasdair Spark, at King Alfred's College, who helped me to get the leave I needed to speed up what has been a long process; Sarah Green at King Alfred's library, whose work finding books has been invaluable; June Menzies, who found countless articles and books for me in Canada; Jamie Lehrer, Karen L. Kilcup, and Cheryl B. Torsny, who read through different drafts and gave encouragement and good advice; Clair Willcox and John Brenner at the University of Missouri Press; Val Stevenson; and Laurel Forster, whose companionship on numerous writing retreats and whose advice in the project's final stages proved indispensable to the finishing of this book. Finally, it is a pleasure to thank Richard, Neville, Ralph, and Max Thompson for making the domestic space alive with interest to me, and to acknowledge the contribution that all my friends, and especially two dear comrades, Jane Seymour and Sue Sissling, have made to this project. The book is dedicated to June Menzies, who, in 1989, sent me Susanna Moodie's *Roughing It in the Bush* and, marvelous teacher that she is, inspired me to read it.

Writing
THE PIONEER WOMAN

Introduction

*T*HIS BOOK IS a study of the writing of the white Anglo emigrant housewife in North America and an argument about her significance and interest as a nineteenth- and twentieth-century subject. This particular emigrant figure, in her different guises of westerner, frontierswoman, and, above all, pioneer, has been a profoundly important one for North American women's historians and feminist literary critics.[1] For a popular audience too, she has remained full of meaning, notwithstanding the multiple reinventions of the western past and the recovery of a much more heterogeneous emigrant population than had traditionally been imagined.

Part of my interest in this book has been in examining the debates addressed by recurring arguments about these emigrant women. But to respond to the work of critics, historians, and editors in this field is to be drawn into the consideration of the autobiographical narratives

---

1. A note about terms: where I have been writing about Anglo-European women migrating to the western states of the United States or to Upper Canada, I have referred to them as "emigrants," whether this involved transatlantic travel or not, in the attempt to foreground the movement between one home and another. The use of "emigrant" to describe both those intending to move from Britain to North America and those migrating westward within the United States seems, in any case, to accord with nineteenth-century usage. I have used the term "pioneer woman" to refer to a heroic figure of Anglo-European womanhood that has appeared with great frequency in popular, literary, and historical writing since the mid-nineteenth-century. "Frontier" and "frontiersman" are terms I use to describe a concept of the West rather than a place; "frontier" is rightly perceived to be a term that describes a margin in a process of civilization defined only by reference to Anglo westward settlement. Although my occasional use of the word "West" also privileges westward migration, its vagueness as a term has the advantage of evoking the status of the West as an imaginative idea for writers (whether emigrants or not) with little knowledge of the life and cultures of the regions that they described.

that underpin the late-twentieth-century discussion. It is these narratives that form the major focus of this book. Through reexamining Anglo women's writing of emigration and the scholarly work about it, I address what seems to me to be the subject at its heart: the work of homemaking in all its many dimensions. In foregrounding the world of the domestic, I am not turning aside from the specific contexts of nation, regions, and economic activity "outside"; on the contrary, I am interested in how the writing of "inside" engages with those contexts. But my starting point is the representation of emigrant homemaking.

The argument has long been, of course, that in ways both actual and symbolic, home was precisely what the Anglo emigrant wife was leaving behind as she journeyed to a new and different life. The nature of wives' responses to the loss of home has accordingly been a matter of intense investigation, particularly for feminist writers in the field of women's history; as Lesley Johnson has argued, home has generally been understood as "a place necessarily to be left behind in the formation of the feminist subject." For many scholars, the West, both as a region within the United States and Canada and as an imaginative construction, has constituted a new kind of space where the boundaries of home are dissolved or at least extended. The West has been thought of as a region in which domestic conventions fall away or are adapted in favor of an engagement in something more than what Ruth Moynihan has called "just marginal, domestic or . . . [gendered] concerns."[2]

Over the last decade, of course, postcolonial theorizing of the work performed by women within the project of land appropriation has refocused the discussion of the domestic in the West. In particular, the creation of the home in "new" lands is interpreted not so much as a radical departure from metropolitan norms, but rather as imbricated within the disposition of imperial power and the formation of national identity. Yet even here the implication remains that the move away from home to the "new" domestic space involves the transformation of conventional housekeeping into a domestic practice invested with greater public status and profound social and political significance.

---

2. Lesley Johnson, "'As Housewives We Are Worms': Women, Modernity and the Home Question," 47; Ruth B. Moynihan, Review of Brigitte Georgi-Findlay, *The Frontiers of Women's Writing*, 236.

The work of western and postcolonial historians in formulating the meaning of homemaking for the privileged has informed this study, but both are underpinned by a reading of the domestic that is dominated by an understanding of domesticity—whether it is in some way shaken off or whether it is imported into the new home—as a monolithic ideological system. In this study, however, I have drawn on different readings of what the domestic might mean and, indeed, on different understandings of what happens in the domestic space. First of all, I have started from theories of home that address the situation of the emigrant. Theorists of diaspora such as Avtah Brah speak of the "double, triple or multi-placedness of home" in the literature of migration, whereby homes are "in perpetual suspension" for the migrant subject. Such a formulation of home's meaning is not unique to diaspora theory. The understanding of home generally is now often one that emphasizes the absence and the elusiveness of home as an idea. It is, in Rachel Bowlby's words, "the place that has always been left." It "cannot . . . be understood," as J. Douglas Porteus argues, "except in terms of a journey." We are all, in this sense, migrants moving from home to home, and all inhabitants of domestic spaces haunted by other, past, original homes: "euphemistic" homes as Porteus evocatively puts it.[3] The emigrant home, then, is a space quintessentially unstable in meaning: like all homes it is, at some level, "euphemistic," yet the association of emigration with loss and dislocation gives the emigrant home a particular intensity of meaning.

It is not difficult to catch the sense of the home in suspension in representations of Anglo emigrant women in North America in the nineteenth century (the period with which I am largely concerned in this book). William Smith Jewett's treble portrait of the Grayson family, *The Promised Land—The Grayson Family* (1850), which Andrew Jackson Grayson commissioned to celebrate his family's arrival in California, though it offers a thick texture of interpretation of the emigrant experience, produces also, in the figure of Mrs. Grayson, a homemaker in transit; a figure redolent of what Homi Bhabha, theorizing the "third

---

3. Avtar Brah, *Cartographies of Diaspora: Contesting Identities,* 94, 205; Rachel Bowlby, "Domestication," 75; J. Douglas Porteus, "Home: The Territorial Core," 387–88.

space" of the migrant, has called the "enigmatic interest of the in-between."[4]

There is none of the subversive potential sometimes attributed to "the in-between" in this painting. On the contrary, it is everything we would expect of a text informed by the expansionist ethic of mid-nineteenth-century America. The massive landscape of the Sacramento Valley that surrounds the emigrants exemplifies not only the "bright Arcadia" of the emigrant imagination but also the familiar American fantasy of an endless open space of opportunity. In their different ways, all three of the family figures, their faces separately bathed in light, express the most optimistic gloss that could be placed on westward migration at the midcentury. Mr. Grayson, though dressed for adaptability and action in the buckskin of the pioneer, remains nevertheless the grave and dignified patriarch of the "civilized" family. His rifle recalls his ability to join battle when necessary while his pose reassures us that he does not seek out conflict.[5]

If Mr. Grayson reminds us that the frontiersman need not abandon himself to the wilderness of desert or backwoods, the figure of his wife, in her sober but elegant dress, foretells the importation of "civilization" intact from the home they have left behind. Their Californian West will be domesticated with Mrs. Grayson's help and without any compromise of the well established social structures and practices of the East. Mrs. Grayson, posed as an emigrant madonna, holds her son in her arms and he, dressed in princely fur and velvet, provides an image of the nature of the dominion over the "new" lands to be realized in the future. A confident depiction of an unproblematic process of land conquest, indeed: all traces of former inhabitants, all signs of the purposes of that conquest, are erased. Even the rupture that the Graysons have themselves experienced in leaving home, while it has begun to transform father and son, has left Mrs. Grayson superbly and reassur-

---

4. Homi K. Bhabha, Keynote Address, "Empire, Design and Identity"; see Janice T. Driesbach, "Portrait Painter to the Elite: William Smith Jewett," for details of Grayson's commission and Jewett's career.

5. William and Mary Howitt, "The Emigrant," 135; a discussion of the painting that focuses on this expansionist aspect of the painting, although with different emphases to the argument here, may be found in Dawn Glanz, *How the West Was Won: American Art and the Settling of the Frontier*, 61–63. For a discussion that links the painting of western landscapes to traditions of American landscape in general, see Alan Wallach, "Thomas Cole and the Course of American Empire."

ingly unaltered; she guarantees the doubling of their old home in the new home in the West.

And yet, in the midst of all this convention and complicity, the figure of Mrs. Grayson has a curiously compelling presence. Dressed and posed as she is for the drawing-room, she is differently placed to her husband and child. While their pose and their dress not only match but summarize their respective positions in relation to land they anticipate dominating, Mrs. Grayson's recall an absent context. She does not seem, in her black silk and lace, less the likely settler or the adventurous migrant than her husband, less willing or less committed, but her position, nevertheless, appears strange in the context of the plunging landscape around her. The viewer is caught between imagining the absent home into which she so evidently fits, and considering how to judge her situation—somberly dressed for the drawing room and yet out-of-doors, composed as on a sofa and yet out in the open—in such an undomestic context. The premise of the painting may be that the new land is a place where the woman and her family will be as much "at home" as before. Yet we cannot look at Mrs. Grayson without striving to imagine what has happened in the home into which she has "fitted," without wondering at the way in which she has departed from it, or without puzzling as to its relationship with an as yet unbuilt western home. The representation of the homemaker in transit between a past and future life makes home and homemaking powerfully present and yet elusive in content.

The portrait of Mrs. Grayson leaves us in no doubt as to the importance of notions of homemaking within the project of settlement, and it suggests how notions of home could be explored against such a background. It is not, however, a text that addresses the life and work of the everyday. The interest of the body of Anglo emigrant writing with which I am concerned here lies precisely in its exhaustive discussion of the daily domestic routine.

Critics within the present generation of historians of women in the North American West have increasingly turned their attention away from the examination of the routines of the domestic. Their interest tends to lie in women's participation in public life of the world "outside" rather than with the delineation of an "inside" they suspect to be confined and isolating for women. Indeed, scholars such as Susan Lee Johnson and Katherine Jensen comment with some exasperation on

William S. Jewett, *The Promised Land—The Grayson Family* (1850). Daniel J. Terra Collection. Terra Museum of American Art, Chicago, Illinois.

some of their scholarly predecessors' "dogged devotion to the heroics of everyday life" and the "protracted argument about the survival of domesticity in the frontier West."

In historical writing informed by postcolonial theory, meanwhile, though the detail of the work of the domestic space has become increasingly interesting, it is exemplified by its work of repression: in Homi Bhabha's words, home is the site of "the normalizing, pastoralizing and individuating techniques of modern power." In Rosemary Marangoly George's *The Politics of Home,* homemaking, in the colonial context and generally, is suffused by the processes of exclusion and inclusion: "Home is neither where they have to take you in nor where they want to take you in, but rather the place where one is in because an Other(s) is kept out."[6]

6. Susan Lee Johnson, "'A Memory Sweet to Soldiers': The Significance of Gender," 266; Katherine Jensen, "Commentary," 35; Homi K. Bhabha, *The Loca-*

However, while the reading of the domestic in fields that address the situation of the Anglo emigrant tend to make it consonant with the inflexible reproduction of dominant ideologies of patriarchy, industrial capitalism, or colonialism—privileging instead the fluid situation of the "unhomed"—other fields (social anthropology in particular) have invested the domestic with some of that fluidity that we have tended to attribute to resolutely undomestic spaces: to contact zones, crossroads, and indeed frontiers. Domestic space in social anthropology may be a site of activity that is interpretative of formations within the culture, rather than merely reflective of them. This is the domestic space as an arena in which, in Janet Carsten and Stephen Hugh-Jones's words, "the to and fro of life unfolds, built, modified, moved or abandoned in accord with the changing circumstances of their inhabitants." This is not to deny the potential of this, as any other colonized space to be the minefield that Smadar Lavie and Ted Swedenburg describe as the "[zone] of loss, alienation, pain, death."[7] But it is an arena that is not merely deterministic, and it is in such a light that I want to read the wealth of domestic description in Anglo women's emigrant writing. The domestic life and domesticity written in the texts that I examine here is not encompassed by constructions of convention and unconvention alone. These texts write new homes according to conventional understandings but they also incorporate a fine descriptive detail that sometimes unravels convention; they embrace the tropes of nineteenth-century writing of domesticity, but in placing them in an unfamiliar context they may destabilize their meaning.

This theorizing of space used interpretatively, along with the theorizing of borderlands and diaspora, has generally been used, at different levels of intensity, to release the socially insignificant and politically disempowered from readings that reiterate their vulnerability and replicate the subjugation visited on them by the socially and politically powerful. The focus has been upon uncovering the agency and the identities of those who inhabit socially marginalized spaces, and not on

---

tion of Culture, 11; Rosemary Marangoly George, *The Politics of Home: Postcolonial Relocations and Twentieth-Century Fiction,* 26.

7. Janet Carsten and Stephen Hugh-Jones, "Introduction: About the House: Levi-Strauss and Beyond," 1; Smadar Lavie and Ted Swedenburg, *Displacement, Diaspora and Geographies of Identity,* 15.

rehearsing the relatively privileged (if often financially stretched) situations of Anglo emigrants choosing to try their fortunes on a colonized "frontier." As Donald H. Akenson has suggested, "the term diaspora threatens to become a massive linguistic weed." Rey Chow's critique of the indiscriminate use, within academia, of the terms of dislocation and exclusion to describe the subject position of emigrant writers prone to appropriating the terms of exile is apposite here. Emigrants to the American West and Upper Canada were often encouraged, supported, and sometimes even subsidized by governments.[8] The texts with which I am concerned emphasize the distance between their "new homes" and "the world." They fail to acknowledge that land has been "cleared" of others' homes for their benefit.

They are also, as we shall see, soaked in references to contemporary discourses of race and racial difference. One cannot, as Elsa Barkley Brown argues, "write adequately about the lives of white women . . . *in any context*, without acknowledging the way in which race shaped their lives." Their very insistence on difference signals, of course, the process by which these women's identity "achieves its positive through the narrow eye of the negative."[9] To read the nineteenth- and early-twentieth-century texts of Anglo female emigration is to find self-serving allusions to emigration as a kind of enslavement alongside disapproving comments upon slavery, to read quiescent elegies to the disappearing race of Indians set beside the figuring of the Indian woman as an ideal "angel in the house," to see a less hierarchical borderland celebrated by writers who racialize working-class fellow-settlers and laud domestic "whiteness" to the skies. Most of these texts address a nativist and racist agenda in explicit terms: vituperative in their comment on Irish fellow emigrants, sentimental about "primitive" Mexicans and "disappearing" Indians.

The emigrant writers with whom I am concerned were clearly making, in their writing of the new home and in their writing of their own

---

8. Donald H. Akenson, "The Historiography of English Speaking Canada and the Concept of Diaspora," 382; Rey Chow, *Writing Diaspora: Tactics of Intervention in Contemporary Cultural Studies*, 13.
9. Elsa Barkley Brown, "Polyrhythmns and Improvisation: Lessons for Women's History," 88; Stuart Hall, "The Local and the Global: Globalization and Ethnicity," 21.

experience, what Nancy K. Miller calls a "gesture of personal territorialism." The "imperiousness" of their "determination to strike a note" recalls their compromising imperial context.[10] Yet these women were often economic migrants. Miller's terms suggest the shifting ground on which such women claimed a role as social actors and a voice as autobiographers, reminding us that a "gesture of personal territorialism" is, after all, only a gesture. There is a strain in this assertion of identity and, in examining the autobiographical writings of these women, I have tried to catch that strain between the privileged subjectivity accorded to and claimed by the Anglo female emigrant on grounds of her origins, racial and regional identity, and in some cases class, and the position of the unhomed emigrant.

We are accustomed to thinking of women's autobiography as having a peripheral presence, especially in the nineteenth century when women's appearance in any public sphere was considered neither modest nor even likely in most circumstances to be interesting. In the nineteenth- and early-twentieth-century literature of emigration to North America we have the appearance—in autobiographies, memoirs, guides, travelogues, journals, and letters—of a thick texture of description of the writers' experiences in the home. Current critical understandings of the nineteenth-century female autobiographer take us in certain directions in addressing such an autobiographical practice. We may explain the appearance of this domestic detail in autobiography as reflective of the restricted route through which women could write their lives: a domestic life was all women were authorized to write. Sidonie Smith suggests, in her discussion of Elizabeth Cady Stanton's 1898 autobiography, that it was necessary to "embrace the cultural identity of a bourgeois woman": "To counter any reading as a *lusus naturae,* a self-asserting but monstrous woman, [Stanton] positions herself squarely inside the enclosure of domestic space, the territory of embodied childhood and true womanhood." Yet, at the same time, as Mary Jean Corbett's study of Victorian women autobiographers shows, that "embrace" also involved "[defending] the privacy of the domestic sphere": a woman was expected to emphasize her self-sacrifice in the

---

10. Nancy K. Miller, *Getting Personal: Feminist Occasions and Other Autobiographical Acts,* xiv, 141.

domestic realm but "good taste" dictated that its details were largely omitted.[11]

In Anglo emigrant women's autobiography we find a writing of the domestic sanctioned by the crucial importance of homemaking within the project of emigration and settling land, and a detail of the everyday round written to prove participation in that project. To this extent, it may seem to share the subject-position of the authoritative colonial housekeeper described by Rosemary Marangoly George. But George's reading of the writing of colonial housekeeping sees it as a celebration of a practice of management. Emigrant autobiography records the writer's own performance of work.

In wishing to reflect on the meaning of autobiographical representations of the domestic work of the Anglo emigrant housewife, I am, of course, retracing the steps of what Krista Comer has rightly called the groundbreaking study of emigrant women's writing, Annette Kolodny's *The Land Before Her*. Kolodny's is an argument about the projection of "the Victorian values of a genteel east into an imagined bourgeois west," and an argument about how the transfer and, in some cases, adaptation of those values is written in a series of texts. She evokes a world of gendered values through which middle-class Anglo-American women imaginatively organized the unfamiliar spaces of the West. Her emigrant autobiographers, in short, write back to the center: to other women, to prospective female emigrants, to the market for writing about the domestic.[12]

Like Kolodny, I imagine a close and diverse relationship between the writing of women's emigration to the North American West and the center, and a continual referencing of metropolitan discussions of domesticity in emigrant autobiography. That relationship, though, is, in my view, one that is always more provisional, more "multi-placed" and less firmly tied to understandings of the West than that which Kolodny describes. A case in point is Kolodny's interpretation of Eliza Farn-

---

11. Sidonie Smith, *Subjectivity, Identity, and the Body: Women's Autobiographical Practices in the Twentieth Century*, 27; Mary Jean Corbett, *Representing Femininity: Middle-Class Subjectivity in Victorian and Edwardian Women's Autobiography*, 58.
12. Krista Comer, "Literature, Gender Studies and the New Western History," 118. Annette Kolodny, *The Land Before Her: Fantasy and Experience on the American Frontiers 1630–1860*, xiv.

ham's 1846 autobiography, *Life in Prairie Land*, a text to which she accords paradigmatic status in terms of its projection of a fantasy of satisfying domesticity onto a western landscape and its mission to soothe the fears of prospective migrants. Kolodny's sense of the text as writing an experience of feminine self-discovery and recuperation in the West is underpinned by her reading of Farnham's life: Farnham's response to domesticity in the West may be understood, in Kolodny's view, by reference to her disturbed early life in the East. The domesticated and feminized West of *Life in Prairie Land* is the representation of a scene of personal recovery that parallels a national fantasy of regeneration in the West. Kolodny quotes Farnham as follows: "[The West] presents itself to my mind in the light of a strong and generous parent, whose arms are spread to extend protection, happiness, and life to throngs who seek them from other and less friendly climes . . . those who go there will find abundance for the supply of their natural wants, but because the influences with which it will address their spiritual natures are purifying, ennobling, and elevating."[13]

Certainly, Farnham had a troubled history and, in important ways, she did reinvent herself in Illinois, living close to her immediate family for the first time (after a childhood of something close to abandonment by her family), and marrying Thomas Farnham, who was speculating in land and involving himself in the legal and business affairs of a new settlement. To this extent, this was, as Kolodny argues, the mythology of a "new home" and a new start realized.

Life in Prairie Land does not, however, tell the whole story. This is scarcely surprising; as Timothy Dow Adams argues, we, as readers, "[begin] with the assumption that the complete truth is not possible"; "even if writers could isolate 'the truth' of their past . . . how could writers separate poetic truth from factual truth, psychological truth from family truth?" Actually, Farnham's circumstances were characterized as much by loss and despair as by escape and recovery: she and her husband lived in Tremont, Illinois, for barely four years, during which time both the sister with whom she had been lovingly reunited and her first child died. Thomas Farnham left the marital home in Tremont after three years, in 1839, to lead an expedition to Oregon; though

13. Kolodny, *The Land Before Her*, 109, Eliza W. Farnham, *Life in Prairie Land*, xxxiii.

the couple went back to New York together in 1840, by the time *Life in Prairie Land* was finished, during 1845, Thomas Farnham had left altogether.[14]

To be aware of the gap between what Farnham writes and what seems to have happened is to be prompted to reflect on passages in *Life in Prairie Land* that seem to address her painful experiences obliquely: the narrative, for example, of the drawn-out death of a housewife who has been left alone on the prairie when her husband travels away in chapters 3 and 4 of the second part of the book. More important, though, this tenuous relationship between her circumstances and the autobiography is suggestive of what it was possible to discuss in an emigrant narrative. Kolodny sees *Life in Prairie Land* as a work of nostalgia for tranquillity in domesticity. Equally, it was possible, in the writing of the emigrant woman (in autobiography or in other forms), to depict the female subject—a married woman—as bitterly unhappy. Here, apparently, was an unusually flexible female subject.

The writing of emigrant women's experience had, it seems, a range of uses beyond the discussion of emigration and domesticity in the West. Farnham produced her narrative four or five years after leaving Illinois. She had, by the time she was writing *Life in Prairie Land*, moved into a situation almost aggressively opposed to the fantasy of domestic seclusion she depicts, a situation on which she is silent in the text. *Life in Prairie Land* was actually written during the time in which Farnham had become the first matron of an American women's prison; as matron of notorious Sing Sing she was engaged, in idealistic and unconventional ways, in the reformation of "bad" women into "good" ones. Looked at against this background, *Life in Prairie Land* seems to be directly responsive to debates about women that were circulating at the center. Farnham's representation of herself as the emigrant housewife may, of course, have been tactical: an attempt to situate herself within a domestic context at a time when she was leading a controversial public life, living apart from her husband and often away from her son. The book may also have been an attempt to reassure those who observed her work educating "fallen women" in Sing Sing that she was

---

14. Timothy Dow Adams, *Telling Lies in Modern American Autobiography*, 14, 9; see John Hallwas's introduction to *Life in Prairie Land* for a discussion of these biographical circumstances.

committed to a conventional model of feminine behavior. Equally, it may have been an attempt to illustrate her view, using the West, that environmental changes in the circumstances and surroundings of women (such as those that she instituted in the prison) could profoundly affect behavior. Farnham was unusual in believing that the recovery of the "fallen" woman was possible.[15]

What Eliza Farnham's *Life in Prairie Land* and the circumstances around its writing make clear is that the figure of the emigrant woman could speak as much to debates about women, work, and the domestic as to issues around emigration and the West. Of course, such debates circulated in a transatlantic as well as a local context, beyond national boundaries to an Anglophone cultural West taking in North America and Britain. The circulation of texts as well as money and populations between Britain and the United States, Britain and Canada, and Canada and the United States produced a complex discourse of emigrant domesticity that cut across national identity. Thus it is significant but not surprising to find Caroline Kirkland, in 1839, modeling her account of life in backwoods Michigan, *A New Home, Who'll Follow?* on a British text of provincial life published twenty-five years earlier, Mary Russell Mitford's *Our Village;* nor to find Eliza Farnham using the same tropes to depict "bad" domesticity as her British contemporaries; nor to find Caroline Kirkland's narrative, published in Boston, and Susanna Moodie's *Roughing It in the Bush,* published in 1852 in London and then in the United States, linked by Moodie's reviewers within the context of a commentary on the fate of the emigrant woman.[16]

As Akenson suggests, the virtue of placing the processes of migration at the center of our enquiry lies in the way it enables us to "escape the tyranny of the nation-state," but plainly, to look at emigrant writing about homemaking within an Anglo–North American and transatlantic context leaves out a great deal that has been very important in U.S. and Canadian scholarship in the field of western studies, not least the relationship between "the frontier," however that term is understood, and

---

15. For details of Farnham's prison work, see W. David Lewis, *From Newgate to Dannemore: The Rise of the Penitentiary in New York, 1776–1848* (Ithaca, N.Y.: Cornell University Press, 1965), 177, 237–50.

16. These are issues that form the focus of chapters 4 and 5. Reviews that compared Caroline Kirkland and Susanna Moodie are cited in Carl Ballstadt, Editor's Introduction, lvii, n. 66.

national identity. Certainly, some histories and literary histories in the United States have chosen to ignore national boundaries in favor of a scholarship that emphasizes a common pioneering womanhood within North America. Most, however, have made a precise link between emigrant women's writing and national development. In Canada, meanwhile, there has been, in addition, a tradition of formulating a Canadian difference that has lent different emphases to the writing of women's experience. The whole world of American expansion—the doughty emigrants, the wild West, the Indian wars—has been contrasted to Anglo-Canada's own colonial and national experience of tentative contact with "wilderness" and a less aggressive appropriation of land.[17]

As we shall see, the emigrant texts discussed here are engaged in describing national and colonial expansion; they are indeed often involved in the imaginative recreation of national history. Important though this plainly is, however, the context of emigration draws us to attend, at the same time, to the complicated as well as painful contexts of economic migration, back-migration, and movement between old and new homes, East and West, North America and Britain. The texts discussed in this study are very much the productions of an era of migration. They have their own complicated histories of migration: some appear at the center in published forms for transatlantic distribution, others are locally distributed. Others still are circulated around families until they are incorporated into local, national, and international publications. They are still continually circulating: recovered and published, in some cases reprinted many times, incorporated into fictions, imitated.

Reading autobiography, as Nancy Miller writes, "entails learning to make out the texture of one's experience . . . beneath the other's imprint."[18] The passionate engagement of scholars in this field is very evident to the reader of the commentary on emigrant women's auto-

---

17. Akenson, "Historiography of English Speaking Canada," 386. Marcia Kline in *Beyond the Land Itself: Views of Nature in Canada and the U.S.*, is unusual in making an explicit comparison between emigrant women's texts in Canada and the United States; her conclusion, in any case, is that the texts exemplify national differences. Some American discussions of pioneer women foreground environment rather than nation, for example, Carol Fairbanks, *Prairie Women: Images in American and Canadian Fiction*, but, as we shall see in chapter 1, many scholars in the field suggest that precise place is relatively insignificant to the formation of the pioneering spirit in women.

18. Miller, *Getting Personal*, 139.

biography. It is with the content of that engagement and its participation, through readings of emigrant autobiography, in a tradition of imagining the female emigrant as a "pioneer woman" that I begin. Pioneering womanhood is almost synonymous with the opportunity for self-expression. In chapter 1, I consider the precise dimensions of the self sanctioned within the discourse of pioneering. If the freedoms of the "frontier" seem literally to authorize women as writers, Elinore Pruitt Stewart's apparently expansive *Letters of a Woman Homesteader*, published in 1914, demonstrates the limits on self-expression at any particular historical moment. It also makes evident how closely the figure of the pioneer woman could be involved in contemporary national debates about women. In chapter 2, I go back to nineteenth-century sources in order to show how it was not so much the experience of "pioneering" that enabled women writing in the nineteenth century to embark on autobiographies and indeed to represent particular kinds of experience of the domestic in autobiographical form; rather it was the discourse of emigration. I argue that, in many ways, emigrant autobiography was an unusually capacious form of autobiographical utterance, even in the high summer of the so-called "cult of domesticity."[19]

In chapter 3, I move on to address how the discourses of domesticity are nuanced and, to some extent, reconfigured by the context of the backwoods. The world of colonial domestication in textual form is certainly in evidence, but so is a grating between domesticity and the subject position of the emigrant. The result is not the radical femininity celebrated by many western historians, but instead a writing that presents a rather less self-congratulatory domestic womanhood. From looking at how the tropes of domestic discourse are both rewritten and problematized in emigrant autobiography, I turn, in chapter 4, to the representation of tasks that do not feature in the literature idealizing domesticity: the "dirty work" of domestic life. It has become a truism that what happens within the home reflects, matches, even produces dominant power structures within society. The question posed here is this: if conventional writing of housekeeping encodes the values and

---

19. The use of the term "cult" to describe the practice and ideology of domesticity is, of course, Barbara Welter's, from "The Cult of True Womanhood, 1820–1860."

processes of the capitalist economy, what values and processes are delineated in the writing of backwoods domestic work?

In chapters 5 and 6, I move on to look at a more specific relationship between the home and "outside." How does the local, increasingly theorized as the domain of women, appear in emigrant autobiography? Women, especially women in the nineteenth-century rural community, are argued to be particularly sensitive to issues of community and to the calibrations of social life. We have become practiced in finding that emphasis in the works of New England regionalists writing later in the nineteenth century, and our knowledge of the importance of women's networks draws us to assume that in the West, of all places, women craved and embraced communal life, whether in the conventional form of a new settlement or in the "frontier" context of, say, a cattle ranch. The question of community and the representation of the local is examined in chapter 5 in the context of a discussion of Caroline Kirkland's *A New Home, Who'll Follow?* Much of the critical commentary on women's apparent communitarianism has tended to draw our attention away from the specifics of local and regional differences. In chapter 6, I question how far the representation of the West by women is sensitive to regional difference. In particular, how are the social and economic activities that define a certain type of western community written in autobiographical narratives that foreground the everyday domestic routine?

Much of this study is a discussion of emigrant women's writing in terms of what is and what cannot be expressed, what is forensically described and what is ignored. In the last chapter, I look at an autobiographical oeuvre—the writing of Anne Langton—that has somehow proved less resonant, less inspiring, less easy to incorporate into narratives of the pioneer woman. Langton's case draws to our attention the processes by which emigrant women's narratives may be preserved and recovered, and our unbending, even ruthless determination to find those images of pioneer womanhood that, in Julia Hirsch's words, deliver "some critical truth to which we can assent."[20]

I have already quoted Miller's comment on how we try to make out the "texture of our own experience" beneath the "imprint" of these emigrant texts; certainly my desire to find meaning in the description

---

20. Julia Hirsch, *Family Photographs*, 106.

of the domestic in these texts arose at a point when I found myself compelled and yet puzzled by the activities and patterns of the domestic space. Miller's argument that we read autobiography "struggling to recognize . . . the sound of another's voice," seems particularly apt. We do so, as she suggests, in order "to walk away and move on" ourselves.[21]

21. Miller, *Getting Personal,* 139.

1

A Tradition of Pioneers

*I*N THE LAST twenty years, Canadian and American scholars of women's history in the North American West have often been engaged in recovering the pioneer woman from the periphery of the dominant scholarly narratives of western "development." The pioneer woman's marginal position—even her disappearance—within the field of western history is attributed to a male-dominated understanding of the western past and a scholarly tradition from which the experiences of women have simply been expunged. Susan Armitage and Elizabeth Jameson, for example, have written of a western "Hisland": "From Daniel Boone to John Wayne, our national folk-lore is replete with white male 'rugged individuals' finding their selfhood in the freedom of an untamed land. . . . Women have been virtually absent from traditional Western history."[1]

This highly generalized argument about women and the West is not a new one—Elizabeth Ellet wrote in 1852 about the "oblivion" threatening the stories of pioneer women—but it has been and remains persistent. Susan Lee Johnson, in a recent essay about writing western history, argues that "no place has been so consistently identified with

---

1. Susan Armitage and Elizabeth Jameson, *The Women's West*, 3. Many studies emphasize the absence of material and the "loss" of western women prior to the period of the study in question. See for example Christiane Fischer, *Let Them Speak for Themselves: Women in the American West, 1849–1900*, 12; Elizabeth Hampsten, *Read This Only to Yourself: The Private Writings of Midwestern Women, 1880–1910*, 15; Linda Rasmussen, *A Harvest Yet to Reap: A History of Prairie Women*, 5, 8–9; Glenda Riley, *The Female Frontier: A Comparative View of Women on the Prairies and the Plains*, 1; Lillian Schlissel et al., *Western Women: Their Land, Their Lives*, 1; Veronica Strong-Boag and Anita Clair Fellman, *Rethinking Canada: The Promise of Women's History*, 1.

maleness." Katherine Morrissey is prompted to point out that the lives of western women (whether housewives or women in paid work) have been obscured by the way in which the very geography of the West is understood by reference to the economic activity of men. And certainly, it does remain the case that emigrant women are usually considered separately from men. It is still unusual to find general histories of the West that use women's circumstances (as opposed to, say, miners' or farmers') to drive the argument.[2]

All this can confidently be argued, and yet, within and beyond the context of academia, the figure of the Anglo pioneer housewife scarcely seems in need of recovery. She has a long-standing presence in North American culture and is as easily recognized as those other figures through which the West is narrated: the trapper, the cowboy, the speculator, the Indian, the revivalist preacher, and indeed such figures of wayward femininity as Calamity Jane. In countless westerns, she stands on the threshold of the cabin, looks out of the window, hovers at the table. Though she is often situated on the border of the main action of western history—the occupation and breaking of land—her occupation of the familiar region of "the frontier" is incontrovertible.

Even in the last decade, as the focus of scholarship has shifted away from the recovery of Anglo figures to the researching of other peoples and other groups participating in the formation of diverse Wests, the Anglo pioneer housewife remains significant for scholars. As "civilizer" she occupies a well-defined position: as a figure bent on shoring up the conquest undertaken by Anglo men, as a player within the contact zones of an ethnically diverse West, or as a figure ideologically constrained within her civilizing role.[3]

Thus, though we have never defined the West through her presence or her activity, the pioneer woman nonetheless remains the object of considerable cultural attention. There may be more cowboys in the writing of the West (and in western states and territories themselves) than housewives, more sheriffs than mothers, more miners than brides, but still we scarcely need to regard the wealth of material about

---

2. Elizabeth Ellet, *Pioneer Women of the West*, vi; Johnson, "Memory Sweet to Soldiers," 225; Katherine Morrissey, "Engendering the West," 138–40.
3. The direction and interests of the scholarly field investigating western intercultural contact are examined in, for example, Virginia Scharff, "Else Surely We Shall All Hang Separately: The Politics of Western Women's History."

the pioneer woman as a minor accompaniment to a dominant discourse. The task is rather one of addressing the debates that cluster around this figure, and it is with this task that I am concerned in this chapter.

There has, of course, been a long-standing assumption that the figure of the pioneer and the writing of Anglo women emigrants project a different perspective on emigration and the West. As we shall see in the next chapter, the possibility that, because of their allegiance to family bonds, Anglo emigrant women would cast a shadow over or undermine the whole project of settlement was voiced on both sides of the Atlantic from the early to mid-nineteenth century, in all kinds of cultural forms. The figure of the wife was, in particular, regularly and precisely positioned as expressing a more or less negative response within the process of decision-making preceding emigration. Meanwhile, the "at once sad and resolute" Anglo pioneer woman so famously described by de Tocqueville as the victim of "fever, solitude and a tedious life," her looks "impaired and faded," was also, as Carol Fairbanks notes, a ubiquitous figure, the object of sympathy.[4]

In some appearances, the pioneer woman signified a "real" West as opposed to the West of fantasy and boosterism; the doughty, even grim figure whose presence defined the limitations of and indeed the constraints upon the fantasy of pioneering. Indeed, the assertion that women constituted a special case has been the selling-point for many an emigrant autobiography: Elinore Pruitt Stewart's *Letters of a Woman Homesteader* and Agnes Morley Cleaveland's *No Life for a Lady,* for example. This has been accompanied by the suggestion that women's reminiscences reveal a stark reality beneath the mythologizing of emigrant life, as, again, is suggested by such titles as Henrietta Jones's *Sketches from Real Life* and Ann Ellis's *The Life of an Ordinary Woman.*

In recent scholarship about emigrant women's writing, women's position in the West has been theorized in terms of opposition to dominant ideologies underpinning western expansion. Brigitte Georgi-Findlay, for example, argues that the "masculinist frontier myth . . . assigned [women] to the margins of a cultural plot." Krista Comer, following Annette Kolodny, finds "a counter-discourse" within emi-

---

4. Alexis de Tocqueville, *Democracy in America,* 203; Fairbanks, *Prairie Women,* 5.

grant women's writing "which broadly critiqued the idea that female-gendered nature was 'there for the taking.'"[5]

Without a doubt one can find emigrant women's writing that is at odds with aspects of settlement as it was ruthlessly managed in the nineteenth century, and that is critical of some dimensions of the work of colonization: indifferent to frontier mythologies, at odds with the project of land appropriation. However, this general argument that women's writing consistently produces a different, if not an alternative, discourse of the West, for all its rhetorical power, is not supported by the content of many emigrant autobiographies. To read a narrative such as Nannie T. Alderson's *A Bride Goes West* or Susan Allison's *A Pioneer Gentlewoman in British Colombia,* for example, is to find the familiar open space of frontier mythology where a new self may be formed and individual impulse rules. They are "frontier" narratives. Allison, an emigrant to the Far West in the late 1850s, produces a blithe and untroubled account of her life as "my camping days . . . the wild free life I ever loved till age and infirmity put an end to it." Although the ranching frontier of 1880s Montana described by Alderson is a harsher environment (and Mr. Alderson failed to make his fortune or even survive), she nonetheless lauds to the skies the informality and egalitarianism of a frontier West, and is at pains to emphasize the excitement inspired by the "new" space. Alderson's narrative ends in piercing nostalgia for a disappeared world that marks the difference between the daily routine worked on the ranch as opposed to in the town: "The years since then have been close packed and strenuous as before. But after my husband's death, I was no longer a bride who went West, nor a woman who was helping to open up a new country; I was merely an overworked mother of four, trying to make ends meet under conditions that were none too easy."[6] Narratives such as these appear to have no interest in adapting the usual story of life as a western emigrant in order to produce a distinctly feminized version. On the contrary, they record a pioneer woman's embrace of that life in terms we can only recognize as highly conventional.

5. Brigitte Georgi-Findlay, *The Frontiers of Women's Writing: Women's Narratives and the Rhetoric of Expansion,* x; Comer, "Literature, Gender Studies and the New Western History," 118.
6. Susan Allison, *A Pioneer Gentlewoman in British Columbia: The Recollections of Susan Allison,* 21; Nannie T. Alderson, *A Bride Goes West,* 263.

The thread that draws the writing of the pioneer woman together is not its "different" gendered response to western space and its meaning. Rather, it is a set of assumptions, expressed in the comments of Mollie Dorsey Sanford, who prefaces her diary of life in Nebraska in the late 1850s and 1860s with the following suggestive terms: "[The journal] is of more value to me than it could possibly be to my children, but I desire that it shall be kept in the family and treasured as a relic of by-gone days, not for any especial merit it possesses, but because I do not want to be forgotten. While I do not *pose* as a heroine, I know that I have had peculiar trials and experiences, and perchance *some* thing I have said or done may be a help to my posterity, for trials and tribulations come to all."

Sanford's claim for the value of her diary rests not so much on its status as a "relic" of frontier life—albeit a relic to which her descendants may be expected to accord some respect—as on its comment on behaviors associated with "heroines" and its discussion of "trials and tribulations" of general relevance to other women. This engagement with issues of womanhood is equally evident in more recent historical descriptions of the Anglo pioneer. Julie Roy Jeffrey's comment, for example, a century later in one of the first histories of the "female frontier," *Frontier Women*, also emphasizes the proposal of a different order of female heroism, the search for models of behavior, the positioning of experience against ideals, and a transgenerational lesson for the reader:

> During the course of doing the research for this book and writing it, my attitude toward my subject shifted, and I think it is important to explain this shift. My original perspective was feminist; I hoped to find that pioneer women used the frontier as a means of liberating themselves from stereotypes and behaviors which I found constricting and sexist. I discovered that they did not. . . . Though my own ideological commitment remains the same, I now have greater sympathy for the choices these women made and admiration for their strength and courage. I have continually wondered whether any of us would have done so well.[7]

The writing of the pioneer woman is certainly not always so aspirational in its discussion of female behavior, nor can western women's

---

7. Julie Roy Jeffrey, *Frontier Women: The Trans-Mississippi West, 1840–1880*, xv–xvi.

history be summarized by reference to this preoccupation. Dawn Lander, for instance, argues that the figure of the lonely female pioneer functions to crush ambition in other women: "The contemporary significance of the received tradition concerning white women in the American wilderness is that it denies feminine wanderlust, keeps women in the home, and reinforces contemporary racial taboos." It is rather the sense of the intense relevance of this figure to women in general that Lander's passage shares with other representations of the pioneer woman. John Faragher, for example, who was fiercely criticized by some historians for his vision of the repressions of western farming life, writes of the way in which his perspective on women in the West is "very much part of my struggle with the contemporary woman's movement."[8]

Insofar as the context of the writing of and about pioneer women is as much concerned with general arguments about womanhood as with arguments about the West, it tends, by that token, to pull against the historicization of women's participation in Anglo settlement. Sandra L. Myres's *Westering Women and the Frontier Experience, 1800–1915,* for example, illustrates the way in which the "female frontier" is untangled from the specificities of precise context:

> Obviously, frontier women needed a great deal of patience, and a sense of humor, as they tried to adjust themselves to frontier conditions and hoped for a better future. Indeed, wrote one, "given the sparse comforts [and] meager advantages, women possessed little else but hope." And hope they did. Despite the dirt floors and canvas ceilings, the snakes and centipedes, the sagging roofs and leaning walls, women described their first frontier homes with

---

8. Dawn Lander, "Eve among the Indians," 77, 211; John Faragher, *Women and Men on the Overland Trail,* xi. For examples of the criticism handed out to Faragher, see, for example, Sandra Myres's comment in "Women in the West," which compares "the more recent feminist stereotypes of frontier women" of Faragher with "old nineteenth-century myths" (182); or Riley's references, in *The Female Frontier,* to the "puerile stereotypes" to be found in the work of contemporary scholars as well as in pre-1970s representations (1). A similar case in Canada is discussed in Aileen Moffatt, "Great Women, Separate Spheres and Diversity: Comments on Saskatchewan Women's Historiography," in which she argues that Sara Sundberg's essay on the pains of western farming for Anglo emigrants, "Farm Women on the Canadian Prairie Frontier: The Helpmate Image," which was included in the first edition of Strong-Boag and Fellman, *Rethinking Canada,* was dropped from the second because of its negative image of pioneer women.

a sense of accomplishment in their ability to cope with unusual situations.

The passage is characteristic of Myres, not only in the breadth and richness of its range of reference, but also in its use of a thick texture of examples to support a central point. Myres's text, published in 1984, was, of course, a synthesizing project of great importance in the field, but at this and other points in her narrative she does not hesitate to illustrate her conclusions by setting quotations from interviews given by women in the 1940s cheek by jowl with a letter written home to relatives in 1861. The lives, for example, of the second-generation migrant, the successive migrant, and the back-migrant, and the importance of the nuclear and the extended family in the process of emigration and settlement are subsumed within a totalizing argument about female experience—in this case that "women did not seem to think that they had suffered unduly."[9]

It is instructive, I think, given the radical changes in women's studies and women's history since Myres's work was published, in particular the rejection of essentializing notions of womanhood and the questioning of the concept of "progress," to find this tradition of writing the pioneer woman continuing into the 1990s in a more recent anthology of early Californian women's writing: Ida Rae Egli's *No Rooms of Their Own*. Here the writer of the volume's Foreword, J. J. Wilson, drives home the transhistoricity of female experience and of the didactic meaning attached to it:

> The title of this collection is, of course, derived from Virginia Woolf's influential book . . . but I keep hearing another oft-repeated phrase of hers, an injunction that we should all be "thinking back through our mothers." Today, as we stand at the frontier of a new century, let us take courage from the words of one of our mothers, Sarah Royce, written about the day of her setting out:
>
> "I would not consent to delay our departure for fear of the weather. Had I not made up my mind to encounter many storms?

9. Sandra L. Myres, *Westering Women and the Frontier Experience, 1800–1915*, 143, 145. A related argument is made in the context of a more general discussion in Elizabeth Hampsten, "Considering More than the Single Reader," 135.

If we were going, let us go, and meet what we were to meet, bravely."[10]

If the writing of pioneer womanhood is often concerned with an argument about a feminine ideal generated from a "real" experience of lighting out from constraint, what are the dimensions of that ideal? Lillian Schlissel, writing in 1981, catches the characteristic flavor of the "true" pioneer woman—and, by implication, the "true" woman—in the following: "Sometimes . . . young girls reached out for the new freedoms the frontier offered. They rode and hunted; they expanded their lives with an eager acceptance of new roles and new expectations. Quite simply they saw the needs of the new land and they did what had to be done." This ideal of womanhood is not, of course, the invention of late 1970s Anglo-American feminist history. Nannie Alderson's pioneer woman is as pragmatic, as active, and as eager to cast off the constraints of convention as Schlissel's. She writes that in Kansas, "I felt that the very air there was easier to breathe. . . . a girl could work in an office or a store, yet that wouldn't keep her from being invited to the nicest homes . . . This freedom to work seemed to me a wonderful thing. I wanted to do something useful myself."[11]

This, however, is precisely the kind of rhetoric that complicates attempts to identify women's writing of pioneering as a counter-discourse. This is a feminized frontier individualism, a separate sphere of activity and fulfillment, an expansion for women that matches the masculine ideal. It is achieved through the literal "going out" to the West to find satisfying and physical work. The idealization of embracing work is not, in itself, particular to the frontier context: not when Schlissel was writing in the first phase of Anglo-American feminism; nor when Alderson was published during World War II at a time when women were encouraged to go out to work to support the war effort; nor indeed during the period when large-scale emigration to the western states took place, when, in the first volume of *The Lowell Offering*, for example, numerous stories describe going to work in the factories

10. Ida Rae Egli, ed., *No Rooms of Their Own: Women Writers of Early California*, x.
11. Lillian Schlissel, "Frontier Families: Crisis in Ideology," 159; Alderson, *A Bride Goes West*, 8.

of Lowell as an adventure much in the same vein as those who praised the opportunities afforded by emigration.[12]

What is distinctive about the discussion of this freeing work that the pioneer woman finds in the West, however, is the frequency with which it is realized in a life conducted within and around the domestic space. "Going out" to work is not precluded, but pioneer women's work is most characteristically pictured as a gargantuan domestic effort. Elinore Pruitt Stewart writes: "I have done most of my cooking at night, have milked 7 cows every day, and have done all the hay cutting, so you see I have been working. But I have found time to put up 30 pints of jelly and the same amount of jam for myself." Writing about eight years earlier, Kitturah Belknap lists the intense activity necessary to maintain the household: "All this winter I have been spinning flax and tow to make some summer clothes—have not spent an idle moment and now the wool must be taken from the sheep's back, washed and picked and sent to the carding machine and made into rolls and then spun, colored and wove ready for next winter. I cant weave so I spin for my mother-in-law and she does my weaving." Bernice White's recollections, quoted by Eliane Silverman, are in the same vein:

> I had a thirty gallon crock. I'd cut all the fat off the pig, cut it into big pieces according to what I wanted, and then put a brine over it . . . Every now and again I'd turn it around. When you'd had threshers for several days, the pork went down. You'd put up a twenty pound roast and it'd be gone. You had to make a lot of other things besides; I used to can a lot of white beans. You'd soak them and cook them with bacon, in the oven with tomato stuff. I'd put them into sealers so you could open them on the day you needed them . . . Pies, pies would disappear . . . A loaf of bread wouldn't go anywhere. And cows to milk, and the chickens, and the children.

The writing about pioneer women's work in recent historical writing strikes much the same note:

> For pure creativity, however, Kitturah Belknap deserved congratulations. Using a Dutch oven, a skillet, a teakettle and a coffeepot,

---

12. See, for example, "The Orphan Sisters" in *Lowell Offering: A Repository of Original Articles,* vol. 1, 263–66.

she devised meals which were just like "at home." . . . Butter for the bread was not a problem for her either. When the cows were milked at night, she strained the milk into little buckets which were covered and set on the ground under the wagon. In the morning she skimmed off the cream, put it in the churn in the wagon. In the morning she skimmed off the cream, put it in the churn in the wagon, and after riding all day she has a "nice roll of butter."[13]

There is, however, the unmistakable flavor of regulation in discussions of this ideal of independence and work. To use Elizabeth Grosz's words, this writing of the pioneer woman "adjudicates what gets included . . . and what does not" in the taxonomy of pioneer behavior. Patricia Limerick, in *The Legacy of Conquest,* makes the boundaries of the ideal very clear: "While individuals may have conformed to the passive, suffering female pioneer, the majority were too busy for such self-dramatization. Cooking, cleaning, washing, caring for children, planting gardens—any number of activities—took priority over brooding." The opposition between realizing the potential of pioneering and any kind of introspective (and, perhaps especially, retrospective) activity has always been explicit. Anne Langton, writing in Upper Canada in the 1830s, makes the point that women occupy a "more natural and proper sphere" in the backwoods "than the one we occupy in over-civilized life," and that it is "her utility" that gives an Anglo emigrant woman her status in Upper Canada.[14]

To perform work that is not "useful" is to be placed beyond the pale of pioneer womanhood. Schlissel's illustration of how emigrant women may fail to change in the face of "the new freedoms the frontier offered" follows this tradition of structuring 'real' pioneer womanhood by showing the perversity of emigrant women unable to embrace useful work: she describes the "haunting photograph" of women apparently so lacking in any sense of how to use their time productively as to have

---

13. Elinore Pruitt Stewart, *Letters of a Woman Homesteader,* 17–18; Kitturah Belknap, "Keturah Penton Belknap," 136; Bernice White quoted in Eliane Silverman, *The Last Best West,* 105–6; Glenda Riley, *Frontierswomen: The Iowa Experience,* 24–25.

14. Elizabeth Grosz, *Space, Time and Perversion: Essays in the Politics of Bodies,* 10; Patricia Limerick, *The Legacy of Conquest: The Unbroken Past of the American West,* 52–53; Anne Langton, *Langton Records,* 71, 220.

undertaken the pointless task of maintaining gleaming aprons, despite being surrounded by mud:

> If a certain hardy independence grew out of the frontier experience of women, it was soon cut off from nurture by attitudes that spoke for Victorian propriety, domesticity, and restriction. The photographs of pioneer women that survive tell us, eloquently, of the struggles of the frontier woman to be all things to herself and to her family. One haunting photograph shows a mother and daughter in Colorado, in boots as thick as any man's, in their barnyard in early spring when the snows are on the ground, feeding their stock, and both wearing white aprons. The effort to maintain those white aprons in all that mud must have been the labor of Sisyphus![15]

So powerful, it seems, is Schlissel's impulse to delineate behavior at odds with pioneer womanhood that she does not want to entertain the notion that the women whom she describes may have been dressing up for the occasion of being photographed. There is instead a kind of exasperation here and, again, this is a long-standing response, easily retraced in nineteenth-century examples such as in this passage from Catharine Parr Traill's 1836 autobiography *The Backwoods of Canada*. Here Traill excoriates the emigrant woman who cleaves to the time-wasting social patterns of a former life:

> I am sorry to observe, that in many cases the women that come hither [to Canada] give way to melancholy regrets, and destroy the harmony of their fire-side, and deaden the energies of their husbands and brothers by constant and useless repining . . . One poor woman that was lamenting the miseries of this country was obliged to acknowledge that her prospects were far better than they ever had or could have been at home. What, then, was the cause of her continual regrets and discontent? I could hardly forbear smiling, when she replied, "She could not go to a shop of a Saturday night to lay out her husband's earnings, and have a little chat with her *naibors,*" while the shopman was serving the customers,—*for why?* there were no shops in the bush, and she was just dead-alive . . . And so for the sake of a dish of gossip, while lolling her elbows on the counter of a village-shop, this woman would have forgone the

---

15. Schlissel, "Frontier Families," 63–64.

real advantages, real solid advantages, of having land and cattle, and poultry and food, and firing and clothing.[16]

This emphasis on the pioneer woman as performing useful work has often produced a very hostile response to her portrayal as the victim of economic and natural forces beyond her control. The much-cited example is, of course, Hamlin Garland's portrait of his mother "imprisoned in a small cabin on the enormous sunburned, treeless plain, with no expectation of ever living anywhere else." Garland's figure has been dismissed as a sexist fantasy, as the rewriting of a misogynistic stereotype that denies the active participation of women in western life.[17]

However, the use of Garland, his Naturalist contemporaries, and other western regionalists to argue for the domination of a thinly stereotypical portrait of the unhappy pioneer woman both exaggerates the influence of this literary tradition and ignores the level at which such a figure references the same values of work as more favored representations of the pioneer woman. There certainly seems little reason to focus on Garland's influence given that, powerfully written though they are, his books were popular in short bursts only: during the 1890s and immediately after World War I. At both points his texts appeared at the same time as other popular and much cheerier portraits of the emigrant farmwoman and her descendants. Much more important is the way in which, from Garland to writers such as Ruth Suckow, the focus on women, gloomy or vibrant, is used to highlight "true" values of work under threat from outside interests of big business.

The threat to or the loss of useful work is articulated, for example, in Ruth Suckow's 1924 novel *Country People*, which uses a second-generation Iowan emigrant farmwoman to delineate the threat made to a noble culture of work within the world of the farm by a rapacious commercialism outside. Emma Stille, the heroine, embodies the solid

---

16. Catharine Parr Traill, *The Backwoods of Canada: Being Letters from the Wife of an Emigrant Officer, Illustrative of the Domestic Economy of British America*, 150–51.

17. Hamlin Garland, *Main-Travelled Roads*, ix. See, for examples of the standard critique of Garland within the field, the discussions in Fairbanks, *Prairie Women*, 12–17; Jeanie McKnight, "American Dream, Nightmare Underside," 25; and, in a more general vein, Kathleen Underwood's comment, in *Town-Building on the Colorado Frontier*, on the weak claims of "those [novelists, playwrights and poets] who deserted their home towns" to represent the West (xviii).

values of work that Suckow finds enshrined in the family circle. If, in her passivity and speechlessness, she represents the vulnerability of those values, she is at least committed to them. The men are quickly and irrevocably drawn into the arid relations of agribusiness.

Some appearances of the pioneer woman merely engage in a generalized nostalgic discussion of values of unincorporated work. Carol Fairbanks and Bergine Haakenson, for example, construct the figure as a traditionalist icon, arguing that "though the patterns of these farm women's lives can no longer be repeated, we can carry their solid values and determined optimism with us into the twenty-first century."[18] In other readings of the meaning of the pioneer woman's work, however, her activity has a more powerful construction: it is both traditional in the sense of being individualized and independent, and it is also expressive of engagement in the present.

The writing about food preservation is a good example of this order of work. It appears in all kinds of accounts of women's lives in the West, autobiographical and otherwise. A letter written in 1852 by Abigail Malick strikes the characteristic note: "Now I must tel you what other preserves that I have. I have peaches And citrons And Sweet Aples. Crab Aples Jelley and Tomatoes And Mince And pairs and Aple butter." Many such passages suggest the pleasing skill and self-sufficiency of the preindustrial housewife and vaguely evoke a more general work of preserving the habits of the past. At the same time, they depict a bright perfection of production, without rules and routines, in a domestic context. The image is not really a retrospective one, however. Preserving fruit was a postindustrial phenomenon, and, as Patricia Limerick memorably points out at the beginning of *The Legacy of Conquest*, the "frontier," rather surprisingly, was the land of preserved food.[19]

This is all, at one level, no more than a rewriting of the values of the Protestant work ethic, but the integrity of such work is underwritten in two ways: first by the understanding of its position as within

18. Carol Fairbanks and Bergine Haakenson, eds., *Writings of Farm Women: An Anthology*, xiv.
19. Abigail Malick is quoted in Lillian Schlissel, *Far from Home: Families of the Westward Journey*, 21; Limerick, *The Legacy of Conquest*, 17–18. For a discussion of preserving, see Susan Strasser, *Never Done: A History of American Housework*, 22.

a domestic space that is quite separate from the alienating contexts of postindustrial work; and second by the assertion of its opposition to a stifling domesticity left behind. Thus Glenda Riley, for example, insists that the position of pioneer women in the domestic space insulates them from "outside" and specifically from the order of work generated by new technologies in the West. It is this assumption about the domestic space as not only separate but in some sense independent from "male" activity that prompts Elizabeth Hampsten, writing in 1982 about the private writings of midwestern women, to argue that region—with all its specificities of space, landscape, and economic activity—is a male construct and not relevant to women at all: "To the extent that regional cultural characteristics may be valid, they are more applicable to men's activities than to women's . . . What women do all day long is much the same from one place to another." Hampsten's claim is all the more telling, one feels, given how deeply influential women writers were, from the second half of the nineteenth century—the period with which Hampsten is concerned—in constructing region.[20]

Although the domestic space is separate, it is not thereby altogether sealed. The open spaces of the West generate a domestic practice that extends outward into the community. The changing West in Sara Deutsch's *No Separate Refuge: Culture, Class and Gender on the Anglo-Hispanic Frontier in the American South-West*, for example, where the true pioneers are Hispanic, is one in which domestic relationships radiate, in widening circles, into a relatively autonomous network of women. Deutsch argues that "for almost all women, relations between the sexes within the family were characterized not by rigidity and hierarchy, but by flexibility, cooperation, and a degree of autonomy." Certainly, changes take place "in the wake of male migration," but the

---

20. For contrasting views of the importance of women writers in constructing regionalism, see Richard Brodhead, *Cultures of Letters: Scenes of Reading and Writing in Nineteenth-Century America*, 163–72, and Judith Fetterley and Marjorie Pryse, *American Women Regionalists, 1850–1910*. The wealth of material that Fetterley and Pryse and other anthologists such as Karen L. Kilcup, in *Nineteenth-Century American Women Writers* (Oxford: Blackwell, 1997), have brought to our attention can, at least, leave no doubt of the importance of women writers in the writing of region.

result is that the power of women extends and "the women's world and the world of the village [begin] to merge."[21]

While the western environment produces the conditions where the domestic space of the woman may open outward, the metropolitan domestic space, by contrast, functions, through the "cult of domesticity," to inculcate passive behavior and to confine individualism. References to Barbara Welter's formulation of a repressive eastern "cult of domesticity" are omnipresent in modern scholarship in the field. In *Relations of Rescue,* Peggy Pascoe's study of relations between middle-class Anglo women involved in philanthropic activity and those whom they imagined themselves to be rescuing, the influence of the "cult" is absolute: Anglo women are driven and hampered by a Victorian morality from which they can find only limited avenues for escape, even when shifts in that morality occur within the wider cultural context. By contrast, the Chinese emigrant women whom they purport to rescue are represented as more able and willing to play with new codes and alternative traditions.[22]

Similarly, Sylvia Van Kirk, in *Many Tender Ties,* contrasts the culturally complex role of her native women in the West, deeply involved at all levels in a diverse and changing economic scene, to that of Anglo emigrants. Van Kirk appropriates the (slightly disturbing) term "lovely tender exotics" from mid-nineteenth-century writing to describe eastern women as burdened with cultural expectations that are absolutely and unvaryingly inflexible. It is these expectations that limit Anglo women's appreciation of a developing and dynamic western women's culture, and trap them in misunderstandings of native women that prove profoundly destructive to all participants in the relationship.

To return, then, to the question of the pioneer woman's position with which we began, we may propose that while the figure of the pioneer woman is continually situated at the margins of history and culture, these margins are far from being shadowy cultural spaces. However, in proposing a tradition of writing the pioneer woman that is highly attentive to particular ideals of female behavior generated within

---

21. Sara Deutsch, *No Separate Refuge: Culture, Class and Gender on the Anglo-Hispanic Frontier in the American South-West,* 48, 41–42.
22. Peggy Pascoe, *Relations of Rescue: The Search for Female Moral Authority in the American West 1874–1939,* 192.

a separate space, and to the possibility of "good" work that the pioneer woman's life raises, we easily enter the realms of generalization within the discourse itself, and risk ignoring the ways in which the writing of the pioneer woman has been influenced by the context in which it was produced. And indeed the ways in which more specific anxieties of the historical moment are addressed by the restatement of traditions of imagining pioneer women draws our attention to the interest and complexity within the writing of pioneer womanhood by emigrant writers.

Elinore Pruitt Stewart's *Letters of a Woman Homesteader* is a rewarding example of the way in which representations of pioneer womanhood both respond and write back to the contemporary mainstream in multiple and specific ways. This high-spirited autobiographical narrative, structured as a series of letters to a former employer in Denver, describes the writer's experience on a farm in Wyoming. The letters stitch together portraits of a warm-hearted parochial Anglo-American West, played against explorations of magnificent surrounding countryside, and asserted in contrast to Other populations perceived as more or less racially different. Readings of the text themselves provide a useful illustration of traditions of reading pioneer women's autobiography. *Letters of a Woman Homesteader* achieved a privileged position within the scholarship of the late 1970s and early 1980s when Pruitt Stewart was cited and quoted as a single woman homesteader, approved as physically active, as industrious as her male peers, and as able to realize the frontier idyll of rural self-sufficiency. Thus in Susan Armitage's early work in 1982, Pruitt Stewart is an "especially appealing and articulate spokeswoman of an almost forgotten group, single woman homesteaders." For Lillian Schlissel, she embodies the brave minority of women pioneers "untroubled about Victorian prescriptions of womanly behavior . . . unconcerned about Victorian ideas that a woman needed a man's protection."[23]

The text has been read as Pruitt Stewart asks us to read it: as a transparent record of experience that proves her success in making real the

---

23. The anecdotes of visits that structure much of the text are organized around encounters with families whose "difference" is marked by custom, food, and accent. See, for example, the representations of the German Louderers and Edmondsons (66–69, 122–27), and of the Irish O'Shaughnessys (69–70, 71–73, 88–89); Susan Armitage, "Reluctant Pioneers," 45; Schlissel, "Frontier Families," 161.

ideal of self-discovery and liberation in the West. Indeed, the passionate partiality and idealism of the project of those who have recovered and explicated autobiographical narratives is never more clearly shown than when it is placed against recent discussions of autobiography that subject the creation of a self in autobiographical writing to the most ruthless deconstruction. Narratives of pioneer womanhood are still often viewed by their critics as holding a kind of gold standard of feminine experience.

Unsurprisingly, the research of Suzanne George, described in *The Adventures of The Woman Homesteader,* has uncovered a life quite at odds with the patterns and mood of Pruitt Stewart's work of self-invention, and with the reconstruction of her life developed by this author's late-twentieth-century admirers. Pruitt Stewart (1876–1933) was scarcely the single homesteader that she has been claimed to epitomize. On the contrary, as her narrative shows in the most oblique form, she married within weeks of her arrival in Wyoming and her "single homestead" was built as an extension to her husband's house. As George explains, she was never able to "prove" the land she had bought because it was illegal for a couple to share a homestead when homesteading neighboring properties. Consequently, Pruitt Stewart's homestead passed into the ownership of her mother-in-law. These events not only bear the very patchiest relation to the life described in Pruitt Stewart's *Letters* but actually exemplify some of the most obvious barriers to single women homesteading; as Sherry L. Smith has argued, Pruitt Stewart's case shows the complex strategies used by *the extended family* in attempting to manipulate government regulations.

Commentators on this text and indeed Pruitt Stewart herself underscore the issue of gender and the West, particularly the way in which the western ideal is adapted by a woman seen as a pioneer in every sense. This is a text, however, that relentlessly draws our attention to its status as "the usual story," as the familiar "true picture" of emigrant experience. Emigrant autobiographical narrative, as we shall see in chapter 2, was a generic form that structured a life in very specific ways. Such narratives, closely associated with promotional material, focused on the western experience as new, emphasizing the expectation of progress from hardship toward self-sufficiency; they also produced an informality in composition that could easily be read as the reflection of authentic experience.

Pruitt Stewart is very artful indeed in producing these effects and indeed she does so with such concentration that the narrative of the experiences that she has "as a woman" has to be rearranged. Within what purports to be an everyday outpouring of successive experiences, she delays the telling of her decision to marry her employer until a point in the text when the character of her husband is sufficiently familiar to her readers for the union to be interpreted as the outcome of a love affair rather than as a matter of convenience; it is not until Letter *Eighteen* that she coyly admits the speed of their change in circumstances and the reasons for it: " . . . the haste I married in, I am ashamed of that . . . But although I married in haste, I have no cause to repent . . . The engagement was powerfully short because both agreed that the trend of events and ranch work seemed to require that we be married first and do our 'sparking' afterward." As Suzanne George explains: "It was Clyde [Stewart] who placed the ad between January and March of 1909 . . . 'WANTED—Young or middle-aged lady as companion and to assist with housekeeping on a Wyoming ranch; a good permanent home for the right party.'" Elinore Pruitt arrived at the Stewart ranch in early March 1909 and married Clyde Stewart eight weeks later.[24] Spontaneity and pragmatism were the order of the day in the writing of the West as an informal space, but only in certain contexts. A strategy of marrying and hoping for the best could not be narrated as spontaneous.

The description of the death of her baby in Letter Ten shows Pruitt Stewart manipulating the sequence of events again: "I have been a very busy woman since I began this letter to you several days ago. A dear little child has joined the angels. I dressed him and helped to make his casket. There is no minister in this whole country and I could not bear the little broken lilybud to be just carted away and buried so I arranged the funeral and conducted the service." The death of the first baby of the marriage with Stewart is identified as her own bereavement only at a later point in the narrative—following the description of her marriage as a fortunate event—once that bereavement can be incorporated into the narrative as one of a series of struggles that were an expected if not essential prelude to sufficiency and contentment in the West: "When

---

24. Pruitt Stewart, *Letters*, 184–85; Suzanne George, *The Adventures of a Woman Homesteader*, 11–13.

you think of me, you must think of me as one who is truly happy. It is true I want a great many things I have n't got, but I don't want them enough to be discontented and not enjoy the many blessings that are mine."[25]

Pruitt Stewart, in every sense, authorized herself through retelling an absolutely conventional story of pioneering in the West: the tradition of citing the experience of ordinary emigrants as proof of the dream of prosperity and happiness made Pruitt Stewart an author, and gave her experiences a tangible value. Her earlier attempts at journalism and her later attempts to write outside the genre were, interestingly, less successful in finding a publisher.[26]

The resolutely uncritical portrait of a settled West produced in *Letters* achieved publication and some success at a point when the widespread taste for western writing was being addressed by a range of narratives that showed a frontier experience—perceived to be ending for the male population—revivified in figures of pioneer women.[27] Zane Grey's *Riders of the Purple Sage* and Willa Cather's *O Pioneers!* for example, were both published with considerable success within two years of *Letters of a Woman Homesteader*. These texts did not place their heroines within the same fictional landscapes, but both Cather and Grey showed pioneer women strengthened emotionally by their ability to use the land to make a self-sufficient living. Such texts proved anew the fantasy of independence and self-fulfillment in the West surely otherwise in danger of becoming threadbare by the 1910s.

Pruitt Stewart's feminization of the individualist ethic was no doubt welcome to those readers who fantasized about the fulfillment of that ethic in the West, even in the face of highly publicized wars between big business and workers in the region. The many-faceted attraction of the ubiquitous tales of the West—wild or otherwise—to city dwellers disturbed by the social implications of early-twentieth-century capital-

---

25. Pruitt Stewart, *Letters*, 98, 191.
26. For a brief but evocative discussion of Pruitt Stewart's journalistic endeavours, see George, *Adventures*, 9–10n14.
27. For an interesting discussion of the circumstances of the publication of the *Letters*, see Peter C. Rollins, "Literature to Film: Why Is the Arcadian Vision of Elinore Pruitt Stewart's *Letters of a Woman Homesteader* (1914) Absent from the Film Version?" *Literature/Film Quarterly* 20, no. 1 (1992): 25–35.

ism is well known.[28] At the same time, *Letters* addressed those parts of her audience who feared the absence of sanctions on social behavior far from the center or, for that matter, within the class from which Pruitt Stewart, the self-styled "ex-washlady," came.

In this more general context, Pruitt Stewart's narrative also addressed a contemporary anxiety about forms of work that could be resolved in the imagination of work in the rural West. As Smith argues, the text, working within traditional understandings of the West as a "safety-valve," spoke to urban working-class women, encouraging them "to consider homesteading as an alternative to the limitations and drudgery of wage-earning." Smith also links the appearance of *Letters* in the *Atlantic Monthly* to the "national infatuation with rural life," reflected in the boom in homesteading between 1898 and 1917 and supported by government and popular publications alike. In the following passage, Pruitt Stewart seems to speak to this project, striving to soothe urban anxiety and to offer a fantasy of rural happiness. She expresses the traditional dream of the homesteader, the worker who embraces her labors:

> To me, homesteading is the solution of all society's problems, but I realize that . . . persons afraid of coyotes and work and loneliness had better let ranching alone. At the same time, any woman who can stand her own company, can see the beauty of the sunset, loves growing things, and is willing to put as much time at careful labor as she does over the wash-tub, will certainly succeed; will have independence, plenty to eat all the time, and a home of her own in the end.[29]

Not surprisingly, traditionalism went arm-in-arm with Anglo-Saxonism in this strain of writing about the West. The *Atlantic Monthly* is associated with a regionalist turn-of-the-century discourse that engaged

---

28. For a recent summary of the grim pattern of labor relations in the West during this period, see Carlos A. Schwantes, "Wage Earners and Wealth Makers." Two helpful studies of how the West was used to address capitalism are: Michael Denning, *Mechanic Accents: Dime Novels and Working-Class Culture in America* (London: Verso, 1987) and Christine Bold "Popular Forms I," in *The Columbia History of the American Novel*, edited by Emory Elliott (New York: Columbia University Press, 1991).

29. Sherry L. Smith, "Single Women Homesteaders: The Perplexing Case of Elinoire Pruitt Stewart," 176, 175, 182; Pruitt Stewart, *Letters,* 215.

in a celebration—if not the confection—of traditions shared among "folks" in the "original" spaces of American life.[30] This was a discussion that masked and justified a reactionary, covertly racist political agenda. While Pruitt Stewart's text certainly promotes a collaboration across class difference between Anglo women based on a common femininity, she also traces a boundary that positions the lives of those who are not white Protestants beyond the pale. Thus, while Lynn Z. Bloom rightly argues that *Letters of a Woman Homesteader* is soaked with the longstanding utopianism of representations of the West, this is a very white utopia indeed. *Letters* bears comparison with such texts as Mary Meek Atkeson's *The Woman on the Farm,* published in 1924, in the way it makes explicit the privileged status accorded to the Anglo-Saxon farmer in the West. Atkeson insists, for example, on the Anglo farmwoman as the descendant of the Pilgrim Fathers and her children as agents for the "Americanization of the hordes of foreign immigrants" quiescent in the face of economic inequity : "Factory managers say that very often it is the farm boy or girl working shoulder to shoulder with the low-class Hungarian and the Russian peasant, speaks for law and order and for the true democracy of America which recognizes the rights of the rich as well as the poor." Her argument is that "American country women" want to be "the same" and not "different": "The quaint and colorful peasant costumes of the European nations have their charm and I dare say the women who wear them enjoy it, but no American country woman has any desire to be thus set off in a class by herself by her clothes." Her precise instructions as to how the Anglo farmwoman runs her house, for the benefit of women who apparently "naturally" do it that way anyway, make evident the perceived need to codify the work of the rural woman.[31]

All these issues in *Letters* bear as much examination as those discussions that directly address gender issues in the text. And here, in any case, is the familiar construction of dynamic pioneer behavior. Pruitt Stewart's perfect work for women is very pointedly domestic. It insists on an unproblematic relation of work inside and outside, yet it produces the domestic context in descriptions of homemaking and food

---

30. For discussions of this aspect of regionalist discourse, see Brodhead, *Cultures of Letters,* chapters 4 and 5; and June Howard, "Sarah Orne Jewett and the Traffic in Words."

31. Mary Meek Atkeson, *The Woman on the Farm,* 4, 23, 134.

preparation, and positions paid work as optional and extra. Much of this is standard in the writing of pioneer womanhood, but Pruitt Stewart's text was referencing a particular discussion of women's work when it appeared.

Pruitt Stewart's generation was much engaged in debates about the gendering of work. The separation between men's and women's paid work in the urban context was very marked, and the lower status of women's paid work (held to be merely an extra rather than a breadwinning income) was made very explicit. Leslie Tentler describes, in *Wage-Earning Women*, the way in which subsistence wages for women were justified by assertions that their work in shops and factories was merely a matter of supplementing a family income. In the context of what Alice Kessler-Harris cites as an "exhaustive concern about the conditions of all wage-earners, especially women," "a stream of public studies" (including three published around the time of Pruitt Stewart's publication of *Letters*) investigated the impact of women working "outside" on the domestic sphere.[32] Both Tentler and Kessler-Harris emphasize the hostility toward women working for wages during this period, and the representation of women's work as undertaken for trivial ends and as depriving men of the work that was their right.

The relationship between domestic work and paid work using domestic skills (taking in laundry, selling surplus dairy produce, and so on), and the overlapping of gendered work in a rural western context have both been preoccupations of the scholarship on pioneer women's experience. In essence, the agenda of the historical discussion has been situated in the consideration of the impact of women's economic activity on their power within the family, and has often traced a narrative of gradual progress toward independence predicated on women's ability to earn (for the family) precious cash for the family enterprise.[33] What we find in Stewart is the intervention into the world of "men's work" in a heavily circumscribed form, an intervention that seems to engage quite specifically with arguments of the era about the *restriction* of women's work.

32. Alice Kessler-Harris, *A History of Wage-Earning Women in the United States*, 97.
33. See, for opposing arguments about the position of pioneer women's work, Faragher, *Women and Men on the Overland Trail*, 50–53, 54–57, 62; Riley, *The Female Frontier*, 62–68; Jeffrey, *Frontier Women*, 22, 54.

When, for example, in Letter Three Pruitt Stewart describes undertaking the mowing of grass in her husband's absence, the incident is presented by the writer as signifying an unconventional impulse as far as work and role are concerned. The suggestion is that the skills involved are unladylike: "If [Mr. Stewart] put a man to mow, it kept them all idle at the stacker, and he just could n't get enough men. I was afraid to tell him I could mow for fear he would forbid me to do so." Her own mowing skills have, however, been generated (appropriately) in the circumstances of a penurious and orphaned childhood, and not as the result of ambition, competition, a failure of femininity, or a lapse in male capability. The anecdote in Letter Three involves Pruitt Stewart doing the mowing, though her performance of a man's job is neither seen by her husband, nor is it visualized in the text. Pruitt Stewart's gloss on the incident appears to raise a point about the gendering of work as fixing women in the lower echelons of the work hierarchy ("I was afraid to tell him . . ."). Her concluding remarks, however, take a rather different direction: "I was glad [that my husband was delighted] because I really like to mow, and besides that, I am really adding feathers in my cap in a surprising way. When you see me again you will think I am wearing a feather duster, but it is only that I have been said to have almost as much sense as a 'mon', and that is an honor I never aspired to even in my wildest dreams." Her work, far from making her more "like a man," becomes a performance for which her husband praises her. His approbation transforms her back into a housewife indeed: a figure *wearing* a feather duster—a signifier, presumably of a form of housework that is scarcely work at all. The mowing episode operates, in fact, to diminish the work of women within and outside the home.[34]

Letters depicts a self-regeneration through the energetic performance of work, but women's self-improvement through education appears much more problematic. Pruitt Stewart identifies her own lack of formal education as a badge of sincerity, insisting rather on her transformation from a wash-lady to a home-maker rather than to a homesteader. She writes a neighbor's efforts to "better herself" as trivial, parochial, and a matter of misplaced social ambition:

34. Pruitt Stewart, *Letters*, 15–17.

Sedalia was present and almost caused a riot. She says she likes unusual words because they lend distinction to conversation. Well they do—sometimes . . . There was another lady present whose children were very gifted musically, but who have the bad name of taking what they want without asking . . . While we were all busy someone made a remark about how smart these children were. Sedalia thought that a good time to get a big word in, so she said 'yes, I have always said Lula was a progeny.' [Her mother] didn't know what that meant and thought she was casting aspersions on her child's honesty, so with her face scarlet and her eyes blazing she said 'Sedalia Lane, I won't allow you nor nobody else to say my child is a progeny. You can take that back or I will slap you peaked.' Sedalia took it back in a hurry, so I guess little Lula Hall is not a progeny.[35]

Such passages define further the nature of the "progress" toward homogeneity and shared values that Stewart idealizes in her text. Clearly, in transferring issues around work and women to a mythologized space of the West, Pruitt Stewart's work offered her fretful middle-class urban readers a text that was deeply reassuring in gender terms as well as in terms of class and race.

Not all emigrant women's narratives link tradition and contemporary reference as seamlessly—or as skillfully—as Pruitt Stewart, and few demonstrate so clearly the potentially reactionary character of popular traditions of writing pioneer women. Most, however, like Elinore Pruitt Stewart, produce rhetorical claims of freedom while re-enacting different versions of conventionally sanctioned behavior. Of course, many of the emigrant diaries and letters published over the last decade and a half have been investigated (almost exclusively so, at times) for subversiveness, for signs of straining against the cult of domesticity, for their "reaction to [the] daily role as a woman and . . . subversive action of questioning the script," to quote Judy Nolte Lensink in her edition of a diary that does indeed "question the script."[36] Although I would agree that some emigrant texts are unconventional in the ways in which they open up the domestic life of the emigrant for discussion, where

---

35. Pruitt Stewart, *Letters,* 97.
36. Judy Nolte Lensink, ed., *"A Secret to be Burried": The Diary and Life of Emily Gillespie, 1858–1888,* xix.

emigrant writers seem more obviously to break with convention is in doing so *autobiographically*. It is to the opportunity for the construction of a domestic self offered by this particular form of autobiographical utterance and to the mid-nineteenth century that generated that opportunity that I shall turn in the next chapter.

2

Private Enterprise

The Emigrant Autobiographies of Kitturah Belknap and Susanna Moodie

*T*HE RECOVERY OF the "pioneer woman" has, of course, only been possible because women who emigrated to and within North America in the nineteenth and early twentieth centuries recorded their experience of emigration. These recollections were published in the writers' lifetimes; emigrant writers edited their memoirs for their descendants; descendants preserved and edited emigrant writing not intended for a public audience. This is not a unique phenomenon. There has always been, as Leigh Gilmore points out, a mass of autobiography written by ordinary women, but "the historical communities in which women write, their choices to join different communities or to alter their given relation to a community in profound ways, and their relation to the male writers whose works have come to represent 'autobiography' have made their work obscure to scholars engaged in theorizing the form and mapping the canon."[1] This has certainly been the case as far as studies of emigrant autobiography are concerned; there are autobiographies that are touchstones for arguments about western women—Elinore Pruitt Stewart's narrative is a good example—but though such texts have achieved a level of recognition in the field, they are considered only within the category of western or pioneer women's

---

1. Leigh Gilmore, *Autobiographics: A Feminist Theory of Women's Self-Representation*, 5.

writing. None has achieved canonical status within the field of autobiography criticism.

The last twenty years have produced some strongly defined traditions of reading women's autobiography. There has been a powerful focus on the ways in which women have been restricted, if not silenced, by the limited range of autobiographical expression available to them. In the following passage from *A Poetics of Women's Autobiography,* Sidonie Smith summarizes the range of obstacles facing the female autobiographer:

> [T]he woman who writes autobiography is doubly estranged when she enters the autobiographical contract. . . . [S]he approaches her storytelling as one who speaks from the margins of autobiographical discourse and on the outskirts of it . . . [and] Since autobiography is a public expression, she speaks before and to "man." Attuned to the ways in which women have been dressed up for public exposure, attuned also to the price women pay for public self-disclosure, the autobiographer reveals in her speaking posture and narrative structure her understanding of the possible readings she will receive from a public that has the power of her reputation in its hands.[2]

One way to move out from behind this identification of women's autobiography as disabled has been to concentrate on those autobiographies that reached publication and to investigate the ways in which tensions around prescribed roles are marked within such texts. Thus, until recently, it has been the practice of many critics of emigrant women's autobiographical writing to focus on what these writers have not managed to write. There has been a strong strand in the field that has focused on suppression and concealment in emigrant diaries, as a function of patriarchal relations. Kathleen A. Boardman, for example, in discussing diaries of the overland trails, identifies the texts as "fragmented, misleading or cryptic." "What," she asks, "were they aiming to accomplish and what kinds of questions were they confronting or ignoring?" Suzanne Bunkers, an important critic of nineteenth-century western diaries written by Anglo

---

2. Sidonie Smith, *A Poetics of Women's Autobiography,* 49.

women, raises the same kind of question: "What do Women REALLY mean?"[3]

For some critics of autobiography, Boardman's and Bunkers' questions are naive. There is no experience, no meaning that can be gleaned, no "clarifying moment" in Joan Scott's words, that will deliver a synthesizing conclusion about emigrant women's lives: as Donna Haraway writes, "What counts as experience is never prior to the particular social occasions, the discourses and the other practices through which experience becomes articulated." In any case, the very nature of language dictates that "embedded in the text lie alternative or defined identities that constantly subvert any pretensions to truthfulness."[4] As strategies in which critics try to divine what autobiographers "really mean" have come into question, emigrant women's diaries seem to have attracted less attention; if the diaries cannot help us to understand pioneering, it seems they have little other interest.

The practice of conceiving of women autobiographers as "outlaws"—as Leigh Gilmore puts it—from a "law of genre" suggests that they never participate, through their writing, in the creation of cultural understandings of events and phenomena.[5] Yet emigrant women's autobiographical writing speaks directly to popular understandings of the major national and international phenomenon of the nineteenth and early twentieth centuries: mass migration. Furthermore, it strains against a reading defined by gender alone: its participation within emigration discourse tends to muffle gender difference, to privilege the progress of the individual (male or female), and to valorize a practice of candor about day-to-day life and gender relations.

Scholars have tended to focus on questions about the nature of women's participation in pioneering rather than on questions of genre. In the introduction to the reissue of the first volume of Kenneth L. Holmes's compilation of emigrant narrative, *Covered Wagon Women*, for example, Anne M. Butler focuses on the long-standing question

---

3. Kathleen A. Boardman, "Paper Trail: Diaries, Letters and Reminiscences of the Overland Journey West," 182; Suzanne Bunkers, "What Do Women REALLY Mean? Thoughts on Women's Diaries and Lives."
4. Joan W. Scott, "The Evidence of Experience," 35; Donna Haraway, *Simians, Cyborgs and Women*, 113; Smith, *Poetics*, 5.
5. Gilmore, *Autobiographics*, 21.

of how much women embraced the life of the West: "The more we know, the harder it seems to be to pinpoint the meaning of life for pioneer women in the American West. Did migrant women look to the West with quavering fear or joyful anticipation?" Butler's question is difficult to answer, not only for its preoccupation with truth-finding but also because the texts under consideration are engaged in a different discussion, one focused on the narration of emigration. The narrative of emigration describes setting out from home, arrival, and the recovery and accommodation to a "new home." It was specifically, as Cinthia Gannett has pointed out, the "massive dislocations and disconnections caused by waves of immigration to American shores and by westward expansion [that] cut women off from their primary female-based discursive networks and affiliative bonds" that produced a mass of letters, journal-letters, memoirs, and autobiographies of the emigrant experience.[6]

One might argue that movement in various forms structures all autobiographical narrative, whether this takes the form of physical movement, a dramatic change of life, or a profound psychological shift. Sidonie Smith imagines the very impulse to write autobiography as a physical movement: "Some women did not stay in their appointed narrative silence, but trespassed upon the grounds of the autobiographical 'I.'" Still, the particular and very common occasion of movement through emigration produced an autobiographical discourse with particular emphases: though emigration was a large-scale phenomenon—and was always presented as such in emigrant autobiographical writing—it was represented through the actions of a single individual or a family, the establishing of a new home and the struggling back to equilibrium. The emigrant experience was produced in published and unpublished letters, in travel narratives, in guides to emigration, in autobiographies that contained a jumble of forms, in tracts and advertisements for new colonies. It was indeed the very ubiquity of the descriptions of emigration that necessitated what Steve Clark calls "hyper-empiricism." Identifying themselves as "true pictures" of a special life-event, autobiographical narratives registered truth by insisting on the record of that which might be proved: in Stephen Fender's

---

6. Anne M. Butler, Introduction, 1; Cinthia Gannett, *Gender and the Journal: Diaries and Academic Discourse*, 135.

words, "the concrete . . . the useful . . . the material evidence of actual experience."[7]

While in other autobiographical contexts the detail of domestic affairs is generally considered too insignificant for inclusion, in emigrant narratives the home that has been left behind, and, by contrast, the progress of life of the new home, lie at the heart of the matter. George Poulett Scrope, an active promoter of emigration in the 1830s, makes the family central to his justification for emigration in his introduction to his collection of emigrant letters, *Letters from Poor Persons Who Emigrated Last Year to Canada and the United States:* "In this country a family, instead of being a burthen to a man is a source of profit and wealth to him as well as domestic happiness." The same emphasis on domestic felicity is evident in the comments of his correspondents. James Treasure writes: "I am going to build me a house this fall is I live. And if I staid at Corsley I never should have had nothing."[8]

While some theorists of women's autobiography have used domestic processes (especially spinning and weaving) to theorize women's writing, there is a strong, even dominant, strand within autobiographical criticism that regards the writing of domestic detail in ambivalent terms. Jane Marcus, for example, writes of women autobiographers retreating—"re/signing"—into the invisibility of the domestic: "enacting a deliberate resignation from the public world and patriarchal history, which had already erased or was expected to erase their names and their words, . . . they re/signed their private lives into domestic discourse." In Marcus's discussion, the organization of an autobiography around the routine of everyday life is the consigning of oneself to silence.[9] There are, of course, more affirmative readings of autobiographies of domestic life, which tend to interpret the description of domestic work in relation to a separate interior space of female expe-

---

7. Smith, *Subjectivity, Identity and the Body*, 25; Steve Clark, ed., *Travel Writing and Empire: Postcolonial Theory in Transit*, 2; Stephen Fender, *Sea Changes: British Emigration and American Literature*, 106, 79–80. It was, of course, a convention of emigrant narrative to advertise itself as a "true picture" and to include in titles terms such as "observations" and "notes" that emphasize knowledge gained from experience. See Fender, *Sea Changes*, 79–80 for a discussion of this point.

8. George Poulett Scrope, *Extracts of Letters from Poor Persons who Emigrated Last Year to Canada and the United States*, 13–14.

9. Jane Marcus, "'Invisible Mediocrity': The Private Selves of Public Women," 114.

rience and contact. Emigrant autobiography, however, asks us to read the domestic as of central significance to the project of emigration.

Of course, to consider emigrant women's texts as *only* explicable in terms of emigration discourse would be to diminish them. To quote Donna Haraway again, "the text is always and already enmeshed in contending practices and hopes." Though scholars since Myres have noted the importance of emigration discourse in forming the understandings by emigrants of the move they were making, the "contending practice" within which the narratives of female emigrants are often currently considered is that of travel writing. Brigitte Georgi-Findlay, for example, writing recently in the wake of new western history and drawing on the colonial discourse criticism of, in particular, Sara Mills, subsumes the (published) autobiographical writing of emigrant settlers such as Caroline Kirkland and Eliza Farnham within the discourse of travel writing. It is certainly the case that some middle-class emigrants recast their experiences as a trip—Frances Trollope's *Domestic Manners of the Americans* is a good example—and many of the texts of well-educated emigrant settlers who published their "adventures" intersperse the account of a migration undertaken for economic motives with episodes of leisured observation. As John Thurston argues in an essay about Canadian autobiography in the early nineteenth century, emigration and travel narratives frequently interlock.[10]

More generally, there is no clear line to be drawn between these different forms of movement as they actually take place. As Stephen Fender writes, some emigrants (like travelers) planned a move "that was temporary from its outset: perhaps they had wanted to see something of the world, or to accumulate a specified amount of money." Some travelers, on the other hand, like emigrants, worked in the region they chose to visit. The demands of writing about emigration and travel are similar in many respects: both require, for example, the proof of observations through minute detail. Both provide reflections on the writer's experience of roughing it in an unfamiliar place; both prompt questions on the writer's savoir-faire in dealing with alien situations. In

---

10. Haraway, *Simians*, 124; Myres, *Westering Women*, 14; Georgi-Findlay, *The Frontiers of Women's Writing*; Sara Mills, *Discourses of Difference: An Analysis of Women's Travel Writing and Colonialism*; John Thurston, "Ideologies of I: The Ideological Function of Life Writing in Upper Canada."

either case, we wonder, as Clark suggests, at the motives and personality that have precipitated this casting away from home, and demand, too, that the writer show us clearly the relationship between the place reached and the place left behind.[11]

The writing of experiences of travel and emigration, however, are not the same and some differences are crucial. While both signal involvement in processes of colonial exploration and discovery, emigrant writing records a highly unsettling and unfinished process whereby one life is abandoned and another new life begun. Eric Hobsbawn has written of the ambiguities of migration that it "is not necessarily exile, though there is no sharp line that separates the economic migrant, even the one who eventually stays, from the exile who cannot go back but wants to."[12] There is the explicit issue of economic need for the emigrant, and of his or her superfluity, in economic terms, in the country left behind. Most obviously, there is no immediate prospect of returning home, as from a pleasure trip.

In looking at two very different emigrant autobiographies, the "Memorandum," written between 1835 and 1848, of Kitturah Penton Belknap (1820–1913), which was produced as a record for her family, and Susanna Moodie's *Roughing It in the Bush*, published in 1852, a narrative of emigration from England to Upper Canada during the 1830s published in London, I want to consider the way in which the very different circumstances described in these texts are, in important ways, organized according to contemporary conventions of understanding emigration. Belknap's narrative was a family record while Moodie's was published by Richard Bentley, an arbiter of British high culture of considerable stature, but I do not want, at this stage, to revisit discussions of the distinctions between private and published texts. The distinction is always difficult to draw, given the assumption of audience in the most secret writings, and the use of diaries and letters to create autobiography. In a field such as emigrant writing, it is especially difficult to make such distinctions. "Private" letters and journal letters for families were often apparently intended for reading by a circle extending well beyond the immediate family, by future generations, even, in the case of Martha Farnsworth, by her Sunday school

---

11. Fender, *Sea Changes*, 3; Clark, *Travel Writing and Empire*, 2–4.
12. Eric Hobsbawm, Introduction to "Exile: A Keynote Address," 61.

pupils. Letters and diaries were also an important element of published promotional material about emigration. Published reminiscences were sometimes reworked letters and journals; sometimes, as indeed in the case of Moodie herself, they were a conflation of different kinds of material.[13]

Nor do I want to emphasize the variable of class difference in these two texts, except to point out that the experience of emigration authorized the range of women who were literate. As with the autobiographical writing of male emigrants, who commonly refer to themselves as writers with no pretensions to education, female emigrants exhibit little self-consciousness in writing their experiences on grounds of lack of literary training. It is interesting to note that the letters home that were published in Britain were not edited for misspelling, lack of punctuation, or nonstandard syntax. One of the interests, then, of these emigrant texts lies in the way that they disrupt the categories of middle- and working-class in terms of autobiography. The narrative of Belknap seems to contradict, for example, Regenia Gagnier's argument that working-class autobiography works in a plotless mode quite different from the "bourgeois climax and resolution/ action and interaction model [that] presupposes an active and reactive world not always accessible to working-class writers"; it adheres to a well-defined plot within emigration discourse. Meanwhile, Moodie's *Roughing It* is, almost notoriously, not the text of repressed Victorian middle-class womanhood that many of the studies of Victorian women's autobiography lead one to expect, but rather a narrative that parades a heroic self thwarted not only by fellow settlers but by her husband as well.[14]

---

13. Martha Farnsworth, *Plains Woman: The Diary of Martha Farnsworth, 1882–1922*, x. The complications surrounding the publication of Moodie's narrative make her text an unstable one. For opposing discussions on the form of the text itself, see Carl Ballstadt, "Editor's Introduction," xxiv–xxx, and John Thurston, *The Work of Words: The Writing of Susanna Strickland Moodie*, 134–38.

14. Regenia Gagnier, *Subjectivities: A History of Self-Representation in Britain*, 43. For discussions of autobiogaphy that stress the problem of writing autobiography for women, see, for example, Corbett, *Representing Femininity;* Felicity Nussbaum, "Eighteenth-Century Women's Autobiographical Commonplaces," in *The Private Self*, edited by Shari Benstock (Chapel Hill: University of North Carolina Press, 1988); Carla Kaplan's Introduction in *The Erotics of Talk: Women's Writing and Feminist Paradigms* (New York: Oxford University Press, 1996); and Valerie Saunders, *The Private Lives of Victorian Women: Autobiography in Nineteenth-Century England* (New York: St. Martin's Press, 1989). In the context of a discus-

Instead, I want to consider both texts' engagement with narratives of emigration, starting with their position within the literature engaged in discussing the justification for moving to the backwoods of North America, in making a judgment on the worthiness of the enterprise, and in advising prospective emigrants on how to make the journey and choose a place to settle. There is a mass of literature here: Wilbur Shepperson, for example, estimates that 250 works about emigration to the United States were published by Britons alone between 1836 and 1860. In general, the texts that appeared in Britain, the United States, and Canada were differently nuanced: very broadly, British emigration literature tended to emphasize the prospective emigrant and his family having fallen on hard times and being forced to begin a new life; Canadian texts typically worried at issues around the attractiveness of the colony as a prospect for emigrants; while U.S. texts usually hit a higher pitch of nationalist sentiment, exalting the "abode of benevolent hearts and intelligent minds" available to emigrants. In addition, different publications placed varying emphases on particular elements—issues of political systems or details of the fertility of particular regions, for example—according to their audience.[15]

---

sion of Susanna Moodie, we should also take note of "The Silent Scribe: Susanna and 'Black Mary,'" *International Journal of Canadian Studies* 11 (spring 1995): 249–60, in which Gillian Whitlock draws to our attention the impact of "the surge in abolitionist and early feminist discourses of the 1820s and 1830s" that made "different voices available" to female autobiographers (251).

15. Wilbur Shepperson, *Promotion of British Emigration by Agents for American Lands, 1840–1860*, 14; John Newhall, *Sketches of Iowa or the Emigrant's Guide*, 252. There is a mass of emigration literature. The following is a list of some interesting examples of different strands within Anglo-American emigration discourse: examples of British government-supported tracts are Thomas Rolph, *Comparative Advantages between the United States and Canada for New Settlers* (London, 1842) and Henry Boulton, *A Short Sketch of the Province of Upper Canada* (London, 1826); Morris Birkbeck's colony in Illinois, which generated a furious controversy over actual conditions, was promoted in Morris Birkbeck, *Letters from Illinois* and described by, among others, John Woods in *Two Years' Residence in the Settlement on the English Prairie in the Illinois County* (London, 1822). British apologists for emigration on grounds of political principle include Robert Holditch, *The Emigrant's Guide to the United States of America* (London, 1818), and John Knight, *The Emigrant's Best Instructor* (Manchester, 1814). The travel tale crossed with emigration guide was an important form, as, for example, in John Regan's *The Emigrant's Guide to the Western States of America* and John Howison's *Sketches of Upper Canada Domestic, Local and Characteristic*. There were fictive guides such as John Galt's *Bogle Corbet or The Emigrants* (London, 1831) and William Dar-

In the hundreds of discussions about emigration that appeared in the early and mid-nineteenth century, the focus lay upon the single emigrant and his—or sometimes her—response to this most extreme change of circumstances in which an old life was thrown off and a new life begun.[16] Such comments as the following were common:

> It may be well for the emigrant to make up his mind philosophically in the start, to cheerfully undergo these things, throw aside some of his former habits, forget some of his former easy blessings, and thus be prepared the better to accommodate himself to the new state of things which he is about to experience.

> The effect is very great indeed and you must be armed against it. All is new: you have all at once lost the sight of a 1000 objects that were become dear to you without you at all perceiving it. The voices that you hear are all new to you; the accustomed nods and smiles of neighbors, which made without your perceiving it, a portion of the happiness of your life, are gone forever.[17]

Fender, in *Sea Changes*, formulates this emphasis on an inescapable process of rupture, grinding labor, and eventual accommodation by reference to the stages of "the special drama of the rite of passage:" the

---

ling Stewart's *Sketches of Canadian Life, Lay and Ecclesiastical* (London, 1849). Indicative examples of American emigrant's guides to the Midwest are: Samuel R. Brown, *The Western Gazetteer or Emigrant's Directory* (Auburn, 1817), Daniel Curtiss, *Western Portraiture and Emigrant's Guide: A Description of Wisconsin, Illinois and Iowa;* William Darby, *The Emigrant's Guide* (New York, 1818); John B. Newhall, *Sketches of Iowa or the Emigrant's Guide;* and J. M. Peck, *A New Guide for Emigrants to the West.* See, for a discussion of guides to the Gold Rush West, Ray Allen Billington, "Books That Won the West: The Guidebooks of the Forty-Niners and Fifty-Niners," *American West* 4 (August 1967): 25–32, 72–76. British promotional texts, unless they had a particular republican agenda (as in William Cobbett, *Emigrant's Guide in Ten Letters*), colonial interests (as in the tract of the Anglo-Canadian agent, Thomas Rolph, *Comparative Advantages*), or a strongly Tory outlook (as in Henry Boulton, *A Short Sketch of the Province of Upper Canada for the Information of the Labouring poor throughout England* [London, 1826]) often made no distinction between Canada and the United States. See, for example, Scrope, *Extracts of Letters,* 9.

16. The texts written for a female audience during this period tended to be written in the form of travelogue, as in Catherine Stewart, *New Homes in the West,* or Eliza R. Steele, *A Summer Journey in the West.*

17. Curtiss, *Western Portraiture and Emigrant's Guide,* 204; Cobbett, *Emigrant's Guide in Ten Letters,* 147.

trauma of separation, the borderland state of new arrival, the psychological effort of adapting to change. The argument is helpful in drawing to our attention the way in which, wherever the emigrant appears, he or she is narrated as engaged in a common experience understood by everyone as likely to take a particular and predictable form of test of the individual's ability to survive the traumatic upheaval.[18]

Such a narrative practice recalls the world of travelers, explorers, and adventurers, and the narratives that attempted to write the strangeness of the New World. The narratives of emigration to North America in the early nineteenth century, however, placed particular emphasis on claims of a need to prove what North America was really like for the unexceptional emigrant: the narrative of emigration was a practice of writing that positioned itself in opposition to descriptions provided by unscrupulous agents or writers who might be suspected of having overactive imaginations or ulterior motives. The provision of proof demanded the exercise of a high level of candor about everyday experience from emigrants who had already reached North America, a candor often expressed in innumerable lists. Thomas Hunt, quoted by Scrope, illustrates the point: "We are in a good country for poor folks; we have plenty of good fire and grog. Wheat 4s per bushel, good boiling peas 3s 6d. Rye 3s. Buckwheat 2s 6d. Indian Corn 2s 6d. Oats 2s. Potatoes 1s 3d. Rum 10d per quart . . . We make our own sugar, our own soap, candles, and bake good light bread."[19]

Apparent artlessness also enhanced the value of the words of those assumed to be too unsophisticated to varnish the truth. The narrative, for example, of Rebecca Burlend published in 1848, *A True Picture of Emigration*, though the work of the daughter of a yeoman farmer, made no qualifying comment either on the significance of the writer's class or her gender. Even comments that strained against the main message of promotional texts were left uncensored; the very common point made by emigrant letter writers whose missives were often printed in such promotional texts that the experience of emigration could not be written until there was good news to write lends a peculiar force to the statement of trials suffered. James Grayston, writing in 1878, comments thus: "I dare say you will think it strange that I have not

18. Fender, *Sea Changes*, 13.
19. Scrope, *Extracts of Letters*, 26–27.

wrote to you before now, but I have been waiting to send you better news." Elizabeth Watson, quoted in a collection of emigrant letters edited by Benjamin Smith of Mountfield, strikes a similar note: "I would have wrote before this, but could not write you pleasant news; as Stephen has been so unhappy in a strange country, but is now contented and doing well."[20]

The writing of emigration in the early and mid-nineteenth century was, then, in many ways a democratic practice of writing; it was certainly one that favored a close grain of reference to the everyday. The experience was organized in a predictable form and the story of emigration was very much focused on the fate of individual families. None of these aspects was unfriendly to the interventions of female autobiographers.

Let me return to my examples. Kitturah Belknap's narrative deals with her life as a second-generation Irish-Scandinavian emigrant in a succession of moves from Ohio to Oregon. It opens when she is fifteen with a passage reviewing her parents' life to date. Then, in 1841, she begins the writing of a series of lengthy retrospective entries prompted by important events and transitions and interspersed with passages written much later. The "Memorandum" was first printed in an edited form in 1977 by Glenda Riley in the *Annals of Iowa*. (Riley used the figure of Belknap as a representative frontierswoman in her early work). Two years later, a more complete version, this time without standardized spelling and punctuation, was printed in a compendium of western women's autobiographical writing edited by Cathy Luchetti and Carol Olwell: *Women of the West*.[21]

Both of these versions of the journal make explicit the editors' sense of it as a document that authenticates and supports an understanding of the pioneering experience shared by editors and readers,

---

20. Grayston is quoted in Charlotte Erickson, *Invisible Immigrants: The Adaptation of English and Scottish Immigrants in Nineteenth-Century America*, 218; Benjamin Smith of Mountfield, *24 Letters from Labourers in America to Their Friends in England*, 1, 19.

21. For details of the formation of Belknap's record, see Kenneth L. Holmes, ed., *Covered Wagon Women: Diaries and Letters from the Western Trails*, 189. The diary is also reprinted in Holmes but this version edits out the passages that were not written soon after the events to which they refer. Riley discusses Belknap in *Frontierswomen: The Iowa Experience*, 4, 24–25; "'Not Gainfully Employed': Women on the Iowa Frontier, 1833–1870," *Pacific Historical Review* 49, no. 2 (May 1980), 245, 246, 263.

and that provides evidence of women's whole-hearted participation in the project. Indeed, in the *Annals of Iowa,* the journal's genuine and representative quality and the transparency of its meaning are drawn to our attention in the drawings used to illustrate the material objects mentioned in the text. Luchetti and Olwell's volume presents to the reader photographs of other—we are to presume, in some sense, interchangeable—emigrant families. The value of the narrative is asserted, in both cases, by reference to the conventions of the grand narrative of frontier: covered wagons are mentioned twice in Riley's brief introduction along with Belknap's experience of "wrest[ing] a living from the wilderness" of Iowa. Belknap's working-class origins, cited in Luchetti and Olwell's gloss, further qualify her as a true pioneer. She is the true pioneer defined in 1986 by Fairbanks as "plain and practical."[22]

Such a reading of an autobiographical narrative as the additional flesh that we can arrange on the bones of a familiar history (albeit a history now superseded in scholarly terms) is, of course, anathema to recent autobiographical criticism, for which the unstable quality of the written and read text makes untenable any proposition of a relationship between an outside world generalized in the writing of history and the integrated self conjured up in autobiography. But the method that Riley and Luchetti and Olwell adopt, and indeed the way in which they produce Belknap's text for us, have the virtue of drawing Belknap's method to our attention by replicating it: this is a method of writing which reverses the conventional model of autobiography, showing no interest in those assumptions about the self and its relationship to society that the recent criticism of autobiography has sought to deconstruct.

Episodes from Belknap's childhood, far from narrating the development of a unique consciousness, place her life within a seamless process of transgenerational migration:

> [My mother and father] Emegrated to the State of Ohio in 1818 Crossed the Alegany mountains with a waggon and a three horse team [what you would call a spike team] there was three familys 17 souls in all at Pitsburg they put the familys on board A flat boat and they rowed themselves to Cincinnatti on the bank of the Ohio.

22. Glenda Riley, "Farm Life on the Frontier: The Diary of Kitturah Belknap," 31; Fairbanks, *Prairie Women,* 66.

> They sold their boat and loaded their early possessions in the waggon the Smallest children rode and the rest went on foot . . .[23]

Belknap's experience has a history, but it is of the process of emigration. She does not extend her range of reference beyond the dimension of family by, say, citing economic cause or social context. This is a narrative so focused on the situation (rather than the uniqueness) of the individual that change only occurs when decisions are made by individuals and not in response to external causes or pressures; there is no key to the links between events except the passing of time. Thus, new sections of Belknap's journal begin with such phrases as "and now": "and now I was over fifteen years old and I determined to help my Father clear up that farm: we was only five in the family one brother four years younger than my self. Mother was Strong and well so she could do the work in the house and I set out to work with the little boys I soon found that I could make a pretty good hand."[24]

Neither the writer's motivation in working outside nor custom itself in farm work are glossed for the reader here. We are left to infer that necessity, custom, and individual preference are unified in every decision and action. Where the modern reader is accustomed to following the development of a unique personality, Belknap's narrative requires us, instead, to remember for ourselves the familiar constituents of the pioneer character: decisiveness and stoicism in the face of difficulty, prudence, and industry.

The "true picture" of the practice and efficacy of such characteristics forms a central strand in emigrant autobiography. Here we have Belknap illustrating the concentrated practical effort that was believed to ensure success and indeed the pleasures of a day-to-day pragmatism:

> Now I want to tell you how I make a substitute for fruit. Take a nice large watermelon, cut it in two and scrape the inside fine to the hard rind. It will be mostly water and when you get a lot prepared, strain it thru a sieve or a cloth. Squeeze out all the juice you can, and boil the juice down to syrup. I then took out some good musk melons and crab apples, about half and half, and put them in the syrup and cooked them down till they were done, being careful

23. Kitturah Belknap, "Keturah Penton Belknap," 127.
24. Ibid., 132.

not to mash them. Put in a little sugar to take the flat off and cook it down a little more and you have nice preserves to last all winter (and they are fine when you have nothing better and sugar 12 1/2 c a lb. and go forty miles for it).[25]

It is, of course, this writing of the detail of day-to-day work that was so exciting to the scholars of pioneer women and their writing in the 1970s and 1980s. It constituted the proof of a general principle that, where women were offered an opportunity to do "real" work (in the rural backwoods at least), they could match male heroism in "wresting a living out of the wilderness"; this is the "healthy and useful domesticity" valorized by women's historians of the West. And indeed, in emigrant narratives, though the precise content of tasks may have gendered associations—plowing as opposed to cooking, say—the meaning given to tasks is not strongly differentiated on grounds of gender; on the contrary, the issue is the material success marked by the amount of work done. The list of achievements made by William Clements, for example, an emigrant to Upper Canada quoted in a British emigration tract, illustrates his concentrated industry and the impetus provided by the new context: "I met with good friends that took me in; and I went to work at 6s per day and my board . . . And now I am going to work on my own farm of 50 acres, which I bought at £55, and I have 5 years to pay it in." The same point is made about the availability of work and the rewards of industry in Mary Sackett's journal, written between 1841 and 1842: "Oliver came home about 10, tackled the horses, and took Mama and Caroline over to the claim, so Dick and I am here alone. I mended my dress, then sewed a little on my patchwork, and then churned 5 or 6 pounds of first rate butter. Then I made a custard pudding and buttermilk cake, and boiled some potatoes for supper."[26]

In emigrant narrative, the rewards of emigration are often expressed in images of starvation and domestic plenty. Two of Scrope's correspondents make this point with particular clarity. William Snelgrove writes: "You have a good many cold bellies to go to bed with, I know, or things is greatly altered from the state that it was when I was with

25. Riley, "Farm Life on the Frontier," 42.
26. Jeffrey, *Frontier Women*, 23; William Clements quoted in Scrope, *Extracts of Letters*, 14; Mary Sackett, "Journal 1841–2," 38.

you. But if you were with us, if you liked, for 3 1/2 pence your belly would be so warm that you would not know the way to bed." John Down makes a similar comment: "A farmer took me one day in his wagon into the country . . . and I dined with him . . . they had on the table puddings, pyes, and fruit of all kind that was in season, and preserves, pickles, vegetables, meat and every thing that a person could wish, and the servants set down at the same table with their masters." The detail of available food in women's narratives may be more precise, but the emphasis on listing a superfluity of food to express the contrast between old home and new is the same:

> Now I suppose you Would wish to know What We Had for Dinner . . . Well We had Rosted Ducks . . . and Fat Chickens And Rosted pig and Sausages And green Apl pie and Mince pies and Custard pies and Cakes of difrent kindes Inglish goosburyes And Plums Blue And green gages And Siberia crab Apples And oregon Apples . . . Likewise Buter and Sturson pickls and Beet pickles And Sauce and Bread and Mashed potatoes and Oister pie. And Coffe and Tea to be shore. Now I must tel you what other preserves that I have. I have peaches And citrons And Sweet Aples. Crab Aples Jelley and Tomatoes And Mince And pairs and Aple Butter. And now I will tel you of the Rest of my Winter Suplies.[27]

This is certainly not all there is to say about emigrant women's writing about housewifery, which, as we shall see, has many resonances. But within the conventions of the description of everyday life within emigrant narrative, we are not asked to differentiate between the signs of economic security and independence—the primary motive for emigration—on grounds of gender.

However, when in emigrant women's writing the values of industry and prudence and indeed the self-congratulatory expression of independence characteristic of emigrant narrative seep into the description of realms of experience to which they are not usually applied, the effect is both striking and unusual. This is most evidently the case with regard to the writing of marriage. Belknap's account of the marriage that immediately precedes her move to Iowa beginning with a courtship strikes a highly pragmatic note:

---

27. William Snelgrove and John Down quoted in Scrope, *Extracts of Letters,* 30, 21–22; Abigail Malick in Schlissel, *Far from Home,* 21.

[The] next one that appeared on the sene was a rich young doctor but he was too lazy to practice and he did not know how to do anything else. he had been raised in the South and had Slaves to wait on him So he was no good.

the next was an old Batchelor with a head as red as fire. he had two Sections of Land and lots of money. he Said it was waiting to be at my disposal but he was too stingy to get himself a decent suit of cloaths. So he was shipped prety quick. but not long after one pleasant Sabbath morning we saw a man comeing walking up the road dressed up with a Stovepipe Hat on and I said to Mother, their he comes now . . . [28]

This is not the description of courtship that we expect of a mid-nineteenth-century woman's text. It may be that Belknap offers the passage in witty contrast to the decorous courtship patterns represented in the fictions of her day—popular magazines found wide audiences in the West—where choices were wont to be considered in rather more covert forms.[29] The event is also apparently open to interpretation through quite other conventions. The succession of laughable suitors, each too this or too that, followed by the instantly recognizable chosen one, is a very familiar narrative convention of popular storytelling, as is the broad humor of the conversation in which Belknap and her mother eye up the possible candidates for marriage. Such is the informality of emigrant narrative. Most interesting, however, is the way in which the marriage is perceived as a project characterized by exactly the same processes of independent decision-making and corrective action as were argued to drive economic prosperity.

In some ways, of course, ideas of marriage and emigration operated in a comfortable unison: the idea of marriage itself as a rite of passage, beginning with a loss of contact with loved ones, as well as offering the hope of absolute fulfillment (and the specter of miserable failure), was a common one in the mid-nineteenth century and easily matched by hopes and fears about emigration. We find emigration referred to as leaving the same "world" of social contact from which newly married couples were exhorted to withdraw, as, for example, in the 1876 memoir of William Nowlin (an autobiography probably ghost-written

28. Belknap, "Keturah Penton Belknap," 134.
29. For a discussion of the range and use of magazines in the rural West, see Riley, *The Female Frontier,* 149–51, 174–75.

by his sister), *The Bark-Covered House,* which opens the account of their experience with: "We left our friends weeping, for, as they expressed it, they thought we were going 'out of the world.'" Nor was the parallel between marriage and emigration lost on writers of the mid-nineteenth-century cultural mainstream. One of Lydia Sigourney's most commercially successful poems, "The Western Home," for example, winds together the two occasions of loss. "Women's love" makes the loss of home and the move to "stranger-bands" a worthy sacrifice:

> How beautiful is woman's love!
> That from the play-place of its birth,
> The sister's smile, the parent's hearth,
> The earliest warmth of friendship true,
> The holy church where first it knew
> The balm of Christ's baptismal dew,
> To stranger-bands, to stranger-home,
> O'er desert clime, o'er ocean foam,
> Goes forth in perfect trust, to prove
> The untried toil, the burdening care,
> The peril and the pang to dare.

In texts such as Sigourney's, however, marriage into the backwoods was usually portrayed as a high point of self-sacrifice on women's part; the test of her "perfect trust" in her husband. And of course many images of women in the backwoods emphasized their vulnerability in the face of howling savages and dark wildernesses.[30]

Emigrant women's narrative tends not, however, to use this model of passively sacrificial behavior. Some emigrant autobiography produces narratives of marriage written wholly in terms of the behaviors valorized by emigration discourse: self-sufficiency and decision-making based on experience. Henrietta Jones, for example, in *Sketches from Real Life,* published in 1898, organizes the story of her successive migrations and marriages in a form that insistently links her ability as an emigrant to act independently to her independence within her marriages:

---

30. William Nowlin, *The Bark-Covered House or Back in the Woods Again,* 10; Lydia Sigourney, *The Western Home and Other Poems,* 27–28. The relationship between marriage and emigration is framed within the *rite de passage* in Fender, *Sea Changes,* 139–40, and within the practices of commercialism in Gillian Whitlock, "Outlaws of the Text," in *The Post-Colonial Studies Reader,* edited by Bill Ashcroft, Gareth Griffiths, and Helen Tiffin (London: Routledge, 1995), 351.

When we were alone in the evening husband said, "I don't like the idea of you raising poultry. Why do you wish to do it?" "To have ready money for small demands," I replied. "What will your St. Louis friends say?" "They may say what they choose. I am not ashamed to have them know I am faithful to my duties here as I was there." "Why do you consider it a duty?" he asked. "Because I know how to do it, and there is nothing but pride in the way of doing it, and it will save you one hundred and twenty dollars." . . . In a week I was mistress of the poultry yard. The 1st of March following, when the overplus was sold, the poultry yard had a credit of ninety-nine dollars and fifty-five cents and I had the satisfaction of hearing my husband say, "The farm has met its own expenses this year." Neighbors asked the secret of my success in the poultry line, and I answered, "Constant watchfulness and care."

Emigrant independence and pragmatism is perhaps more frequently written into women's autobiography through the relegation of the husband to the background of the narrative. This has been picked up in discussions of another emigrant autobiography: Caroline Kirkland's *A New Home, Who'll Follow?* Caroline Gebhard argues that Kirkland masks the details of "her own marriage and motherhood" in order to maintain the privacy appropriate to a woman of her class. David Leverenz finds instead the self-obsession of a "Miss Manners of Michigan": "Not until the tenth chapter do we learn that she has her children with her, though she has introduced her prized greyhound . . . Where is her husband in all this?" My suggestion here is that emigration discourse privileged the dynamic pursuit of independence above all else; it is the progress of the individual in the circumstances of emigration that dominates the text.[31]

Of course, it has long been argued that the writing of emigration did not permit the expression of criticism of its dominant values. Certainly, many critics of emigrant women's diaries have started their reading from a position of assuming the sex of these writers hampered them in expressing a predictable sense of trauma at being uprooted. Gayle R. Davis, for example, has argued that diary writing among emigrants

31. Henrietta Jones, *Sketches of Real Life*, 147–48; Caroline Gebhard, "Comic Displacement: Caroline M. Kirkland's Satire on Frontier Democracy in *A New Home, Who'll Follow?*" 158; David Leverenz, *Manhood and the American Renaissance*, 156.

developed because "the move West took women who were accustomed to sharing intimate thoughts and feelings with beloved female companions to often very isolated regions where men were the large majority"; such conditions "threatened" their "identity."[32]

The passage in which Kitturah Belknap relates the death of a child is one that might easily be used to support such an argument. It does indeed produce a fissure within her writing of emigration as a progress of infinite possibility. It does, briefly and in opaque terms, express a broad dissatisfaction:

> I have had to pass thru another season of sorrow death has again entered our home this time it claimed little John for its victim, it was hard for me to give him up but dropsy on the brain ended its work in four short days. When our pastor was here a week before he thot the child was too good for this wicked world. but he little expected to be called to preach his funeral in less than one week. We are left again with one baby and I feel that my health is giving way, a bad cough and pain in my side is telling me that disease is making its inroads on my system.

Yet, this kind of narrative turn is characteristic of emigrant narratives: they focus on the critical moments in the narrative of emigration at which participants must strive to prove their mettle: the journey, the arrival (often at night), the first home, the first winter, the first harvest, and so on. Emigrant women's autobiography often adds to these its own tropes by which to define the experience as a series of tests of the individual emigrant: the first attempts to bake, the need for the writer to work in the fields, the fearful moment of isolation in nature, the sickness of the husband, and, as here, the sickness of children. Successive periods of discouragement at setbacks are part of the structure of the emigrant experience as it was popularly written, if not a necessary prelude to success.[33]

Fender frames such tests as part of the "purifying trials of emigration" of a "conversion experience" "charged with intense drama." This is a construction of emigration narrative that he traces to the practices of rigorous self-examination characteristic of Puritan culture, but, as

---

32. Gayle R. Davis, "Writing for Good Reason," 8.
33. Belknap, "Keturah Penton Belknap," 139.

Fender argues, the experience of emigration is subsequently similarly cast as trial and recovery by emigrants generally; James Thorpe, for example, quoted in a collection of letters, *Twenty Four Letters from Labourers in America to their Friends* edited by Benjamin Smith and published in 1829, writes:

> I often look back on the scenes that we have passed through. While we were passing over the water, our sufferings were great; but that God, that is loving to all that trust in him, has brought us through. I will not grieve your hearts with all our sufferings, for my paper will not hold it . . . but this I can say, that we want for nothing; bless God for it; for we can buy a leg of mutton every day, and green peas or French beans brought to the door.[34]

Interestingly, Belknap was herself a devotee of the rather different practices of revivalism, in which the trials of the spirit and dramatic changes in the subject's psychological state were signs of grace, so there is perhaps a particular religious resonance within the expression of "sorror" in her "conversion experience" of emigration. Significant, too, in this context is the argument made by historians such as Barbara Epstein that a more particular opening for women existed within evangelistic practice of the mid-nineteenth century for bringing tensions within the domestic sphere to the surface.

Conversion, though, supposes an endpoint of acceptance and an evident assimilation into a set of beliefs—or at least an accommodation to the compensations of peas and beans "brought to the door"—but this is an effect that Belknap's narrative does not deliver. It is particularly interesting that it does not do so in the context of a description of the death of a child, for narratives of the death of children were, of course, among the great moral set-pieces of mid-nineteenth-century writing. The meaning to be derived from the deaths of fictional children such as Harriet Beecher Stowe's Eva or Charles Dickens's Little Nell was always clear. Likewise, in prescriptive literature for women, the illness of a child appears as a punishment for neglect of the duties of wifehood as in such mid-nineteenth-century texts as Sara Josepha Hale's *Keeping House and Housekeeping* and Eliza Follen's *Sketches of Married Life*.

34. James Thorpe in Smith, *24 Letters from Labourers*, 42.

By contrast, Belknap's description of her response is inconclusive in moral terms, and it is not positioned within any particular register of moral feeling. Characterized by shifts in tone, it has the flavor of an open-ended consideration of a painful circumstance. It is formal ("a season of sorror"), and elaborately expressed ("death has again entered our home"). It also uses the informal terms of everyday expression ("I feel that my health is giving way") and euphemism ("it was hard for me to give him up"). Certain matters—specifically her health—are signaled as important and yet their position in relation to her bereavement is not unambiguous.

Belknap's shifts in diction are not exceptional. In a comparable passage in Mollie Sanford's journal, we find the use of a number of stylistic strategies to convey unhappiness:

> Baby Charlie lies on Mother's breast, looking as pure and sweet as a cherub dropped from the skies, his night dress thrown from his shoulders, exposing his perfect limbs, his golden hair parted from his bonny brow, his dark eyelashes kissing his rosy cheek ... I do try to feel that it is all for the best to be away off here. I can see and feel that it chafes Mother's spirit. It worries her to think that we are in such straightened circumstances, but my father had to make a change.

The passage shows a shift between the language of sentiment in the conventional scene of the ailing angel of the first paragraph, to a discussion—equally intense—conducted in the language of everyday speech, in the second. In the latter, slightly different registers are adopted to convey the response she aspires to, then her mother's feelings, and finally the argument made by her father.[35]

The elusive quality of passages that deal with specific crises is matched in more general passages of comment on the whole experience of emigration that conclude narratives. For example, Harriet Noble's account of a migration from New York to Michigan in the 1820s, printed in Elizabeth Ellet's 1852 compendium, *Pioneer Women of the West,* includes a passage in a comparable vein:

---

35. Mollie Sanford, *Mollie: The Journal of Mollie Dorsey Sanford in Nebraska and Colorado Territories, 1857–1866,* 38.

> When I look back upon my life, and see the ups and down, the hardships and privations I have been called upon to endure, I feel no wish to be young again. I was in the prime of life when I came to Michigan—only twenty-one and my husband was thirty three. Neither of us knew the reality of hardship. Could we but have known what it was to be pioneers in a new country, we should never have had the courage to come; but I am satisfied that with all the disadvantages of raising a family in a new country, there is consolation in knowing that our children are prepared to brave the ills of life, I believe far better than they would have been had they never left New York.[36]

What is the substance of this tortuous statement? That Noble would not like to repeat the experience of resettlement in Michigan, even if, in doing so, she could regain the youth destroyed by the process? Or that her children have benefited from being withdrawn from New York because they could not otherwise have developed a resistance to the difficulties characteristic of Michigan?

Likewise, Rebecca Burlend, whose narrative epitomizes the success story of emigration, ends with the following: "If our success has been ultimately greater than at one time we anticipated, or even than that of many of our neighbors, as indeed it has, it must be borne in mind that our industry and perseverance has been unremitting. If our cattle and lands have kept increasing, that increase is but the reward for the numberless anxieties we have experienced, and the privations we have undergone. Few would undertake the latter to secure the former." Not only is there no clear moral import to Burlend's comments—the efficacy of "industry and perseverance" is emphasized, but not their virtue—but even her faint praises fail to recall the position of gratitude that might be attached to the prosperous life she has described. She has been changed by emigration, but that process is not summarized by a change in behavior readable in moral terms.[37]

This is a reflection, it seems, of the way in which emigration was perceived as a process with no fixed point of closure. Even in prosperity, even in their sense of their achievement as worthwhile in ab-

---

36. Elizabeth Ellet, *Pioneer Women of the West*, 395.
37. Rebecca Burlend, *A True Picture of Emigration*, 153.

solute terms, there was always the life left behind, forever unrecoverable, always the loss of institutions and people to give meaning to that achievement. Thus, far from it being difficult for women autobiographers to write dissatisfaction with the life of an emigrant, the way in which emigrant narrative tended to leave the jury out on an unequivocal judgment of the experience made its inclusion appropriate. At the same time, representations of the emigrant woman within the more general context of mid-nineteenth-century culture figured the holding of a quite separate view of emigration on women's part to that of men. It is with the working of these two strands of writing emigrant women's dissatisfaction together in mind that I want now to turn to the examination of Susanna Moodie's emigrant narrative.

Susanna Moodie (1803–1885) was born into a family of some social and intellectual ambition. When her father, Thomas Strickland, died in 1818, his estate collapsed, and the family was left in a deteriorating financial and a precarious social position. The Strickland sisters proceeded to write for annuals and magazines for small sums. In 1830, Susanna married John Dunbar Moodie, a half-pay officer who had returned to Britain from a sojourn in South Africa to find a wife. They left for Upper Canada in 1832. They were not successful emigrants; indeed, they were very unsuccessful ones in economic terms.[38]

First of all, what does Moodie's narrative have in common with Belknap's? Moodie's *Roughing It* exemplifies the generalized emphasis on character-building experience that we find in emigrant autobiography: the focus on rugged day-to-day trials and the emphasis on material hardship. As with all emigrant narratives, it insists on its purpose as a delivery of unmediated truth in order to inform (though recent research has, quite predictably, discovered that it did not do so: "If these sketches should prove the means of deterring one family from sinking their property and shipwrecking all their hopes, by going to reside in the backwoods of Canada, I shall consider myself amply repaid for revealing the secrets of the prison-house, and feel that I have not toiled and suffered in the wilderness in vain." The structure of the text is informal, incorporating fictional tales, poetry, and travelogue into

---

38. For good recent discussions of Moodie's life, see Michael A. Peterman, "Susanna Moodie"; Carl Ballstadt et al., *Susanna Moodie: Letters of a Lifetime;* and Thurston, *The Work of Words.*

the emigration narrative, though Moodie's experience of "the bush" is conceived, generally speaking, in the familiar form of a series of crises and problems.[39] When it was published, critics associated *Roughing It* with other emigration literature, and consequently judged its integrity as an accurate representation of a popular emigrant destination.[40]

What Moodie describes herself achieving through emigration, however, is measured less in terms of prosperity and independence (or, in her case, their notable absence) than of feminine nobility and wisdom. The level of candor that we find in emigrant autobiography is still there, but it is directed toward different narrative ends. The following unequivocal expression of this understanding of her experience is characteristic of the text:

> For seven years I had lived out of the world entirely; my person had been rendered coarse by hard work and exposure to the weather. I looked double the age I really was, and my hair was already thickly sprinkled with grey. I clung to my solitude. I did not like to be dragged from it to mingle in gay scenes, in a busy town, and with gaily-dressed people. I was no longer fit for the world; I had lost all relish for the pursuits and pleasures which are so essential to his votaries; I was contented to live and die in obscurity.

Of course this virtuous withdrawal from the world is the stuff of spiritual autobiography, the most common form in which women's autobiography was published during the early and mid-nineteenth century,

---

39. See, for an interesting example of the discussion of such a gap with regard to Moodie, Carl Ballstadt, "'The Embryo Blossom': Susanna Moodie's Letters to Her Husband in Relation to *Roughing It in the Bush.*" It is this hodgepodge of generic forms that has lead John Thurston, in "Rewriting *Roughing It*" in *Future Indicative: Literary Theory and Canadian Literature,* edited by John Moss (Ottawa: Ottawa University Press, 1987), and then subsequently in *The Work of Words,* to argue that we cannot treat Moodie's text as authored by herself or as a "stable" text. Clearly, I have not followed this argument, or indeed Michael Peterman's description, in *"Roughing It in the Bush* as Autobiography," of the text as "casual or covert autobiography" (39), taking the view that the same might be said for many texts and that the development of the book through stages and the active participation of a publisher need not be a mark of incoherence or instability of any kind.

40. See, for example, the comment in the review of the *Observer* that "all those who desire to emigrate to Canada should peruse this book" (February 15, 1852), 6; and the *Boston Daily Evening Transcript*'s description of it as "the light literature of colonization" (July 6, 1852), 2.

though a narrow enough field for all that. And certainly a few Victorian autobiographies—and, of course, many, many novels—written by middle-class women cast their spiritual struggle, as Moodie does, in terms of the form of the social persecution following loss of income and status, and in terms of the humiliation of having to undertake demeaning or even manual work. Moodie's narrative is comparable, in this sense, to a metropolitan text such as Mary Barber's autobiography, *Breadwinning or the Ledger and the Lute,* in the way that it explores the middle-class nightmare of crushing poverty. *Roughing It* describes the dimensions of that nightmare loss of caste in uncompromising terms: "The tears sprang to my eyes, and I thought, in the bitterness of my heart, upon my own galling poverty, that my pockets did not even contain a single copper, and that I had scarcely garments enough to shield me from the inclemency of the weather. By unflinching industry, and taking my part in the toil of the field, I had bread for myself and my family." Writing, to this extent, within the conventions of spiritual autobiography, Moodie stresses in particular the psychological damage wreaked by having to move outside the family circle, comparing her changed circumstances to death: "After seven years' exile, the hope of return grows feeble, the means are still less in our power, and our friends give up all hope of our return; their letters grow fewer and colder, their expressions of attachment less vivid; the heart has formed new ties, and the poor emigrant is nearly forgotten. Double those years, and it is as if the grave has closed over you, and the hearts that once knew and loved you know you no more."[41]

However, if the unhappy experiences of emigration are interpreted by Moodie as producing this kind of spiritual crisis, her narrative scarcely has the self-abnegatory assumptions of the spiritual autobiography. We have already noted that emigrant women's narratives, while stressing crisis, draw away from moral closure, and Moodie, certainly, is famously complacent as far as her own moral position is concerned. Her trials are offered as evidence of an *undeserved* pain and ill-fortune, and not as signposts to an elevated spiritual state. Thus she claims sympathy for a worldly predicament and describes that predicament in the detail

41. Susanna Moodie, *Roughing It in the Bush, or Life in Canada,* 501, 474, 115. For a discussion of Victorian spiritual autobiography written by women, see, for example, Corbett, *Representing Femininity,* especially chapter 2, and Linda H. Peterson, *Victorian Autobiography: The Tradition of Self-Interpretation* (New Haven, Conn.: Yale University Press, 1986).

characteristic of the emigrant's narrative where setbacks are expected but not attributable to moral fault.

This kind of narrative of undeserved sorrow and anomie also owes something to the discourse of British back-migrants hostile to emigration, with its emphasis on the threatening and malevolent presence of fellow settlers and its sharply unfunny satire on North American manners. But where these anti-emigration narratives were written largely to justify a return to the Tory fold in Britain, and, no doubt, to pander to class fears about the consequences (or even the possibility) of more democratic political structures, Moodie's whole experience of backwoods life remains focused, as in the conventional emigrant narrative, on tests of the individual.[42]

More influential here perhaps were the popular representations of women objecting to their husbands' decision to emigrate—hence their undeserved suffering. A separate response and an independent objection to emigration were quite frequently attributed to women in the nineteenth century in mainstream cultural texts (as opposed to the narratives of emigrants themselves). This kind of response could take misogynistic forms. William Cobbett's emigration tract, for example, complains that women's objections to leaving home blight the optimism of their more dynamic husbands. The emigrant husband, he argues, must prepare himself: "To be reminded every time the flies settle on the preserved peaches that they do not do this in Old England; and to have to show your wit by observing that it would difficult for them to do so in England; and to add the question, whether it were not as well to be annoyed by flies in the eating of preserved peaches, as not to have any peaches to eat?" Annette Kolodny quotes Timothy Flint making a similar comment, with respect to the United States, about "modern wives who refuse to follow their husbands abroad, alleging the danger of the voyage or journey or the unhealthiness of the proposed residence, or because the removal will separate them from the pleasures of fashion and society."[43]

42. See, for example, such texts as William Savage, *Observations on Emigration to the United States of America Illustrated by Original Facts;* "Ex-Settler," *Canada in the Years 1832, 1833 and 1834, Containing Important Information and Instructions to Persons Intending to Emigrate Thither in 1835;* John McDonald, *Narrative of a Voyage to Quebec and Journey from Thence to New Lanark and Upper Canada.*
43. Cobbett, *Emigrant's Guide in Ten Letters,* 35; Kolodny, *The Land Before Her,* 85; Kolodny's quotation is from Timothy Flint, *Biographical Memoir of Daniel Boone* (Cincinnati: N. and G. Guilford, 1833), 115.

By the middle of the nineteenth century, when Moodie was writing, the expression of a *justified* criticism of emigration was commonly attributed to women. The British painter Richard Redgrave's *The Emigrant's Last Sight of Home* (1858), for example, depicts the father of the family stretching his arms out expansively in a gesture that is both a farewell and a welcome to rural life. The gesture recalls the English assumption that structures of a traditional English village life might be replicated in the new land.[44] His wife, meanwhile, sitting with her children in his shadow, wears an expression of gloom that seems to suggest impatience at her husband's facile optimism as well as resignation. She has already turned away from the village scene, and directs her gaze at her husband's back. Comparable relations of feeling are imagined in a contemporaneous American painting, James F. Wilkins's *Leaving the Old Homestead* (c. 1853). Here a rather more dignified husband stands armed with a rifle and a bundle, directing a contemplative gaze into the distance. But, once again, it is the figure of the wife who draws the problematic aspects of emigration to our attention. Not only does her mourning recall the familiar notion of emigration as "leaving the world" of familiarity and comfort, but in following her husband, she is sacrificing an apparently idyllic home with no apparent cause beyond her husband's impulse.

It is this reading of female experience of emigration as an exile enforced (with whatever good intentions) by men that is taken into autobiographical form by Moodie, combined with the conventions of spiritual autobiography and emigrant narrative and used to produce a self well-justified in its assertiveness. As we have seen, emigrant narrative allows Moodie to examine the experience of emigration without any sense that her independent understanding need be muffled by the language of self-abnegation or organized according to conventions of depicting women's lives as *happily* devoted to self-sacrifice. Accordingly, *Roughing It* makes a clear distinction between her own views and her husband's, justifying the former in the depiction of subsequent disastrous events; indeed, she goes to some lengths, in her "true picture," to prove Mr. Moodie's behavior to have been misguided.

44. For a discussion of this assumption and its implications for emigrants to rural America, see Charlotte Erickson, "The Agrarian Myths of English Emigrants," in *In the Trek of the Immigrants,* edited by O. Ander (Rock Island, Ill.: Augustana Library Publications, 1965).

Richard Redgrave, *The Emigrant's Last Sight of Home* (1858). The Tate Gallery, London.

Buttressed by the focus on self-sufficiency in emigrant narrative, Moodie portrays herself not merely working to enable her husband to fulfill his duties as a soldier but taking over their farm in his absence, supporting the family through writing, and indeed ensuring his subsequent employment as a civil servant by writing to the lieutenant governor to ask that her husband remain in the militia. Her explanation, in chapter 12, of their emigration as driven by Mr. Moodie's fears for their financial security is succeeded by her commentary on the nature of his mistake, which lies in his failure to listen to "the voices of the soul" to which women were, of course, felt to be especially alert: "All who have ever trodden this earth, possessed of the powers of thought and reflection, of tracing effects back to their causes, have listened to [the] voices of the soul, and secretly acknowledged their power: but few, very few have had courage boldly to declare their belief in them: the wisest and the best have given credence to them, the experience of every day proves their truth."[45]

45. Moodie, *Roughing It,* 206.

James F. Wilkins, *Leaving the Old Homestead* (c. 1853). Missouri Historical Society, St. Louis.

Moodie's self-portrait of undeserved suffering in Canada also comes very close, at certain points, to producing, in autobiographical form, the idealized victimhood imaged in contemporary poetry. At a time when settings that glamorized Woman's sacrifice of a social existence through marriage were popular, the forests and prairies of North America offered an exemplum of physical and psychological isolation. The frustration of exile from public life—especially at the hands of male decision-makers—doubtless had many resonances, not only for middle-class female readers constantly exhorted to focus on the domestic but also for those women writers whose interventions in the world of literary endeavor were achieved at the cost of a marginalized and restricted personal life.[46]

46. See, for example, the discussions of Alan Richardson and Marlon B. Ross in *Romanticism and Feminism*, edited by Anne K. Mellor (Bloomington: University of Indiana Press, 1988), 13–25 and 26–51 respectively; and Angela Leighton, *Vic-*

A poem such as Lydia Sigourney's "Western Emigrant" that depicts emigrant life in North America as exile is not far from the accounts of less enthusiastic travelers and back-migrants (male or female) alike. Sigourney writes of the "dark forest shutting out the day," of a "lone hermit home," "rugged" and made with "shapeless logs." Plenty of anti-emigration writers made a similar point, of course. Edward Talbot's *Five Years' Residence in the Canadas*, for example, strikes similar notes: "The backwoodsman who buries himself in the pathless savannas or the drearier forests of the western country . . . is surely an object of pity to the poorest inmate of a hospital or workhouse . . . he is absolutely excluded from human society . . . nor is he animated by any hope beyond the anticipations of the merest physical gratifications."[47]

The difference between Talbot's shudder and "The Western Emigrant," however, lies in the way in which, in Sigourney's poem, these objections, though not actually voiced by the appropriately submissive figure of the wife, are feminized. Sigourney depicts the wife as absolutely out of place in the backwoods. When, later in the poem, she depicts the emigrant observing his wife, her terms suggest a well-born lady transported to an inappropriate and featureless setting:

> Wife! did I see thee brush away a tear?
> Twas even so. Thy heart was with the halls
> Of thy nativity. Their sparkling lights,
> Carpets, and sofa, and admiring guests,
> Befit thee better than these rugged walls
> Of shapeless logs, and this lone hermit home.

---

torian *Women Poets: Writing against the Heart* (London: New Harvester, 1992). This construction of the problems of "entering the public sphere" as a woman is traced with specific reference to Moodie in Misao Dean, "Concealing Her Blue Stockings: Femininity and Self-Representation in Susanna Moodie's Autobiographical Works," in *Re-Siting Queen's English: Text and Tradition in Post-Colonial Literatures*, edited by Gillian Whitlock and Helen Tiffin (Amsterdam: Rodopi, 1992).

47. Lydia H. Sigourney, " The Western Emigrant" in *Zinzendorff, and Other Poems*, 246–48; Edward Allen Talbot, *Five Years' Residence in Canada including a Tour through part of the United States of America in the Year 1823*, 135. Shannon Russell deals with this kind of poetic comment on emigration in a different argument in "Recycling the Poor and Fallen: Emigration Politics and the Narrative Resolutions of *Mary Barton* and *David Copperfield*," 49.

The effect of passages such as this is to erase the economic motive that constituted the most powerful justification for emigration and to construct it as the result of the husband's egotistical and irresponsible impulse. Meanwhile, the wife's "gentle smile" and her attention to her "waking infant" absolve her from the kind of accusations made by the Cobbetts and Flints that women whined after the superficial luxuries of "the world." Whatever her unhappiness, there is no hint of any deterioration in this emigrant woman's commitment to her role as a mother.

The bitter twist in "The Western Emigrant" lies in Sigourney's revelation that the backwoodsman himself has doubts as to the wisdom of his decision. At the end of the poem, he dreams of the deep pleasures of the life left behind. His mind returns to glowing scenes of "his own native city": the horse and the dog that he loved, the friends who always welcomed him, the stimulation of discussion, and the beauty of the scenery. In his dreams (listening, in Moodie's terms, to the "voices of the soul") he endorses the loyalty to home that is deeply felt by his wife.

Moodie's reworking of this view of exiled womanhood in *Roughing It* writes a comparable narrative of gender relations for her British (and subsequently American) readers. As in "The Western Emigrant," Moodie argues that the conflict between her husband's view and her own exists at the superficial level of conscious behavior. No spoken argument is written into the text, as it is in her quasi-autobiographical novel of emigration, *Flora Lindsay,* which opens with the bullying tactics of the eponymous heroine's husband and an explicit discussion about money:

> "Flora, have you forgotten the talk we had about emigration, the morning before our marriage?" was a question rather suddenly put to his young wife by Lieutenant Lindsay, as he paused in his walk to and from the room . . .
> "I am afraid, dear girl, you are destined to learn a practical illustration of the meaning [of the word emigration]. Nay, don't look so despondingly. If you intended to remain in England, you should not have married a poor man."

Nonetheless, by the time we reach the chapter in *Roughing It* in which the case for and against emigration is rehearsed, we already know that the writer's arguments have been defeated and her desires ignored.[48]

In drawing on a cluster of overlapping discussions of emigration, then, Susanna Moodie produces a very distinctive autobiographical self. The much-quoted warning of Gayatri Spivak, however, that we need to "wrench ourselves away from the mesmerizing focus of the 'subject constitution' of the female individualist" is at its most persuasive in the case of Moodie, though no less appropriate in Belknap's. Theorists of settler culture suggest that Anglo settlers may be seen, in some ways, as the alienated victims of the imperial ambitions of a governing elite. However, while the situation of emigrants is undoubtedly a complex one, attributing to economic migrants the positions of exile and victimhood seems to me problematic, if not, to use Leela Gandhi's word, "facile." Belknap's writing of a conventional emigrant identity and Moodie's representation of herself as a doughty but unwilling emigrant, an exile dragged from her home, produce, after all, an "alibi," in Jane Marcus's terms, by which these writers can "slip out of the confines of history and social responsibility." The accompanying silence, in these emigrant texts, on the issue of appropriation of land and its implications for those outside the colonizing group draws us back to the social politics of these texts, and to the discussion of complicity. However, as we shall see in the next chapter, complicity in the project of appropriation and colonization of land sat less comfortably with the subject-position of the emigrant housewife than with that of the mournful exile.[49]

---

48. Susanna Moodie, *Flora Lindsay or Passages in an Eventful Life*, 1–2.
49. Gayatri Spivak, "Three Women's Texts and a Critique of Imperialism," 177; Leela Gandhi, *Postcolonial Theory: A Critical Introduction*, 169; Jane Marcus, "Registering Objections: Grounding Feminist Alibis," 14.

3

Recipes for Success

Catharine Parr Traill's Empire of Woman

*E*MIGRATION DISCOURSE promoted the place to which the emigrant moved by describing it as an open space for the pursuit of personal ambitions, as an Eden cut off from "the world," as a space of equal opportunity. Those less impressed by the prospects offered by emigration wrote of a wilderness, a rural nowhere struggling (without obvious success) to form a "civilized" community, a graveyard for the aspirations of the sophisticate.[1] For all the rhetoric of escape, recovery, exile, and loss, however, these Anglo emigrants were participating, in different ways, in the population of land appropriated by Britain and the United States. Populating land sparsely settled or emptied of its previous inhabitants was, of course, as literally women's work as men's. But middle-class Anglo women might, in addition, participate more actively in the settlement of Upper Canada and the western territories of the United States than by child-bearing alone. In their homemaking and their contacts with others within the home, they could transmit

---

1. See Fender, *Sea Changes*, 47–63, for a discussion of the inventories of resources and costs, natural bounty, and the mythology of the Golden Age to which emigration discourse refers; writing hostile to emigration is discussed in chapters 13–15. Wilbur Shepperson's *Emigration and Disenchantment: Portraits of Englishmen Repatriated from the United States* is also a helpful source. The conventions of writing about Canada are discussed not as anti-emigration discourse but in comparable terms in Douglas Owram's *Promise of Eden: The Canadian Expansionist Movement and the Idea of the West, 1856–1900*. As discussed in this chapter, some of the writing promoting Upper Canada is close to anti-emigration discourse in mood and emphasis, for example, Howison, *Sketches of Upper Canada;* Talbot, *Five Years' Residence in Canada*.

those societal values by which an imperial power might wish to be defined.

Some scholars have constructed the work of childbearing, homemaking, and social activity performed by middle-class white colonists as bearing symbolic meaning: women were acting as "the necessary guarantors of permanent settlement" through the provision of a second generation rather than by exerting power. Others have focused on the way in which Anglo women were themselves oppressed within the hierarchy that their behavior was expected to support. Indeed, it is sometimes argued that the colonial context produces an exaggerated patriarchy: Beverley Gartrell asserts that the colonial woman is wholly defined by her husband's status; Callaway that "women were placed in a confined location within alien culture, deprived of their usual responsibilities."[2]

Increasingly, however, since the mid-1980s, another strand of scholarship has recovered an enthusiastic dedication on the part of the middle-class Victorian female civilizer to the task of enforcing Anglo bourgeois values upon less dominant groups: "natives," "savages," working-class settlers, non-Anglo-European immigrants. The empire of Woman could, indeed, extend from any home outward into any space; Woman might, as Mary Louise Pratt evocatively puts it, "collect and possess everything" from the private space of her "personal, room-sized empire" to the "world she explored . . . in circular expeditions" to and from home. Hers was a power and influence that might be dispensed as firmly in the rural spaces of the West as in the urban "frontiers" left behind, though, as John Faragher notes, the West seemed to offer "a unique stage"—in the sense that it was perceived to be an open space—for the exercise of the "civilizing force" of women. However, this work of enforcement—of domestication—for all its possibilities for public work, was centered upon domesticity.[3]

2. Heath Dillard, "Women in Reconquest Castile," 71; Beverley Gartrell, "Colonial Wives: Villains or Victims?" 166; Helen Callaway, *Gender, Culture and Empire*, 233. Georgi-Findlay, in *The Frontiers of Women's Writing*, investigates the spaces, confined and liberatory, available to women within the project of western settlement, but the complex position of the colonial housewife in terms of the organization of private and social space is set out with particular suggestiveness in Hilary Callan, Introduction, 1–13.
3. Mary Louise Pratt, *Through Imperial Eyes: Travel Writing and Transculturation*, 160–61; John Faragher, "History from the Inside-Out: Writing the History of

Hilary Callan has suggested that in the colonial context, the home was particularly powerful because it was "projected 'outwards' . . . as a vehicle for the dissemination of civic or national virtues." Rosemary Marangoly George, in her discussion of the "authoritative" female colonist, casts the colonial home as a space intensely engaged in the work of controlling the colonized, as "policing" behavior and boundaries between races. In these readings, the colonial home is not only significant, it is crucial in exemplifying and imposing imperial values.[4]

Such constructions of colonial housekeeping are clearly relevant to the consideration of Anglo emigrant domesticity: both colonial involvement and emigration, and their representation, intensified the meaning of the home and made the transfer of domestic values into the "new" space profoundly significant. The distinction between the figure of the colonizer and that of the emigrant settler is, at some points, after all, a difference of emphasis. We assume, in the case of the former, that the man of the family has been invested with governmental responsibility in a way that the emigrant was not, but middle-class emigrants frequently took on civic and governmental responsibility. Among the writers considered in this study, Susanna Moodie's husband became the sheriff of Belleville, Anne Langton's brother became a colonial administrator and politician, Christiana Tillson's husband took on a range of offices and socially significant roles in Alton, Illinois, and Caroline Kirkland's husband anticipated taking a major role as a decision-maker in the community in which he had invested heavily. While the colonist was paid to exert considerable influence on his surroundings, the middle-class emigrant was expected to do the same. However, both might live a rather less triumphant existence as the evidently superfluous population

---

Rural Women in America," 539. The discussion of contact between reformers and the objects of their work are described in these kinds of terms by Christine Stansell in *City of Women: Sex and Class in New York 1789–1860* (Urbana: University of Illinois Press, 1987), chapter 4, especially 64–68. For recent work on the middle-class experience of working-class domestic space that raises questions about the politics and imagination of the working-class "lair," see Carolyn Steedman, "What a Rag Rug Means," and Martin Hewitt, "District Visiting and the Constitution of Domestic Space in the Mid-Nineteenth-Century" in *Domestic Space: Reading the Nineteenth-Century Interior*, edited by Inga Bryden and Janet Floyd (Manchester: Manchester University Press, 1999).

4. Callan, Introduction, 9; George, *Politics of Home*, 235.

of their place of origin. Such inexperienced administrators as Dunbar Moodie strained to assert authority.

In discussing the domesticity constructed in Anglo emigrant women's writing, I want to consider the extent to which it occupies this same kind of ground: the assumption of imperial privilege and the strain of asserting its signifying practices. The description of domestic practices is certainly used, in Anglo emigrant women's texts, to express the authority of the Anglo "gentlewoman," but that description exposes the difficulty experienced by the emigrant in importing such practices into the "new" community. Not only were they generated in the metropolitan and suburban context, and thus simply difficult to fulfill in the backwoods, but also they became problematic in ideological terms. Thus, though it is argued that the practices of domesticity were imported without much difficulty by some colonists, the writing of domesticity by emigrant settlers suggests a less seamless transfer than some scholars suggest.

I want to pursue questions around the representation of domesticity through the work of the Anglo-Canadian emigrant writer (and Susanna Moodie's sister), Catharine Parr Traill (1802–1899). Traill's writing was much concerned with the domestic experience of women in Upper Canada, both in *The Backwoods of Canada*, published in 1836, an autobiographical narrative derived from and organized as a set of letters, and in *The Female Emigrant's Guide,* published in 1854, a compendium of advice and information authorized by reference to the writer's own experience. These are confidently imperialistic texts to the extent that they celebrate the process of British domination of Canada. The process of appropriation of the backwoods that they describe does not include the work of subjugating others in any direct sense; nonetheless, the "civilization" of the Indians is perceived to be a triumph of British effort: "Many of them can both read and write fluently, and are greatly improved in their moral and religious conduct. They are well and comfortably clothed, and have houses to live in. But they are still too much attached to their wandering habits to become good and industrious settlers. . . . Certain it is that the introduction of the Christian religion is the first greatest step towards civilization and improvement."[5]

5. Traill, *Backwoods of Canada,* 59–60.

At the same time, both *The Backwoods* and *The Female Emigrant's Guide* take the predictable rhetorical position that female emigrant experience occupies a place on the margins of discussions about the advantages of emigration, and that, by implication, women themselves are easily sidelined in the context of a project dominated by male ambition and responsibility. There were indeed very few female guides (and Traill's own text soon lost the reference to gender in its title), though, as we have seen, arguments about the extent of women's commitment to emigration were current within Anglo-American culture during this period, and one might expect that Traill was interested in addressing that discussion. Nonetheless, Traill, in her explorations of emigrant homemaking and housekeeping in Upper Canada, makes an unequivocal claim for her commentaries to be integrated into the discourses of imperial self-justification available to British and American colonizers alike. Certainly, she emphasizes the sacrifice of comforts and pleasures demanded of the emigrant: "Those who can afford to live in ease at home, believe me, would never expose themselves to the privations and disagreeable consequences of a settler's life in Canada." But her work elides the gap between mainstream assumptions about the rupture of emigration, the process of colonization, and a quietly triumphant creation of the nation.[6]

In general, Traill's critics have responded to her work by asserting her representativeness as a successful early Canadian. She has often epitomized an unproblematic transformation of British immigrants into Canadians and the possibility of a natural emergence of a national cultural life. Carl Ballstadt, for example, shows the British outlook fostered by Traill's early pre-emigration reading giving way to a more "affirmative" and, in Ballstadt's argument, better work:

> Although *The Female Emigrant's Guide* has elements similar to *The Backwoods*, it exhibits differences in both content and tone. After more than twenty years as a resident of Upper Canada, Traill wished to remedy the other book's deficiencies in instruction by providing more essential information . . . and less personal narrative, but a comparison of the two books shows a marked advance in the degree of Traill's Canadianization, as well. The promise of the

6. Traill, *Backwoods of Canada*, 9–12, 218; Catharine Parr Traill, *Female Emigrant's Guide*, 1–5.

earlier book has been realized and is conveyed in a very affirmative attitude towards the new country.[7]

Traill seems, then, a particularly useful example of the way in which the emigrant writer might be assimilated within the imperial project, indeed might embrace it. And, looking at *The Backwoods* and *The Female Emigrant's Guide*, we encounter two texts dominated by botanical passages typical of the categorizing activity that both veiled and satisfied the appropriative passion and the hierarchical assumptions of the imperial project, and exemplified a model of gendered behavior that underwrote the structures of imperial life. Pratt has argued that botanical researchers made a "display of self-effacement"; in nineteenth-century Canada, British women of education apparently grasped, with some confidence, the opportunity to write within a suitably "self-effacing" genre. The association, indeed, between a perfumed upper-class femininity, botany, and the justification for colonial possession could scarcely be made clearer than in the following passage of Traill's *Backwoods*, which not only emphasizes "our" possession of the plants in its triumphant listing, but organizes that list by reference to the political structures and self-justificatory assumptions of the British colonizers:

> The flowers that afford the most decided perfumes are our wild roses, which possess a delicious scent: the milk-weed, which gives out a smell not unlike the night-blowing stock, the purple monarda, which is fragrance itself, from the root to the flower, and even after months' exposure to the wintry atmosphere; its dried leaves and seed-vessels are so sweet as to impart perfume to your hands or clothes. All our Mints are strongly scented: the lily of the valley is remarkable for its fine smell; then there is my queen of the lakes, and her consort, the water-king, with many other flowers I cannot now enumerate. Certain it is that among such a vast assemblage of flowers, there are, comparatively, very few that are gifted with fragrant scents. Some of our forest-trees give out a fine perfume. I have often paused in my walks to inhale the fragrance from a cedar swamp on some sunny day when the boughs were still wet with the dew-drops or recently fallen shower.[8]

7. Carl Ballstadt, "Catherine Parr Traill," 179. Ballstadt surveys traditions of Traill criticism up to the early 1980s here.
8. Traill, *Backwoods of Canada*, 205. Pratt argues, in *Through Imperial Eyes*, that botany is a male discourse (56), though see Lawrence Buell's argument in

This is the stuff of imperial self-justification, but there is nothing unfocused about this kind of writing in terms of the promotion of the colony. In a study of how Canada was formulated as a nation through scientific discourses, Suzanne Zeller has discussed the particular ways in which Canadian colonists cultivated the wilderness for the benefit of British readers who might thereby be encouraged to emigrate and populate the country. Botanical description was used to stress Canada's stability and manageability. Traill's text exemplifies the point: her description of her own "discovery" of scented flowers advertises the possibility of a leisured and refined life in the colony. It seems designed to allay the fears of wildness that Traill attributes to female prospective emigrants. She is also setting out a model that carefully proposes different degrees of civilization between Britain and Canada in a form that could flatter both places: Britain has a civilization to be imitated, while Canada has the potential to produce a different—in particular, larger—but comparable civilization. Again, this is characteristic of Canadian botanical writing, according to Zeller, for at least as important as the promotion of Canada to potential middle-class emigrants as "a hardy new northern variation of the British nation" was the promotion of the colony as full of agricultural produce ready to be tapped by British entrepreneurs. And indeed Traill herself, involved as she was in sending plants back to the laboratories of Britain, took part in a direct way in this work of appropriating Canadian resources.[9]

The cultivation specifically of flowers had a particular resonance, expressing a gentle and wholly unproblematic form of land control. Gardening and colonization made an especially apt and resonant—and self-justificatory—comparison for the colonizer: tending the garden expressed the continual effort in keeping "nature" at bay and also suggested attractive, blameless aspects of the task of "civilizing" the colony. While, as Ann Schteir argues, "male botanists made grand treks in search of rare and new specimens," Victorian women were

---

The Environmental Imagination: Thoreau, Nature Writing and the Formation of American Culture, 43. In Canada, the botanical work of Lady Dalhousie and her circle, Harriet Sheppard and her husband, William, and Anne Marie Percival (as well as that of Traill) is considered noteworthy.

9. Suzanne Zeller, *Inventing Canada: Early Victorian Science and the Idea of a Transcendental Nation*, 91, 271. Zeller refers to Traill's work for "a professor at the University of Edinburgh" (195–96).

perceived to be more appropriately engaged with "the local terrain of garden, woods, or seashore." This is Traill's approach, as she directs the "ladies who belong to the higher class of settlers": "to the natural history and botany of this new country, in which they will find a never-ending source of amusement and instruction, at once enlightening and elevating to the mind . . . To the person who is capable of looking at the beauties of nature, and adoring the creator through His works, are opened stores of unmixed pleasure."[10]

Still, for all their usefulness as metaphors estheticizing colonization, neither botany nor gardening held the charged position in terms of Woman's "mission" that was accorded to the task of supervising the private space.[11] It was as a purveyor of information on housekeeping that Traill made her name. Traill's work is full of instruction on how to run the home and, especially, on how to prepare food in different ways. The world of domestic management could, of course, be as heavily laden with the priorities and assumptions of the colonizer as botanical management. Indeed, the wording of the subtitle of *The Backwoods of Canada, Letters from the Wife of an Emigrant Officer, Illustrative of the Domestic Economy of British America*, draws our attention to the different dimensions of the domestic sphere and its widening, from the domesticity of the home to the domestic politics of internal government, and indeed to the "domestication" of colonized lands. Domesticity was foundational within the ideological assumptions of industrializing and

---

10. Traill, *Backwoods of Canada*, 11–12; Ann Schteir, *Cultivating Women, Cultivating Science: Flora's Daughters and Botany, 1760–1860*, 191. See also the discussion of parallels between the cultivation of gardens and the domestication of women in Leonore Davidoff and Catherine Hall, *Family Fortunes: Men and Women of the English Middle Class, 1780–1850*, 188–92.

11. *Woman's Mission* was, of course, the title of a best-seller in the mid-nineteenth-century literature of domesticated womanhood. Sarah Lewis's interpretation of the "mission" and its ramifications for the home are set out in Elizabeth K. Helsinger, Robin Lauterbach Sheets, and William Veeder, *The Woman Question: Society and Literature in Britain and America, 1837–1883*, vol. 1 (Chicago: University of Chicago Press, 1983), 3–20. For a discussion of the mission's more radical dimensions, see, for example, Caroll Smith-Rosenberg's "Beauty, the Beast and the Militant Woman: A Case Study in Sex Roles and Social Stress in Jacksonian America," *American Quarterly* 23 (1971): 562–84. Studies of the American and Canadian West have often focused on the racism implicit in the mission, as in, for example, Pascoe, *Relations of Rescue* and Linda Kealey, ed., *A Not Unreasonable Claim: Women and Reform in Canada, 1880–1920* (Toronto: Women's Press, 1979).

colonizing Britain and North America: in its emphasis on the efficacy of self-sufficiency and separate activity, its obsession with the precise measurement, careful management of time and control of workers, and its exhortations to defer pleasure in favor of a concentration on work.[12]

Traill's instructions for culinary preparations show the domestic, colonial, and national agenda locked together, particularly with respect to arguments about the necessity for surveillance and control of work in the private as well as the public space. Lydia Maria Child's exhortations in *The Frugal Housewife* to gather up "fragments of time as well as of materials" are much quoted in the context of such arguments. Traill's account of her method for boiling maple sugar, for example, is strongly reminiscent of the obsessional insistence in Anglo-American domestic discourse on the need for a single-minded dedication to the individualized task; on the process, conducted in private, of learning and executing the task to a standard conclusion; on the purity or brightness of the result, without taint of waste, dirt, or the signs of exertion on the body of the housewife.[13]

> This spring I have made maple-sugar of a much finer color and grain than any I have yet seen . . . which . . . induces me to give the plan I pursued in manufacturing it. The sap having been boiled down in the sugar bush from about sixteen pailsful to two, I passed it through a thin flannel bag, after the manner of a jelly bag, to strain it from the first impurities, which are great. . . . A few minutes before it comes to the boil, the scum must be carefully removed with a skimmer or ladle, the former is best. I consider that on the care taken to remove every particle of scum depends, in a great measure, the brightness and clearness of the sugar. The best rule I can give as to the sugaring-off, as it is termed, is to let the liquid continue at a fast boil: only be careful to keep it from coming over by keeping a little of the liquid in your stirring-ladle, and when it boils up to the top, or you see it rising too

---

12. Jeanne Boydston gives a helpful summary of the arguments of social historians and theorists of housework in the preface to *Home and Work: Housework, Wages and the Ideology of Labor in the Early Republic*. See also Faye Dudden, *Serving Women: Household Service in Nineteenth-Century America*, chapters 4 and 5, especially 156–61; Davidoff and Hall, *Family Fortunes*, 392–96.

13. Lydia Maria Child, *The American Frugal Housewife*, 3. For discussions of the cleanliness demanded of the bourgeois housewife, see Leonore Davidoff, "The Rationalization of Housework"; Karen Halttunen, *Confidence Men and Painted Women: A Study in Middle-Class Culture in America, 1830–1870*, 102–6.

fast, throw in a little from time to time to keep it down; or if you boil on a cooking-stove, throwing open one or all the doors will prevent boiling over. . . . [T]he sugar need never rise over if common attention be paid to the boiling; but it does require constant watching: one idle glance may waste much of the precious fluid. I had only a small cooking-stove to boil my sugar on, the pots of which were thought too small, and not well shaped, so that at first my fears were that I must relinquish the trial: but I persevered, and experience convinces me that a stove is an excellent furnace for the purpose, as you can regulate the heat as you like.

Beyond its reference to the tenets continually reiterated within domestic discourse, the passage also addresses an equally important question about the efficacy of civilized values in Upper Canada. Traill's discussion of maple sugar, appearing alongside another appendix containing official information about emigration, advertises the way in which those civilized values can be exemplified even in the apparently ramshackle context of the colonial domestic space. It shows their supremacy, moreover, with an example, maple sugar boiling, where the reader might expect that local expertise would prevail. A communal version of sugar boiling described earlier in *The Backwoods* is the "pretty and picturesque" object of touristic interest. But, as we see in this later instructional passage, the task may literally be domesticated, in the sense of removing it from its usual context of communal activity, as well as in the sense of tracing within it those Anglo-American domestic practices that exemplify the priorities of the mid-nineteenth-century middle class.[14]

While we fix our attention on those scenes of observation and local color that allow Traill the subject-position of the elite civilizer, her work conforms to the patterns of colonial discourse and produces the order of domesticity that postcolonial critics have drawn to our attention. It may not reach the high pitch of emphasis on control that may be found in the material discussed by George, but as David Spurr points out, while colonial discourse may be "marked by internal repetition" it is not a "monolithic system."[15] We do not, however, have to drift very

14. Traill, *Backwoods of Canada*, 253, 263, 130.
15. David Spurr, *The Rhetoric of Empire: Colonial Discourse in Journalism, Travel Writing and Imperial Administration*, 1–2.

far from such scenes to find domestic description where Traill struggles to position herself in such unambiguous terms. This is because her work speaks, in direct and indirect terms, to the idea of emigration as a downward trajectory in social terms. She was, after all, an emigrant self-avowedly escaping from a troubled economic situation in Britain; indeed, she was someone who was involved in "downward" migrations across class and space throughout her life.[16]

Her father, Thomas Strickland, was a man whose upward social mobility necessitated shifts across class and region, but that mobility failed to establish his family's social position in provincial England with anything like the firmness required for the attribution of unambiguous social status. His fall, worse still, from financial security and his subsequent death in 1818 left his wife and children in a precarious social and economic situation. Traill's marriage in 1832 to an indebted half-pay officer of good birth but economic insecurity—a man with no economic alternative but to emigrate—seems rather of a piece with her earlier life. Hers was an experience that typified the circumstances in which emigration might carry a social stigma.[17]

Once settled in Canada (after 1832), Traill's experience of emigration altogether failed to conform to those formulas of the promotional literature that she herself, interestingly, had rehearsed in an early fiction published in 1826: *The Young Emigrants*. The Traills' farming was not successful and by 1835 they began to try to sell up. (It was while they waited for the sale that Traill managed, with the help of her sister Agnes Strickland, who was by now a successful popular historian, to publish *The Backwoods of Canada*). Three years later, in 1839, the family managed to move to Peterborough, described by one of Traill's emigrant contemporaries, John Langton, in a letter home as "a very pretty, picturesque, thriving village . . . with near thirty genteel families within visiting distance," and even by a more disinterested traveler as "stated . . . to be the most brilliant and polished [community]

---

16. For biographical material I have drawn, in particular, on Ballstadt, "Catharine Parr Traill"; Rupert Schieder, "Editor's Introduction"; Thurston, *The Work of Words,* especially the discussion of the Strickland family.

17. For signs that emigration held a stigma, see, for example, the representation of the emigrant woman in the review of Moodie's *Roughing It* in *Blackwood's Edinburgh Magazine* 71: 355; G[?] H[?], *The Emigrants: A Tale of Truth* (Eton: E. Williams, n.d.); Wilbur S. Shepperson, *British Emigration to North America: Projects and Opinions—The Early Victorian Period,* 38.

in Canada." But for all the colonial boosterism of Peterborough, the Traills were no more successful here than before. Thomas Traill tried to deal in land and got further into debt, to the point that, by 1846, the family was virtually destitute. By this time, at forty-four and after fourteen years of marriage, Catharine Parr Traill had given birth to nine children, seven of whom had survived. In 1846, a friend helped them to resettle on Rice Lake, but Thomas Traill suffered from depression, family members suffered sicknesses, and their income remained precarious at all times.[18]

Traill's economic insecurity and downward mobility are clearly traced in the generic forms of her output. She made an income through writing before her marriage, publishing didactic tales for children between 1819 and 1831. Though she apparently forged some helpful connections in the process, this kind of writing was nevertheless marginal in literary terms. *The Backwoods of Canada*—subtitled *Letters from the Wife of an Emigrant Officer*—situated her as part of a future if not present elite; these letters appeared closer to the leisured writing of a lady to her mother than to work undertaken for money. Her botanical work was, as already discussed, imbricated in the formulation of Canada as a space by the center.[19] But her return to writing in the early to mid-1850s (fifteen years after publishing *The Backwoods*), with *Canadian Crusoes*, marked a return to the semi-literary genre of children's didactic literature. The instructional *The Female Emigrant's Guide*, which followed in 1854, took her a step further down into realms beyond the literary: the world of the instructional guide and the cookery book.

Certainly, *The Female Emigrant's Guide*, with its emphasis on passing on information, especially recipes, expresses, as we have seen, the assumptions of colonial discourse and the subject position of the colonial civilizer. The discussion of food that dominates the text is plainly expressive of what is cast as civilized social behavior in any society, and the emphasis both on transmitting national practices in the cooking

---

18. W. A. Langton, *Early Days in Upper Canada: Letters of John Langton*, 21; Patrick Shirreff, *A Tour through North America*, 123.

19. I refer here to the early botanical activity in which Traill was involved. From the late 1860s, finally on an even keel financially, Traill published several distinguished works of botany, for example: *Canadian Wild Flowers* (Montreal: John Lovell, 1868) and *Studies of Plant Life in Canada, or Gleanings from Forest, Lake and Plain* (Ottawa: A.S. Woodburn, 1885).

and eating of food, and on marking the limits of possible adaptation may be viewed as lying firmly within the remit of the civilizer. The need for recipe books was a function of the large-scale migrations that institutionalized the appropriation of land: it was the fragmentation of community through mobility nationally and emigration internationally on a huge scale in Britain and North America that had first generated the market for recipes. Women were moving away from the informal help with housewifery traditionally available within families.[20]

Susan Leonardi's well-known argument that recipes actually work to construct an imagined community supports the notion that recipes are involved in nation-building and the codification of behavior in the new space of the colony. Anne Goldman sharpens Leonardi's point in a discussion of the housekeeping of the colonized, arguing that "a cookbook . . . may reproduce . . . those cultural practices and values that provide a community with a means of self-definition and survival . . . [and] an individual authority as well." It is also, of course, a community imagined by and through the lives of women.[21]

If we look, for example, at Traill's recipe for "Sweet Fruit Cake," we can see this kind of community-building at work, in Traill's assumption that the reader is sensitive to the cultural meaning for Anglo emigrant women of baking and serving puddings, cake, and bread, and aware of the contexts in which these foods are produced. The important information imparted is not so much how to make the cake, but rather how middle-class British social practices of which her reader is the supposed inheritor are ideally pursued—the social ritual of the "furnished" tea table, the rejection of conspicuous consumption ("costly luxuries"):

> Sweet Fruit Cake
>
> This is made by rolling out a fine short crust very thin, and spreading about an inch thickness of apple-marmalade, made by boiling down dried-apples to a pulp; over this lay another thin crust of pastry: it should be baked in shallow tin-pans, and, when quite cold, cut into squares, or vandyke-shaped pieces, by cutting squares from corner to corner. This is sold in the confectioners under the

---

20. See Eileen Fordyce, "Cookbooks of the 1800s," 101–3.
21. Susan J. Leonardi, "Recipes for Reading: Summer Pasta, Lobster à la Riseholme and Key Lime Pie"; Anne Goldman, "'I Yam What I Yam': Cooking, Culture and Colonialism," 187.

name of mince-pie, and pie-cake. . . . Canada is the land of cakes. A tea-table is generally furnished with several varieties of cakes and preserves. I have given you as many receipts as will enable you to make a selection: if you require more costly luxuries, there are plenty of good receipts to be had, by referring to any of the popular cookery-books.[22]

However, Traill's final point about "the popular cookery-books" demonstrates the difficulty she encounters in locating recipe-writing securely within colonial discourses. At the time when Traill's text was published, the publication of recipes situated the author within the borderland of the socially insecure, hence Traill's claim that, though she has produced recipes of a kind, her guide is not a recipe book: "As this work is not intended for a regular cookery-book, I have limited myself as to such cakes as are in common use in the farm houses."[23]

The form not only placed the author within a liminal position in literary terms but also brought her uncomfortably close to an audience with mere aspirations to a secure social status. It was not just that the woman who wrote recipes admitted to a knowledge of cooking more extensive than might be expected of a member of the middle classes, or that writing in such a sub-literary mode was an activity plainly directed toward generating income. The writing of recipes in a colonial guide such as, for example, Flora Anne Steel's and Grace Gardiner's later *The Complete Indian Housekeeper and Cook* evades these associations by focusing almost exclusively on knowledge of recipes as necessary simply for the instruction and supervision of servants. The position of the genteel backwoods housewife could not be cast in such a way with any conviction.

The very content of cookery writing was closely associated with social aspiration and upward mobility: cookery books were engaged in instructing women with class aspirations (such as a housewife on the margins of the middle class or a woman aspiring to "service" in a bourgeois household), by setting out, as exactly as possible, the requirements of

---

22. Traill, *Female Emigrant's Guide*, 104.
23. Ibid. Sarah Freeman's discussion in chapter 8 of *Mutton and Oysters: The Victorians and their Food* is suggestive in this context, as, at a more general level, is Roland Barthes, "Ornamental Cookery," 78–80.

polite society. While Traill's class origins entitled her to offer recipes in the context of the "improvement" of fellow settlers, nevertheless, her emigration, obviously undertaken for no other reason than the pursuit of secure social status and greater financial security, closed the gap between herself and other aspirants. With her sweeping description—"Canada is the land of cakes"—Traill firmly bends her recipe for sweet fruit cake toward the genre of travelogue and, by implication, an audience with no need to migrate.

Traill's apparent emphasis on matters of caste was not simply the sensitivity of a déclassé economic migrant. It was probably also, in part, an attempt to participate in a discussion of emigration, conducted within the ruling classes of Canada, which was strongly and explicitly directed toward the fixed maintenance of class difference. In the writing of *The Backwoods of Canada*, we find Traill signaling that participation by prefacing her text with a flattering reference to William Dunlop's "witty and spirited pamphlet," *Statistical Studies of Upper Canada. For the Use of Emigrants by A Backwoodsman*. This may have been an attempt to sell more copies on the back of Dunlop's popular text, published four years before Traill's. Certainly, it seems evident that Traill, turning to publication with the need to raise cash in mind, had every reason to identify a niche in a buoyant market for emigrant narratives.[24] This she did in claiming to be writing a "woman's version" of a guide for middle-class emigrants. But Dunlop's text was a confident paean to an unbridgeable class distinction in the colony, and thus his guide erased the class mobility that was for many the object of emigration.

William Dunlop and his text occupied a far more privileged position than Traill and *The Backwoods;* a position of influence and comfort to which, one imagines, the Traills aspired. Dunlop himself arrived in Canada in 1813 at age thirty-four, after pursuing a military career. He moved in Tory governing circles, and, at various points, took jobs as a government agent, while at the same time continuing the literary journalism of his pre-Canada years, setting up a Tory literary circle in

---

24. Traill, *Backwoods of Canada*, 4. Her hopes, if such they were, were justified, as the publisher of *Backwoods*, Charles Knight, reprinted it five times and issued a new edition in 1846. *Backwoods* went through three reprints between 1846 and 1849 in an edition published by Nattali and Bond before appearing in an edition bound with Charles Grenfell's *The Oregon Territory* in 1860.

Canada in 1836.[25] In *Statistical Sketches* he takes care to make clear that he can afford to parody advice books for "backwoodsmen." Small wonder that Traill pulls away from the world of recipe writing; Dunlop specifically identifies the recipe as a means to satirize the practices of the "lower orders" in Canada and to cast doubt on the idea of "civilizing" them into bourgeois practices: "Cut the steak about a quarter of an inch thick, wash it well in a tub of water, wringing it from time to time after the manner of a dish-clout; and when it boils, put in the steak, turning it for about a quarter of an hour then put it in a deep dish and pour the oil over it, till it floats—so—serve it." Instead of the homilies upon the need for prudence and industry that were continually restated in the guidebooks of the day (and, of course, in Traill's work), we have Dunlop's exquisitely patronizing "I have no acquaintance with prudence, yet I sincerely wish her all manner of success in her patriotic and philanthropic undertaking." In place of the detail of how to achieve success as an emigrant, he writes: "I shall not waste my reader's time nor my own with estimates of the result of farming pursuits or how they ought to be set about."[26]

Dunlop's point, however, for all his jokes, lies in the portrait this highly confident colonist produces of two classes of Anglo-Canadians in antithesis to one another. In Dunlop, we see a quasi-gentry in Canada (of which he, of course, is part) indifferent to the material result of prudence and industry. His description of this type of colonist settling in the new home both parodies the guidebooks and advertises the emigrant gentleman's life of ease: "Having settled yourself and got things into some kind of tolerable order and comfort, you will next begin to think how you may amuse your leisure hours." The less prosperous settlers are described in altogether different tones: "The original shanty or log house-hovel, which sheltered the family when they first arrived on their wild lot, still remains, but has been degraded into a piggery." Dunlop's Canadian settlers are seemingly inescapably uncivilized. They are,

---

25. See, for biographical material about Dunlop, William Hugh Graham, *Tiger Dunlop* (London: Hutchinson, 1962), and Gary Draper and Ros Hall, "William Dunlop," in *Dictionary of Canadian Biography*, vol. 7 (Toronto: University of Toronto Press, 1988), 259–63.

26. William Dunlop, *Statistical Sketches of Upper Canada For the Use of Emigrants by a Backwoodsman*, 56, 105. Traill writes in the same vein on prudence and industry; see for example *Backwoods of Canada*, 89–90, 149–51.

for all intents and purposes, the lazy "natives" represented in countless colonial texts.[27]

Dunlop's commentary was not unusual in content. It appeared at a point when Anglo-Canadian promotional writing tended to dwell on the distinctive concerns of the colonial ruling class with regard to the likely future social composition and cultural status of Canada. The Canadian government, burdened with the responsibility of replicating the social systems of the Mother Country, perceived a difficulty in manipulating an emigrant population that was both unpredictable in size and largely impoverished. They feared the advent of disproportionate numbers of destitute members of the "laboring classes" who had been "shovelled out" of their native land and who arrived on Canadian shores too poor to travel out of the port, much less set up a farm and become part of a colonial quasi-feudal social structure.[28]

It is not my purpose here to discuss the arguments about the substance of this fear, but its presence is very evident.[29] While the U.S. government was similarly concerned that the western states should be settled in such a way as to develop quiescent as well as prosperous societies, the difference in the arguments of the two governments lay in the level of anxiety that the Anglo-Canadian ruling classes were prepared to express on the issue of class.[30]

Though Dunlop simply insisted that there were two classes in Canada and that a chasm existed between them, other writers considered the possibility that Canada might just, in the end, be better suited to the working classes. Traill's brother, Samuel Strickland, in *Twenty-Seven Years in Canada West* makes the common observation that it is for "the artizan, the hand-loom weaver, and the peasant" that Canada is "a true land of Goshen." While "the man of education and

---

27. Dunlop, *Statistical Sketches*, 32, 104.
28. See Norman MacDonald, *Canada: Immigration and Colonization, 1841–1903*, for a description of some of the difficulties experienced in the 1840s.
29. Howison, *Sketches of Upper Canada*, 169–70; Talbot's comments, in *Five Years' Residence*, about Canada as being in a "state of helpless infancy" are very similar.
30. See the discussion of U.S. government attitudes in Andrew R. L. Cayton and Peter S. Onuf, *The MidWest and the Nation: Rethinking the History of an American Region*, where they argue that "right from the beginning of settlement in the North West Territories, the character of the people who would settle the region was a central issue" (xvii).

refinement" might strive to "keep the balance steady" and to "hold offices in the colony," he might equally feel culturally stranded within an indigenous working-class culture.[31]

Traill, of course, had every interest in asserting that class difference in Canada was fixed; if this was the case, then no matter how straitened her circumstances, her identity was secure. Certainly, we find her restating the rejection of Canada as the context for a refined life in *The Backwoods*. She claims that she would find it "difficult to send [my little friend Emily] anything worth [her] attention" from Canada.[32] To claim that civilized life was impossible was to justify her own stripped-down fortunes as inevitable. But here the discourses of domesticity were at odds with the position within a colonial hierarchy in which she was striving to place herself.

To withdraw into domestic seclusion was, of course, one of the great ideals of the era, and the backwoods home, like the rural and suburban home, seemed, to many writers of domesticity, a perfect context. Catherine Stewart, for example, in *New Homes in the West*, addresses herself as follows to "those who awake from the pleasing dream of happiness and security, to the stern reality of a frowning fortune"; the wistful victims of the urban marketplace might be found in "asylums of peace and beauty . . . where nature seems waiting to open her stores of rich abundance; and to form new hopes, new associations, and new homes."[33]

This was a model that was not only popular but also had the virtue of placing the straitened circumstances of an emigrant such as Traill in the flattering light of a worthwhile lifestyle choice: Traill lauds to the skies the uncluttered domesticity of the backwoods, free of what Sara Josepha Hale styles "empty ceremony, formal parade and idle displays"; the focus on child-rearing: "Here" Traill writes, "there is nothing to interfere with your little nursling. You are not tempted by the pleasures of the gay world to forget your duties as a mother; there is nothing to supplant him in your heart." In the same vein, Traill idealizes migrants enjoying a life of frugal self-sufficiency, without recourse to competitive consumerism: "The dresses of the children were of a coarse sort of

31. Samuel Strickland, *Twenty-Seven Years in Canada West*, xi.
32. Traill, *Backwoods of Canada*, 216; see also subsequent comments, 146, 218, 228–29.
33. Stewart, *New Homes in the West*, iv.

plaid, the produce of the farm and their mother's praiseworthy industry. The stockings, socks, muffatees, and warm comforters were all of home manufacture. Both boys and girls wore moccasins, of their own making: good sense, industry and order presided among the members of this little household."[34]

But withdrawal in this sense went hand in hand with the embrace of domestic practices of the utmost simplicity. This was a model of transatlantic significance, as powerful in the British context (where no "new homes" were available) as in North America. Mrs. Ann Martin Taylor, for example, one of the most influential domestic writers of early-nineteenth-century England, looked back with approval to a time "when females of rank and influence were not degraded by dressing the fatted calf, and baking cakes upon the hearth . . . who looked well to the ways of her household, and ate not the bread of idleness." And indeed, Traill draws on the same biblical reference in *The Backwoods*, where she cites "the prudent mother of King Lemuel": "'She layeth her hands to the spindle and her hands hold the distaff.' 'She seeketh wool, and flax, and worketh willingly with her hands.' 'She looketh well to the ways of her household, and eateth not the bread of idleness.'"[35]

The return to rural simplicity was also often depicted as a kind of secularized fortunate fall. A scene in Ebenezer Bailey's *Young Lady's Class Book*, for example, illustrates the way in which financial ruin makes domesticated rural release possible. A young married man is "ruined" and has to move to a cottage in the country. On his arrival home with a friend on the first day of his new life, he steels himself for a disconsolate greeting from his wife. But the trials of the simple country life have apparently passed unnoticed: his wife runs out in uninhibited excitement, having prepared a meal in a holiday spirit:

> She came tripping forth to meet us. She was in a pretty rural dress of white; a few wild flowers were twisted in her fine hair; a fresh bloom was on her cheek; her whole countenance beamed with smiles . . . "My dear George," cried she, "I am so glad you are at home! I've set out a table under a beautiful tree behind the cottage;

---

34. Sara Josepha Hale, *Keeping House and Housekeeping*, 124; Traill, *Backwoods of Canada*, 217, 220.

35. Mrs. Ann Martin Taylor, *Practical Hints to Young Females on the Duties of a Wife, a Mother, and a Mistress of a Family*, 1; Traill, *Backwoods of Canada*, 149–50.

and I've been gathering some of the most delicious strawberries, for I know you are fond of them, and we have such excellent cream, and everything is so sweet and still here."[36]

Part of the attraction of this kind of withdrawal lay, however, in its apologists' sense of rural space as a context in which problems of contact and differentiation could simply be edited out of the picture. In Fanny Fern's *Ruth Hall,* for example, the eponymous heroine's rural idyll is characterized by her freedom to enjoy an egalitarian informality in her relations with those country people who live around her. This, however, was a difficult ideal to depict in an emigrant colony where replicating the social system left behind was central to the establishment of power and the assertion of class identity. And Traill faced some difficulty in her attempt to delineate a simple and informal domesticity within the rural backwoods. We find her using the tropes of domestic discourse with their convoluted codifications of class difference; she describes a rigidly correct behavior in class terms. But, set in the context of the austere values of domestic simplicity, the effect is far less distinct than we perhaps expect.

In Traill's passage of advice on borrowing in *The Female Emigrant's Guide,* for example, we see exemplified the difficulties of using such tropes to position herself securely in relation to others, much less to produce the scenes of exclusion of Others associated with colonial domesticity. What we find here is a catalogue of possible problems that emphasizes the status of privately owned and exclusively used objects as signifiers of middle-class domestic practice. There are, Traill argues, "kindly, well-disposed neighbours" who understand bourgeois codes about borrowing. The description of this group is passed over quickly in favor of a taxonomy of those who are "not over-scrupulous" about what they have borrowed: those who may cause "much heart-burning in the lender and some unpleasant wrangling" before returning goods; those who borrow items rather than buy them for themselves; the servants whose borrowing approximates stealing; and those who victimize those better off than themselves by constantly harassing them for clothes. The passage culminates in the following example of unacceptable borrowing behavior:

36. Ebenezer Bailey, *The Young Lady's Class Book,* 67.

> Another woman came to borrow a best baby-robe, lace cap and fine flannel petticoat, as she said she had nothing grand enough to take the baby to church to be christened in. Perhaps she thought it would make the sacrifice more complete if she gave ocular demonstration of the pomps and vanities being his to renounce and forsake. I declined to lend the things, at which she grew angry, and departed in a great pet, but got a present of a handsome suit from a lady who thought me very hard-hearted. Had the woman been poor, which she was not, and had begged for a dress for the little Christian, she should have had it, but I did not respect the motive for buying finer clothes than she had herself for the occasion.[37]

Traill's discussion of borrowing is expressed in the fine distinctions of acceptable and unacceptable relations that are characteristic of an era sufficiently nervous about the manifestations of social mobility in any context to regulate every instance of social behavior. The difficulty here, of course, with lending—or indeed not lending—the "best baby-robe" lies partly in the form in which the request from a less prosperous woman is couched: she shows no awareness of the style of interaction required. Certainly we understand that there is no consciousness on the part of the would-be borrower of the possible objections (for Traill) to her baby looking the same as a baby born into a higher caste. Nor does she, it seems, understand the symbolic value placed upon certain objects of ritual, especially in the bourgeois home.

Lori Merish takes up the latter point, using Caroline Kirkland's *A New Home, Who'll Follow?* and the discussion of borrowing in that text to argue that in a narrative structured around "the opposition between lower-class vulgarity and upper-class civility," it is the overdetermined relationship with objects that marks out the class identity of the narrator. She identifies Kirkland as being preoccupied with objects, arguing that "in such texts . . . the home is sacralized as a sphere of regenerate sentiment, and domestic artifacts are endowed with characterological import and serve to metynomically designate 'civilized' or fully 'human' emotional states." Merish argues that Kirkland's class operated to create Michigan as a consumer society, and that Kirkland's comments about objects express her sense of their

---

37. Traill, *Female Emigrant's Guide,* 25, 27.

civilizing influence within the private home. The point may remind us of a long scholarly tradition of hostility to Victorian middle-class consumerism, especially as practiced by women, that has located everything from greed to emotional deprivation in the acquisition of objects for the overstuffed domestic shrine. However, this hostility is heightened when it surfaces in arguments about the backwoods, where a style of urban consumerism is imaged as a blight of middle-class colonization. Ironically, given Merish's stringent critique of Kirkland as an urban consumer importing her acquisitive, status-conscious class behavior to the democratic, informal backwoods, many emigrant women writers (Kirkland included) were themselves wont to point out how useless those objects signifying class status were in their "new home." Traill also, in a story called "The Lodge in the Wilderness," made much of the incongruity and unwieldiness of such objects—china, furniture, pianos—transported with great difficulty to the backwoods.

Merish's argument assumes that middle-class emigrants were actually able to maintain a life in some sense separate from the local community and also that their social practices were soon dominant. The scholarship of backwoods communities does not necessarily bear this out, however, and the practice of borrowing as interpreted by different social groups is very much a case in point. John Faragher's *Sugar Creek* describes the practice of barter in backwoods Illinois whereby small farmers could elude participation in the eastern economy by using the "social exchange network," a "web of common obligations . . . demonstrating the mixture of private and communal that characterized the back country economy." It is certainly easy to see how antithetical such economic practices might appear to the bourgeois emigrant intent on creating a more substantial profit, on finding a self-sufficient living by managing others' work, and, most of all, looking to assume a role of social authority. It is also possible to imagine how the practice of borrowing might signify the workings of a more or less tightly knit backwoods community from which the middle-class emigrant might either wish to separate herself, or, conversely, feel herself excluded. Hence we have Traill's embattled narrative where borrowing appears to be institutionalized across class boundaries and her "correct" behavior works to isolate her socially and mark her out as "very hard-hearted." The right course of action with regard to borrowing is not, after all, very easy to define; Traill's middle-class neighbor chooses a different response.[38]

At the same time, Traill could also associate the fellow settler's request not so much with backwoods economic practices but with its opposite, the commercial context of getting loans; that is, with the world of business from which the domestic was argued to be free—and indeed never freer than in the backwoods. This was the understanding of borrowing that apologists for the domestic sphere at its most aggressively separate adopted, describing the practice as an undesirable model of contact even between ladies and outlining an etiquette that highlights the important but obscure distinctions to be made between this and the commercial practices of borrowing. Eliza Farrar advised as follows: "If you happen to borrow a little money from a friend, be very prompt and exact in repaying it, taking care to make up the exact sum in clean bank bills and as little copper as possible; fold the whole up in a piece of white paper, and direct it, so that it may be ready to be transmitted at a moment's notice." In Traill's introduction to her anecdote about borrowing, we find her making precisely the same point that, in exact measurement, all possibility of the taint of profit (on either side) is expunged: "It is best," she writes, "to keep a true account in black and white, and let the borrowed things be weighed or measured and be returned by the same weight and measure. This will save much heartburning and some unpleasant wrangling with neighbors." In this light, we might argue that it is not the consumerism of the middle class that is at issue here, but precisely the opposite: the commercialism of the backwoods population.[39]

There are difficulties, then, in adapting discourses of domesticity to represent a distance between the middle-class emigrant and her so-

---

38. Lori Merish, "'The Hand of Refined Taste' in the Frontier Landscape: Caroline M. Kirkland's *A New Home, Who'll Follow?* and the Feminization of American Consumerism," 495, 514. For critical comment on Victorian middle-class consumerism see, for example, the discussions in Thad Logan, "Decorating Domestic Space: Middle-Class Women and Victorian Interiors," and Grant McCracken in *Culture and Consumption: New Approaches to the Symbolic Characteristics of Consumer Goods and Activities,* that link accumulation of objects to a sense of lack. Catharine Parr Traill, "Forest Gleanings No. XIII: The Lodge in the Wilderness," 496. John Faragher, *Sugar Creek,* 136.

39. Eliza W. Farrar, *The Young Lady's Friend,* 277; Traill, *Female Emigrant's Guide,* 25–26.

cially inferior neighbors. The consonance between domesticity and the subject position of the colonizer that the whole discussion of colonial domesticity and domestication proposes presupposes a stable hierarchy and rigid power relations between different players. The emigrant writer's attempt to marry the position of the middle-class emigrant woman with the realization of domestic virtue seems only to serve to open up the difficulties of both: on the one hand, the maintenance of boundaries between opposing groups cannot apparently be resolved through the performance or the codification of domestic behavior; on the other, the failure of the other group to recognize the meaning of the practices of domesticity drives home the consequences of erasing the distinctions valorized by domestic discourse.

For Merish, the allegiance to objects expressed in these episodes may be understood as fetishization of things, but this is, to my mind, a very austere position. As Csikszentmihalyi and Halton argue, objects are especially important to those who, like emigrants, have "witnessed the dissolution of many relationships, the decay of many forms of structured order." Objects' vulnerability to damage gives them special importance. To lend such a valued thing threatens the loss of memories, the chipping away of identity. Even the other "lady" in Traill's passage chooses to buy the would-be borrower new clothing for her baby, rather than lend a garment of her own.[40]

This fear about dissolving identity is an important facet, I suspect, of these emigrant writers' depictions, in episodes of borrowing and elsewhere, of the absence of shared understanding of the meaning of objects. In Traill's passage, the writer describes a lack of appreciation of the meaning of the object on the part of the fellow-settler. The following interchange from Caroline Kirkland's *A New Home, Who'll Follow?* shows a version of the figure where neither party can find significance in a treasured object:

> "What on airth's them gimcracks for?" said my lady, as a nest of delicate japanned tables were set out upon the uneven floor. I tried to explain to her the various convenient uses to which they were applicable; but she looked very scornfully after all and said "I guess they'll do better as kindlins than anything else, here." And I began

40. Mihalyi Csikszentmihalyi and Eugene Rochberg Halton, *The Meaning of Things: Domestic Symbols and the Self*, 83.

to cast a disrespectful glance upon them myself . . . wondering in my own mind how I could have thought a log house would afford space for such superfluities.

In this context, not just borrowing but the very possession of objects becomes difficult to codify, and the "psychic energy" projected onto these objects is dispersed.[41]

Finally, of course, borrowing relates to a merely temporary arrangement of possession and holds within it a possible loss. Within this transaction of lending and borrowing, neither party possesses the object securely. Pratt has written of the way in which "the difference between equal and unequal exchange is suppressed" in the colonial encounter.[42] Here, however, borrowing—a temporary exchange—articulates the unstable relations between groups with opposing economic and political interests, an absence of consensus about value across different social groups, and the tenuousness of the identity and status affirmed so confidently elsewhere in the text. Traill's empire of Woman is partly the representation of a securely dominated colonial space. It is also a shared borderland of mutual incomprehension.

We cannot ignore the extent to which texts such as Traill's were drenched in the assumptions of the mid-nineteenth-century empire-builder; the representation of domesticity that we find in these texts needs to be located within that context. At the same time, the present emphasis in the field on the brooding domination of middle-class mores in the colonial context obscures the representation, in texts such as Traill's, of a conflicted and provisional domesticity. Her writing describes a world where the loss of distinction attendant on emigration is at least as apparent as the authority that it bestows on the privileged settler. The anxious marking of social boundaries is scarcely unusual in mid-nineteenth-century Britain and America. But here, as we see in the troping of borrowing, are conflicted frontiers, and domesticities that fail to resolve questions around the emigrant woman's behavior.

Texts such as Traill's are, as we have seen, deeply engaged with the preoccupations of domestic discourse and the tropes through which

---

41. Kirkland, *A New Home, Who'll Follow?* 42–43; Csikszentmihalyi and Halton, *The Meaning of Things*, 142.

42. Pratt, *Through Imperial Eyes*, 84.

those preoccupations were articulated. In this last chapter, I have considered how the position of the emigrant threatens to unravel the writing of conventional domesticity. These emigrant texts do much more, however, than rehearse the tropes of the discourse of domesticity. In the next chapter, I want to look at some of the less predictable detail of the domestic sanctioned by emigration discourse, and consider how to read it.

4

Domesticity and Dirt

Eliza Farnham's *Life in Prairie Land* and
Christiana Tillson's *Reminiscences of Early Life in Illinois*

*I*N THE LAST CHAPTER, I looked at the gap between the subject position of the colonist and that of the emigrant as it appears in the writing of instructional text, and at some of the problems for the emigrant autobiographer in assimilating those tropes through which the management of others was imagined. In this chapter, I want to look specifically at the representation of domestic work in emigrant autobiography and to reconsider the relationship between the homework written within the mainstream and that which is represented in emigrant texts: Kolodny's scene of the "domestic fantasy" moving West—or at least the West of popular imagination. Writing in 1984, Kolodny argued that, in the mid-nineteenth century, the domestic ideal was perceived to be achievable in the American West with a completeness that was proving difficult at the metropolitan center. At the same time, historians such as Sandra Myres, Julie Roy Jeffrey, and Robert Griswold wrestled throughout the 1980s with the question of whether emigrant women held fast to the domestic ideology of the center and what the western environment may have done to modify conventional beliefs. More recently, postcolonial critics such as Anne McClintock have argued for a more dynamic symbiosis between the "new" and the metropolitan home. McClintock suggests that it was not merely that the Victorian home became "the space for the display of imperial spectacle and the reinvention of race" but that the work of imperialism charged the work of domesticity with ideology: "Imperialism suffused the Victorian culture of domesticity and the historic separation of the private and the public, which took shape around colonialism and the idea of race."[1] I want to pursue the argument about the relationship between the domesticities written in an urban context and those written by Anglo emigrant women. I will suggest that the domestic, as it is represented within emigrant narratives, is not necessarily or in any consistent way inflected by the western scene or the context of emigration. Nor, however, can domestic description in emigrant texts always be attached to the discourse of domesticity.

We may, however, embark on the discussion by looking at how the conventional practices of domestic discourse, as they were continually rehearsed in narratives set in an urban and suburban context, could not only be reexemplified in scenes of "new homes" in the West but also exactly replicated regardless of context, on either side of Atlantic. There was little perceived need, on the part of apologists for domesticity in any context, to invent new tropes to explicate, rehearse, and justify bourgeois domestic values. A comparison between scenes in Eliza Farnham's *Life in Prairie Land*, published in 1846, and Elizabeth Hamilton's British best-selling tale of provincial squalor, *The Cottagers of Glenburnie*, published four years later, for example, makes evident the transferability (in any direction) not merely of the general values underpinning middle-class domesticity but of specific scenes to illustrate them. In both texts there are pivotal episodes dealing with the experiences of a displaced middle-class woman living as a temporary boarder in the remote household of a farmer. Processes of food preparation constructed as dirty are used to signify an unbridgeable gap between middle-class female boarder and farming family and to justify a separation between them: no relationship whatsoever can apparently be sustained between the very white and spotless figure of the temporarily homeless visitor and her hosts. The response to perceived squalor, in both cases, is the heroines' horrified withdrawal into "rooms of their own": separate and private spaces within the house that they have "scoured," "washed," and "thoroughly cleansed" into a "snug, neat little home."

---

1. Kolodny, *The Land Before Her*, chapter 8. See, for example, the discussions in Myres, *Westering Women*, 6–7; Jeffrey, *Frontier Women*, 7–12; and Robert Griswold, "Anglo Women and Domestic Ideology in the Late Nineteenth and Early Twentieth Century," 15–22. Anne McClintock, *Imperial Leather: Race, Gender and Sexuality in the Imperial Contest*, 36.

In the familiar figure of separation between classes and sexes in the middle-class home, in creating "a room of her own," in a "[cleansed] snug neat little home," both Farnham and Hamilton imagine a means whereby the housewife is both active and hardworking, and also hermetically sealed within the home. As Jane Marcus points out, in the context of a discussion of the great apologist for rooms of one's own, the consideration of the terms on which the perceived privilege of a private space rests—the exclusion of others and the refusal of the possibility of the needs of others for similar benefits—is omitted in the claim for a separate space of their own. Yet, as Marcus goes on to point out, the room of one's own, while "a space where one can escape from being the object of the gaze of others," is nevertheless "merely for privacy in confinement to police one's own prison as it were, not to stretch into space without boundaries."[2] Whether or not we choose to read this self-imposed withdrawal sympathetically, the point remains that, in scenes such as these, the actual context of the North American backwoods was scarcely relevant.

At the same time, though, it was not unusual for mid-nineteenth-century writers of domesticity to use the figure of the untutored emigrant wife to warn of a national need for domestic expertise and to evoke domestic incapability, as in the grim comment of Catherine Beecher in *A Treatise on Domestic Economy:* "A pupil of the writer, at the end of her schooldays, married and removed to the West. She was an entire novice in all domestic matters; an entire stranger to the place to which she removed. In a year she became a mother, and *her health failed.*" Similarly, Eunice Bullard Beecher's narrative of the life of a western minister's wife, *From Dawn to Daylight or the Simple Story of a Western Home* (1859) puts words of despair at domestic duties (as opposed to, say, the commoner lament at loss of family) into the mouth of the overtaxed emigrant heroine: "None can tell, but those who have been tried, how soon the strongest constitutions droop before the difficulties and hard labor incident to limited means, and in the generally unhealthy climate of the new states. I could point to many, many graves . . ." Such comments, however, were using backwoods isolation merely to accent representations of the predicament of the

---

2. Marcus, "Registering Objections," 183.

untrained and unsupported housewife in ways that were affirmative to the calls from domestic education current at the time.[3]

Generally, there was no shortage of representations of setting up home in any circumstances as a series of trials that could be resolved through seclusion, a renewed focus on the skills of housekeeping, and the meticulous supervision of servants. Nor was this a subject that precluded description of the tedium, even misery of learning to keep the first "new home," though that description of woe might be muted or resolved through depictions of, for instance, the love of children. This kind of material was, of course, very apposite for the portrayal of emigrant domesticity. It does not undermine the ideal, but it elaborates on the painful discipline it forces on the housekeeper.

Keeping House and Housekeeping, the work of Sara Josepha Hale, a writer sometimes regarded as the high priestess of domesticity, is a good example of a strain of metropolitan domestic writing that lingered on the description of the sacrificial aspects of setting up home. It concerns the situation of an attractive but domestically untutored young wife who learns, through a series of increasingly humiliating trials, to reject an outside world of social contact and to embrace domestic responsibilities in the form of household work and a renewed focus on child and husband. The tests of this pettish young wife are the standard ones in this body of more or less didactic domestic writing: she fails to discipline or to inspire servants to provide a good table, and she cannot take the reins herself, in terms of cooking and entertaining. At first her husband indulges her incompetence, but her failures soon become exasperating to him. Meanwhile, the wife is tempted to overspend, especially on fashionable clothes and unnecessary items, and her negligence enables her servants to overspend. The point at which this incompetence threatens the stability of the home and the devotion of the husband occurs in the form of the child falling ill. The young wife emerges from this crisis with new priorities, born again in a willingness to learn the

---

3. Catherine Beecher, *A Treatise on Domestic Economy*, 42; Eunice Bullard Beecher, *From Dawn to Daylight; or the Simple Story of a Western Home*, 59. For discussions of domestic education, see Strasser, *Never Done*, 185–95; Laura Shapiro, *Perfection Salad: Women and Cooking at the Turn of the Century*, 27–33, and Jean Boydston, Mary Kelley, and Anne Margolis, *The Limits of Sisterhood: The Beecher Sisters on Women's Rights and Women's Sphere*, 13–14, 115–24.

tasks of housewifery—here, as is often the case, exemplified by cooking. In doing so, she removes any possibility of the servants ever gaining ascendancy over her again by learning their skills. She disdains to spend time with her friends now, preferring to withdraw into seclusion.

Sara Josepha Hale's narrative has a dour air, as do such very similar tales as Mrs. Graves's "Emily Howard" in *Girlhood and Womanhood* and Eliza Follen's *Sketches of Married Life*. Less admonitory are the semiautobiographical reminiscences of Caroline Gilman in *Recollections of a Housekeeper*, the episodes concerning the eponymous hero's marriage to Dora in *David Copperfield*, and the strand of Louisa May Alcott's *Good Wives* that deals with the housewifery of Meg Brooke.

If these didactic narratives reach their resolution in the restatement of an ideal of domestic behavior, they also make the extent of the sacrifice evident to the reader. They construct domesticity as dictating an absolute loss of freedom, tawdry as these narratives seek to prove that freedom to be. Further, those narratives or episodes that do not end with the death of the irresponsible housewife (as in the case of Dora Copperfield, for example) close without any prospect of the housewife regaining another order of freedom. In the austere world of Hale and Graves in particular, there is no good going out, no harmless amusement to leaven the weight of responsibility. Alcott's Meg Brooke loses what she must in order to run a happy home, but her reform brings other losses too: the reformed Meg is no longer interested in the world outside at all, and, when her husband looks to discuss the election with her, she can only try (unsuccessfully) "to look deeply interested, to ask intelligent questions, and to keep her thoughts from wandering from the state of the nation to the state of her new bonnet."[4]

Domestic life is painful in these texts, for the protagonist may be wounded to the point of disintegrated self-respect. Caroline Gilman's narration of problems in separating her work in the kitchen from the work of managing the dining room are just demoralizing. Her problems mark her even so: "When my husband looked at me for the first time alone, at his table, he perceived that the kitchen fire, added to the effects of weeping, had deepened my complexion beyond the delicacy of beauty, and as I was assisting him to a potato, detected a spot of

---

4. Louisa May Alcott, *Good Wives*, 199.

'smut' (pot black) on the finger on which he had placed a pearl ring."[5] Much worse is the agony of Sara Hale's heroine, who experiences the nightmare of risking all, financially and socially, to cut a social dash. She throws a party à la mode in her home, only to see her aspirations laid waste in the deeply humiliating failure that it becomes.

Narratives such as these raise the work of housekeeping in general to a high pitch of anxiety, locating crises and trials in the everyday. The heroine is subject, at every turn, to the unforgiving and absolute judgment of others—husband, relatives, visitors, employees—on her person and her home. The fact that there are no excuses—only failings in skill and experience—produces a world of inescapable correction. Emily Howard's husband in Mrs. Graves's *Girlhood and Womanhood* is plainly to be understood as impatient and fastidious, yet his reported remonstrances blend with the authorial voice in repetition of the terms of domestic virtue: "She was wholly unfitted to contend with impertinence and inefficiency of hired menials. In order to produce neatness and regularity in the daily routine of her husband's household, she knew not how much was necessary, what vigilant attention and what unremitting superintendance in every department." The women in Graves's text all learn "the duties of their sex and station," but the very day-to-day quality of their trials at the hands of others has the effect of arousing our pity for the heroine who has not, after all, "failed" on purpose.[6]

The same mid-nineteenth-century tropes of domestic disaster are used across the range of North American emigrant texts: the dinner as debacle (in Farnham), the first humiliating attempt to cook (in Moodie), the failure to make servants serve (in Kirkland and Moodie), the use of a series of domestic disasters as a plot mechanism (in Farnham, Kirkland, and Moodie). Likewise, the inflexible and punishing judgments of others upon the forlorn housewife's efforts reappear, as when Moodie, in *Roughing It*, shows herself compromised by the blackened, half-raw result of her bread-baking:

> "It is the bread," said I . . . "Dear me it is all burnt!"
> "And smells as sour as vinegar," says he. "The black bread of Sparta!"

5. Caroline Gilman, *The Recollections of a Housekeeper*, 23.
6. A. J. Graves, *Girlhood and Womanhood or Sketches of My Schoolmates*, 75, 81.

> Alas! for my maiden loaf! With a rueful face I placed it on the breakfast table. "I hoped to have given you a treat, but I feel you will find it worse than cakes in the pan."
> "You may be sure of that," said Tom, as he stuck his knife into the loaf, and drew it forth covered with raw dough. "Oh, Mrs. Moodie, I hope you make better books than bread."

The dully routine nature of the behavior demanded of the housewife is emphatically set out, here by Kirkland:

> The inexorable dinner hour, which is passed *sub silentio* in imaginary forests, always recurs, in real woods, with distressing iteration, once in twenty-four hours, as I found to my cost. And the provoking people for whom I had undertaken to provide, seemed to me to get hungrier than ever before. There was no end to the bread that the children ate from morning till night—at least it seemed so; while a tin reflector was my only oven, and the fire required for baking drove us all out of doors.[7]

As I have suggested, the backwoods context accentuated the issues raised by setting up home. The housework demanded of the backwoods housewife—washing clothes, scrubbing floors, and cooking food with little or no help—was of a type that might have intimidated even the well-prepared middle-class bride. Where, in stories set in city and suburb, help is always eventually forthcoming, here fellow settlers revel in seeing middle-class women do their own work: in *Roughing It*, Susanna Moodie describes the "sneering laugh" of her neighbor, Mrs. Joe: "'Well, thank God! I am glad to see you brought to work at last. I hope you may have to work as hard as I have . . . I rejoice to see you at the wash-tub and I wish that you may be brought down to your knees to scrub the floors.'"[8]

However, while we can argue that the backwoods home worked well as a context for picturing the pains of setting up home, the representation of the emigrant, as we have seen, favored a detailed domestic account but not one that delivered a sense of closure. Scenes of continuing travails of the emigrant housewife were more appropriate to such an emigrant narrative's emphasis on the process of adaptation and

---

7. Moodie, *Roughing It*, 114; Kirkland, *A New Home*, 49.
8. Moodie, *Roughing It*, 149.

acceptance than to cozy domestic scenes. Thus, where in the work of writers such as Hale and Graves the central figure, once able to run her home, is always shown as enjoying, as a result, the increased love of her husband and children, the same soothing equation does not operate in *Life in Prairie Land*, *A New Home*, or *Roughing It*. The emphasis on the values of privacy, separation, and hierarchy are certainly maintained, but the ideal home remains unrealized and the compensations of self-sacrifice in consequence are suspended in a vague future rather than being, as it were, proved by the text.

Not only is the fantasy of smooth-running domestic happiness never realized in these texts, but it is displaced in curiously disembodied forms. Gillian Brown has argued that this is characteristic of nineteenth-century texts of domesticity; she suggests that these texts characteristically omit "women's agency from her own labor, disconnecting her labor from her body." This is not the case in emigrant texts, which in any case glorify work and are prone to dwell on the effort involved. The fantasy of effortless work appears in these texts as just that: invisible action performed by invisible or disappearing housewives. Farnham's rendition, in *Life in Prairie Land*, for example, of perfect baking goes so far as to attribute willpower to a pie (for whose "conduct" the hostess must "apologize"), and jokingly describes food gathering of its own accord: "Dishes now began to drop around upon [the table]. They appeared at random, of all ages, colors and sizes, just as the congregation gathers at a country meeting-house." Many emigration tracts held up the prospect of what Morris Birkbeck chose to refer to as the "pleasurable exertion" of New World labor, but Farnham's domestic scene moves beyond pleasurable exertion into a parody of automatic performance.[9]

In a similar vein, Farnham describes the perfect home in her sister's "Prairie Lodge" as a place where work is so effortless that its results are indistinguishable from the work of Nature. Farnham's sister, for example, has no need actually to make curtains as the flowers around the windows of "Prairie Lodge" are decoration sufficient or, indeed, superior to that which she might strive to produce: "These windows

---

9. Gillian Brown, *Domestic Individualism: Imagining Self in Nineteenth-Century America*, 64; Farnham, *Life in Prairie Land*, 36; Birkbeck, *Letters from Illinois*, 24.

are not so bare in the summer. I have a flowering scarlet runner that clusters very thickly over them, and makes a more beautiful drapery than your damask and gossamer."[10]

This second scene, though it deals, albeit in a more serious tone, in the same wish-fulfillment as the tea-time episode, is more darkly nuanced by the association that Farnham claims between her sister's natural domesticity and the figure of an "Indian princess." This comparison has been read by Dawn Keetley "as some kind of metaphor for white freedom" that becomes available as Native American nations were forcibly removed. But the association goes further than this. By the end of Part One, "Prairie Lodge"—the site of the domestic ideal in the text—itself disappears from the text. The sister styled an "Indian princess"—and as an ideal housewife—dies as well.[11]

Farnham is not the only mid-century emigrant writer to link the domestic angel (a figure that, in any case, as Vanessa D. Dickerson points out, occupies a strangely anomalous position as a heavenly figure presiding over an enclosed earthly space) with the doomed Indian woman. In Kirkland's *A New Home,* for example, we have the scene of a visit to the home of a French trader and his Indian wife. Keetley argues that this scene visualizes the "veritable chaos" of the "deeper cultural disorder" caused by "mixing" races. For Keetley, the episode seeks to prove the need for what has already been achieved: the colonization of the American West by Anglo-Europeans. All this makes sense, but the scene also, as in Farnham, displaces the housewifely ideal onto the Indian woman: this wife is hospitable, treating her visitors "with much civility," while herself remaining largely silent. Certainly, we seem to have here a variant on the bourgeois fantasy of the worthy poor. Yet this figure of the Indian woman provides precisely the kind of supper endlessly praised in domestic discourse: austere, yet made "luxurious" by the addition of fruit and syrup, the signifiers of the frugal and old-fashioned skills of the cook. Her children, furthermore, are "shy innocents": they "(exhibit) none of the staring curiosity which is seen peeping from the sun-bleached locks of the whiter broods of the same class of settlers." The Indian

10. Farnham, *Life in Prairie Land,* 33.
11. Farnham, *Life in Prairie Land,* 32; Dawn E. Keetley, "Unsettling the Frontier: Gender and Racial Hegemony in Caroline Kirkland's *A New Home, Who'll Follow?* 32.

wife is even a doughty supporter of that favorite middle-class Anglo-American cause, temperance; she is represented disapproving—with a modest silence—of the maltreatment of Indians at the unscrupulous hands of her husband, a man who accelerates and anticipates Indian downfall by selling them whiskey. As in *Life in Prairie Land,* the ideal is located in the figure of a marginalized and "disappearing" race.[12]

In sum, then, tracing the relations between mainstream domestic discourse and texts written about backwoods domesticity produces a melange of scenes: some lifted from countless other domestic texts, some exaggerated versions of common tropes and plots, and some that are differently nuanced by the context of emigration. This in itself suggests a richer writing of the domestic than is often attributed to these texts. To finish here, however, would be to leave unexamined some of the other—and sometimes most striking—domestic description within emigrant writing. The difficulty with the scholarly emphasis on the cult of domesticity as exercising an ideological stranglehold, paired with the increasing tendency to contextualize domestic description predominantly in terms of class fantasy and imperial strategy (or indeed, as in the case of a writer such as Faragher, in terms of patriarchal structures)[13] is that it has tended to discuss a domesticity with a thinner content than that which we find within the texts under discussion. As scholars use structures and formations generated by the relationships and practices of the workplace, the priorities of the capitalist economy, and the ambitions of the builders of empire to understand the world of the domestic, so the domestic space seems, increasingly, to be significant only insofar as it reflects and rehearses those structures and formations.[14] This model of reflection drains the domestic of its vitality and variousness, reducing the domestic to a mere microcosm of a more real world

---

12. Vanessa D. Dickerson, ed., *Keeping the Victorian Home,* xiv; Keetley, "Unsettling the Frontier," 31; Kirkland, *A New Home,* 28–29.
13. See Faragher, *Women and Men on the Overland Trail,* 2–3.
14. Dorothy O. Helly and Susan M. Reverby provide a helpful overview of the public/private debate in "Converging on History," their introduction to *Gendered Domains: Rethinking Public and Private in Women's History.* Also helpful is the broader discussion of Stanley I. Benn and Gerald F. Gaus, in the introduction to *Public and Private in Social Life;* Margaret R. Higonnet's "New Cartographies" in *Reconfiguring Spheres: Feminist Explorations of Literary Space,* opens up the discussion of gender and space.

outside, and it erases much of the discussion of the domestic work in emigrant texts.

The home, as Henrietta Moore suggests, is inhabited by social actors who do not merely follow the rules; their movement through and action in ordered space are simultaneously action and interpretation and intelligible as such.[15] If this is the case, we need not assume that the domestic life of the interior has, as it were, nothing of its own to say. If action in the domestic space may have fluctuating and changeable agendas, then it may create meaning not only with regard to the interior life of the home but also as an expression of interpretations of contemporary cultural practices and formations.

This is the argument I want to make in relation to the domestic work represented in Eliza Farnham's *Life in Prairie Land,* for this narrative seems to me to elucidate the work of emigration as it is performed in the domestic space. In chapter 13 of *Life in Prairie Land,* Farnham speaks, in an account of her organization of setting up home in Illinois, to the western democratic ideal of self-sufficiency and independence. Here we see her own hands marked in the pursuit of the ideal. Farnham's description of cleaning the floor runs thus: "I . . . proceeded to put these cleansing agents to their duty. Their efficiency succeeded my most sanguine expectations. The floor came up from the superincumbent mass, with a distinctness which no one could have anticipated. Blistered hands and lacerated fingers were matters of no moment to one intent upon a great purpose like mine."[16]

On one level, Farnham follows the convention in nineteenth-century domestic discourse of elevating housework above labor: she describes the process as overseen—though in this case as a spatially puzzling interaction between "cleansing agents" and "superincumbent mass" (the elaborate term she uses to name the dirt). Here also is the task of domestication: the transformation of the ground into a clean floor. The work is hard, but Farnham's lofty expression in this passage diminishes its drudgery: her language cleans up her act.[17]

---

15. Henrietta Moore, *Space, Time and Gender: An Anthropological Study of the Marakwet of Kenya,* 78, 85.
16. Farnham, *Life in Prairie Land,* 79.
17. I am indebted to my colleague at King Alfred's College, Professor Christoper Mulvey, for this observation.

And yet the high formality of the language also allows us to read her words ironically, by pointing both to the mock-heroic possibilities inherent in a scene of the writer scrubbing a floor, and to the gap between the construction of domesticity as imposing right order and the work that is actually performed. Significantly, it is difficult to find a parallel with this scene in the mid-nineteenth-century literature of domesticity. Certainly, women writers used mock-heroic language to register the pains of household tasks; as in "The Patchwork Quilt" for instance, in *The Lowell Offering:* "O what a heroine was I in driving the stitches! What a martyr under the pricks and inflictions of the needle, which often sent the blood from my fingers but could not force a tear from my eyes! These were the first lessons in heroism and fortitude." But, as Jeanne Boydston points out, those tasks that actually dominated the routine of the mid-century housewife—she cites the drudgery of cleaning and routine sewing and mending—were not represented in descriptions, mock-heroic or otherwise, of domestic work; such descriptions, as with the above, tended to lead to the struggles of acquiring more elaborate skills.[18] This is certainly true of washing the floor. This seems to be a passage, indeed, that is directed less at the particular project of housework than to the work involved in settlement.

There are the marks of the work of scrubbing the floor on Farnham's hands: her "blistered hands and lacerated fingers" denote hands both clean and marked. Usually, in domestic discourse, we read of marked hands in opposition to the hands of unblemished whiteness that signified the middle-class ideal.[19] Again, the use of a formal diction to describe the blistered hands—the almost religiose reference to laceration and to "a great purpose" in their marking—seems to draw us away from the picturing of class difference that we normally associate with the imaging of work-worn hands in a domestic context.

Interestingly, the description of middle-class hands "blistered" and "lacerated" by the marks of labor appears in several of the emigrant narratives of the era. In Catharine Parr Traill's *Female Emigrant's Guide,* for example, we have the effect of the process represented in very similar

18. Anon., *Lowell Offering* 5, 200; Boydston, *Home and Work,* 82.
19. See Davidoff, "The Rationalization of Housework," 127.

marks. The woman is driven to harvest the fields by the sickness of her husband: "She soon became interested in the work, and though her soft hands, unused to rough labor, were *blistered and chafed* [my italics], in a few hours she had stripped the cobs . . . and thrown them into heaps, running backward and forward from time to time to speak to her baby, and amuse him by rolling towards him the big yellow golden pumpkins." This example shows the blistered hands in association with work *outside* the home; we may place it squarely within the discussion of the physical cost of "roughing it" and the importance of the process of roughing it within emigration discourse. Work in the fields is itself a trope that appears across the range of emigrant women's texts to signify the extremity of females roughing it.[20]

In Farnham's passage, however, that process of roughing your way to independence is—literally—brought home, and a different and unusual kind of true story of emigration is offered for the reader's consideration. Certainly, the "great purpose" of emigration and settlement is a matter of dirt expelled and order asserted. But it is also imaged in a female figure very different from the idealized emigrant discussed earlier: working on her hands and knees, doing "dirty work." Of course, Farnham keeps her hands clean; we do not see reddened or smudged hands here. But the association between "keeping one's hands clean" and "dirty work" is an interesting one. "Keeping your hands clean" is an adage that makes explicit the wedge between principle and politics for the subject in possession of power; "keeping one's hands clean" involves an apparent (if not actual) distancing of the self from the political "dirty work" claimed pragmatically to be necessary for the achievement of policy.[21] Farnham's clean but nevertheless lacerated hands may signify the suffering of the emigrant woman and the implications of settlement brought home. They also bring home the limitations, if not the impossibility, of asserting distance from the "dirty work" of settlement achieved with what is now perceived to be a ruthless pragmatism.

Nancy I. Paxton has written that "tracing how the physical body, as subject and object, writes itself into these texts" helps us to locate

---

20. Traill, *Female Emigrant's Guide*, 114–15. Other examples of working in the fields may be found in Moodie's *Roughing It,* chap. 21; and Burlend, *A True Picture of Emigration,* 91–92.

21. The figure of keeping one's hands clean or getting them dirty is discussed by M. Walzer in "Political Action: The Problem of Dirty Hands."

the "troubled site of 'disruption' and displacement" in autobiographies written in the colonial context. The figure of Farnham's hands—spotless and yet blistered—articulates the conflicted position of the emigrant within colonization: neither personally responsible nor personally fulfilled—and yet inescapably marked by her or his participation.[22]

More dramatically, scenes of eating in the emigrant autobiographies of middle-class women show the body of the writer in revolt. In such episodes, participation in the process of settlement in the backwoods is rewritten as enforced, and individual fulfillment and domestic felicity, the reward for emigration, as a sham. A highly charged version of this kind of scene appears in Christiana Tillson's *Reminiscences of Early Life in Illinois*. The occasion is, once again, a familiar trope of North American travelogue: the meal served in the home of a family of dirty settlers or in a dirty inn. It is the liminal space of the frontier, the edgy encounter between emigrants and settlers understood as an indigenous "native" population. Tillson's response to the prospect of eating breakfast in such a space, an event that she has tried to avoid, is as follows: "Oh, oh, oh! What could I do. I told him [her husband] it would be impossible for me to eat a mouthful in that house, and that what I had already seen the night before was already more than I would stand; but before we were ready to start, breakfast was smoking on the table, and I had no alternative but to sit down."[23]

This is of course the same prospect of closely sharing the communal performance of food with unacceptable others that continually appears in texts of travel and settlement, as for example in *The Journal of Madam Knight* where Sarah Kemble Knight, writing of her business trip from Boston to New Haven and New York in 1704, describes a meal that she is offered in the following terms: "Having called for something to eat, the woman bro't in a twisted thing like a cable, but something whiter; and laying it in the bord, tugg'd for life to bring it into capacity to spread; [which] having [with] great pains accomplished, shee serv'd in a dish of Pork and Cabbage, I suppose the remains of Dinner. The sause was of a deep Purple, [which] I tho't was boiled in a dye Kettle; the bread was India." Anne Royall's *Sketches*

22. Nancy I. Paxton, "Disembodied Subjects: English Women's Autobiography under the Raj," 388.
23. Christiana Tillson, *Reminiscences of Early Life in Illinois*, 50–51.

of History, Life and Manners in the United States strikes a very similar note:

> Meanwhile you are addressed by the mistress of the family, "I reckon you are almost starved," while she is busied in preparing you something to eat; while this is doing, you are suffering the torments of the ordeal from the impertinent curiosity of the whole family . . . At length a small table is drawn into the center of the same apartment you are in, while the noise produced by it jars every nerve in your body. The table is covered, (in many instances, with a cloth black with grease and dirt) ten or a dozen plates, (I'll say nothing of them) are placed on it. . . . At one end of the table is another pile of besmeared, becracked cups and saucers, which seem to maintain their place on the edge of the table by magic.[24]

The writing of the "frontier" in autobiography and travelogue often envisions food in the West as disgusting, especially by reason of its contact with a dirty cook. The appearance of smoking meat is a standard detail, as is the appearance of "dirty" pickles—William Dunlop's description of "the bilious Calcutta-looking complexion, and slobbery, slimy consistency" of Canadian pickles demonstrates the range of racial reference available to the abusive Anglo middle-class emigrant writer.[25] The willingness of "other" settlers to eat such food, their method of preparing it, and its restricted range is one of the standard markers of their lack of civilization.

Looking at the trope of consuming crudely cooked and served meat recalls, of course, Levi-Strauss's well-known analysis of how the method used to cook food may be understood. The issue in descriptions of western cooking is often that the food is insufficiently cooked: not purified, not civilized. Meat is often smoking on the outside, burned and spoiled, prepared without utensils, and being roasted; hardly, in Levi-Strauss's terms, changed in its composition at all. We can find this hierarchy of meat preparation clearly reasserted in the mid-nineteenth-century domestic guide; in, for example, Mrs. Loudon's *The Lady's Country Companion*, which makes it clear that roast meat is less than

---

24. Sarah Kemble Knight, *The Journals of Madam Knight and Rev. Mr. Buckingham*, 14–15; Anne Royall, *Sketches of History, Life and Manners in the United States*, 59.

25. Dunlop, *Statistical Sketches*, 57.

appropriate as a meal if it is not accompanied by foods cooked in more elaborate ways. In Loudon, for example, smoked meats are more praiseworthy, being those that, in Levi-Strauss's construct, are most redolent of the transformations of raw meat into a commodity that may be used at any time, or used in exchange.[26]

The form of food that these emigrant writers of autobiography (and indeed the writers of travelogue) most abhor is that which is not preserved, that which directly expresses the frontier values they laud in principle elsewhere: frugality, pragmatism, informality. Even the treatment and appearance of bakery and dairy foods—the bread cooked in a kettle by the fire that is sometimes so soft inside as to suggest a parallel with the crude process of roasting, the butter in any case uncooked and subject to spoiling—commonly signify a lack of civilization. Anne Norton has made an important argument for the specific associations, in the nineteenth century, of the West of the United States with extremes of masculine appetite both for food and whiskey, and with the subsequent evacuation of food. This she links with westerners' fantasy of themselves as strong by reason of their untutored, aggressive instincts, as close to nature. It is easy to make the connection between appetite and the "land hunger" exemplified in the massive populating of the American West in the wake of the building of the Erie Canal or in the pressure exerted on the government by settlers wanting to "clear" the land of Native Americans. But in Tillson's narrative we have the opposing phenomenon: not eating.

Tillson represents herself waiting at the table for her breakfast and considering a meal that she reads as exemplifying the qualities of western life: disordered, careless, appealing to the crudest appetite. It is, in its form and presentation, redolent of a space both uncivilized and corrupt, and she portrays herself as refusing to consume the food until, almost literally, she is being forced to eat her words. That Tillson means to suggest an experience of extremity is suggested by the textual disintegration at the start of the passage: "Oh, oh, oh!" But, finally, she is made to eat the breakfast; her husband's indifference to her response means she has "no alternative but to sit."

26. J. Loudon, *The Lady's Country Companion; or How to Enjoy a Country Life Rationally*, 67 ff.

Her refusal to eat may be understood in terms of her undoubted sensitivity to any narrowing of distinctions of class: she does not want to consume the same food as those whom she considers more or less savage. There is also an implication that her right to choose is easily ignored because of her status as a woman. As Lillian Furst points out, not eating is "[A] potent means to control one's own life, to negotiate disagreeable situations and to manipulate others. Eating may provide comfort and pleasure as well as satisfying or placating others, while non-eating can be an assertion of will, an expression of one's own preferences in defiance of those imposed from outside." However, Tillson's refusal to eat also evokes a refusal to participate in or tolerate, in particular or general terms, the consumption underway. As with the scenes of blistered hands, this passage's significance seems all the greater when one notes its similarity to passages in, for example, Kirkland's *A New Home* and *Life in Prairie Land*, though Tillson's is different in its representation of herself voicing her refusal.[27]

When Tillson's husband consumes the food without demur, even remarking that "the breakfast seemed pretty good," Tillson is obliged to swallow what is unbearable to her, to literally, as David Spurr puts it, "interiorize savagery"—that of not only her fellow settlers but also perhaps her westernizing husband who can apparently swallow the traces of the Other with pleasure.[28] Here, in Tillson's passage, we have a sense of self in collapse, and the articulation of a moment where the superfluous position of her own values and aspirations in the West is laid bare. If greedy consumption of food epitomized one construction of colonization, surely refusal to eat repellent food evokes others: certainly, a reading of a female alienation and a class-based revulsion that seems familiar from other representations of emigration; but also a rereading of the mythology of independence and self-definition in the West set in scenes of domestic behavior and ritual.

The difficulty of finding boundaries within the spaces, domestic or otherwise, is not only addressed exclusively in relation to the western context. The world of domestic work that Luce Giard describes in "Doing-Cooking" is one that continually resists the drawing of

---

27. Lillian R. Furst, ed., *Disorderly Eaters: Texts in Self-Empowerment*, 153; Kirkland, *A New Home*, 14; Farnham, *Life in Prairie Land*, 75.
28. Tillson, *Reminiscences*, 51; Spurr, *Rhetoric of Empire*, 77.

boundaries: there is within it a process of work "without schedule or salary, . . . without added value or productivity, work whose success is always experienced for a limited duration," of which the traces are continually and altogether erased. I shall consider the issue of routine and the writing of it in chapter 6, but here I want to return to the passage in *Life in Prairie Land* with which this chapter began: Farnham's description of food preparation that justifies her withdrawal from the spaces of her fellow settlers into a "room of her own." It is, as I have already suggested, a familiar trope of nineteenth-century travelogue of North America. This is the moment when both observer-visitor and observed/"native" occupy the undivided space of the rural home, as the latter engages in cooking:

> Opposite the fireplace . . . stands a table, spread with a darkfigured india-rubber cloth. Beside this stands our lady hostess manipulating various parcels of dough; a process rendered particularly interesting from the fact that a current of air enters the fireplace every few moments from the south side and departs at the northern to make the circuit of the room; having during its brief stay taken a heavy freight of ashes and smoke. . . . A very considerable portion of this cargo is deposited upon the table, and the principal object of the woman's labor seems to be to distribute this brown coating fairly through the mass. Each time that the parcels are taken up, the space they have covered is left comparatively clean, and though I will with an earnestness that starts the perspiration that the operator will lay them on the same spot again, yet she fails to do it in every instance . . . How could one ever eat that bread?[29]

The intrusion of industrial modes of work (performed without satisfaction by "hands") into domestic work that was so repellent to the mid-nineteenth-century middle class is clear enough in the reference to "freight," "cargo," and the "labor" of "operators." Nor need the reader strain to find a parallel between this portrait of a "lady hostess" and the ubiquitous hate figures of mid-nineteenth-century literature that represented domestic life; the ugly, red-handed servants who signify the order of labor from which reader and writer separate

---

29. Luce Giard, "Doing-Cooking," 159, 153; Farnham, *Life in Prairie Land*, 73–75.

themselves.[30] There are echoes here, too, of the angry discussion in many travelogues of the failure of settlers to match the mythology of the "new home."

What makes the passage more pointed in its commentary on repugnant values is the ambiguous subject position of the female narrator. This is not the housewife regarding her servant in the hierarchized bourgeois home, but a passive inhabitant of the working-class lair; in this case an Easterner (and a self-styled apologist for a domesticity ideally fulfilled in the West) "come home" to the maternal lap of West, who runs away from domestic work. As Carla Mertes, among others, has pointed out, the great subject of nineteenth-century domestic instruction was the distinction between middle- and working-class women's contact with "dirty" work: the "cult of domesticity . . . functioned as part of middle-class struggle to define and concretize the absolute differences between working-class and middle-class lifestyles."[31] Farnham's passage evokes not only a reversal where the middle-class woman must participate in the life of a working-class woman, where both settler and writer are involved in a domestic task, but also a situation where the task itself, kneading, is plainly difficult to codify in any context.

Farnham's choice of kneading as her focus was not an unusual one. It was, however, a task full of contending meanings. Lilly Martin Spencer's popular 1854 painting, *Shake Hands?* is a good example of a representation of the problematic quality of kneading. It shows a woman kneading bread at a point where the raw dough is wet enough to leave its traces sticking to her fingers. The moment depicted shows the offer, on the part of this figure, of her palm, covered with dough, to someone who—like the viewer of the painting—comes upon her in the kitchen. Her words are "Shake hands?" Must the viewer smile at her jolly informality and demur, or refuse her hand because the work she is doing makes her hands unpleasant to touch—in a sense, dirty? Certainly, dirty work would, as Phyllis Palmer argues, "threaten to taint the character of the woman who does it," and yet this hand is

30. For a discussion of the complexities of the identification between servants' hands and work, see Bruce Robbins's *The Servant's Hand: English Fiction from Below*, Introduction.
31. Cara Mertes, "There's No Place Like Home: Women and Domestic Labor," 66.

Lilly Martin Spencer, *Shake Hands?* (1854). Ohio Historical Society, Columbus.

not precisely "dirty." As Mary Douglas points out, there is no such thing as "dirt," but only a substance positioned in a way that is perceived as inappropriate in cultural terms.[32] Nor is it clear whether we are looking at a healthy woman at work performing a task both simple and redolent of nurture (a task that we might associate with health and capability), or whether the scene is to be understood as taking place in more threatening regions "below stairs."

Certainly, some contemporary reviewers identified the subject of the painting as one of Spencer's unattractively "grinning servants." Are we, then, being welcomed into the heart of the home, or are we intruding on the space of a servant (surrounded by dead animals and having apparently taken a bite from an apple) with a vividly physical presence—plump, uncovered arms—and a gaze of challenging invitation; a woman whose hand we would not expect to shake? This is not a scene, then, that we may see "[concretizing] the absolute differences between working-class and middle-class lifestyles"; on the contrary, it blurs those differences.[33]

The baking of bread has continually been represented as an activity fundamental to the imagination of domestic work as pleasurable and virtuous. But, as Lisa M. Heldke writes, kneading is a part of making bread "in which subjects' and objects' boundaries necessarily meet, touch and overlap"; in kneading, boundaries are broken down between subject and object, between what is "worked" and what is consumed, between what is handled and what is ingested, between what is needed and what is unpleasantly untouchable, at least in its raw state.[34]

Farnham's retreat into a "room of her own" in response to a "dirty" woman is predictable. Perhaps it is also a flight from a task that cannot finally be understood as dirty or elevated, that collapses distinctions between the abject "outside" world of physical drudgery and the ennobling world of secluded domestic felicity. Her flight reasserts the stratification of the domestic space and its work and refocuses the dis-

---

32. Phyllis Palmer, *Domesticity and Dirt: Housewives and Domestic Servants in the U.S., 1920–1945*, 138; Mary Douglas, *Purity and Danger: An Analysis of Concepts of Pollution and Taboo*, 35–36.

33. For a discussion of such reviews, see Elizabeth O'Leary, *At Beck and Call: The Representation of Domestic Servants in Nineteenth-Century American Painting*, 66 ff; Mertes, "There's No Place Like Home," 66.

34. Lisa M. Heldke, "Foodmaking as a Thoughtful Practice," 206.

cussion of housework firmly back on a purification that is both aggressive and self-imprisoning. But the moment of observation of kneading remains a powerfully disturbing one.

To attempt to reread the detail of housework in a text such as Farnham's may seem labored, and yet it is in the performance of the everyday—both in actions and, in Farnham's case, in writing—that, as Michel De Certeau writes, we continually adapt dominant cultural forms to our "own interests and [our] own rules." This is, indeed, the interest of "everyday life." At the same time, Farnham's text evokes what De Certeau calls the "'indirect' and 'errant' trajectories" traced within conventional cultural practices, the "innumerable and infinitesimal transformations of and within the dominant cultural economy" that are made by the individual.[35] It is not a housework that can be read solely through arguments about the transfer or the intensification of domesticity, nor even the West.

In the introduction to this book, I considered the ways in which we might think of Eliza Farnham's writing of a domestic text of the West: as the work of a woman embroiled in a complicated, controversial, and, in many ways, constrained metropolitan public life; of a back-migrant; of a woman nostalgic for a past episode. It is this context, I think, that may inspire us to consider what is unexpected or difficult as well as what is conventional within the domesticity of *Life in Prairie Land*. The work of housekeeping is, as we have seen, a highly significant subject within the discourse of domesticity. In the mid-nineteenth century, at least, emigrant women's autobiography, with its detail of the domestic, addresses the subject of that work with intensity and presses home the breadth and variation of meaning within domestic behavior.

---

35. Michel De Certeau, *The Practice of Everyday Life*, xiv, xviii.

5

"A Space in Which to be Imaginative"

Caroline Kirkland's *A New Home, Who'll Follow?*

*I*N CHAPTER 1, I looked at how space could be imagined in writing about the pioneer woman: what Susan L. Roberson has called "a widening of [the] sense of self." Roberson writes, "At the same time that she was extending spatial, territorial boundaries, going from 'the states' to the territories, the pioneer woman was opening up social and psychological spaces, new knowledges, powers, and discourses."[1] The "territories" of the pioneer woman might also be witnessed extending outward from the domestic space into a social space shaped by and engaged with the communal aims of women. This idealization of a home without confinement and a communal scene in which the domestic is the center is not, of course, peculiar to the writing of pioneer women. In the critical discussion of women's "regionalism," for example, women are perceived to have a sense of the local and a vision of an "elsewhere" to the city, an alternative to the individualism and rigid separation of public and private favored within industrial capitalism. More generally, it has been argued that women perceive and experience space differently, because their lives are more local.

None of these attempts to imagine the relationship between women and space is uncontroversial, of course, but they do strike a chord with the social model aspired to by those concerned with emigration at all levels—governments, speculators, writers, and emigrants

---

1. Susan L. Roberson, "'With the Wind Rocking the Wagon': Women's Narratives of the Way West," 231, 214–15.

themselves. While individual families should be independent, separate, they should not be alone.[2] The preoccupation of an emigrant such as Kitturah Belknap with her ability to stay ahead of the game, her defiantly competitive "they think Im too young to get up a dinner under the circumstance," is matched by her interest in giving meaning to such endeavors and achievements through social activity. The balance, meanwhile, between a society open enough to allow individual self-definition and one sufficiently developed to stop emigrants from "running wild" was, from the start of the movement to occupy new lands, a very important element within thinking about expansion.[3]

The scholarly work on women in western communities has often constructed a model of a female social impulse—a sisterhood—through imagining its absence; in descriptions of oppressive isolation within the process of emigration—the passages describing the midwestern farming family in John Faragher's *Women and Men on the Overland Trail*, for example; in images of the anomie of the displaced emigrant trapped in a confined domestic space and isolated from the arenas of social activity.[4] Representations of this type of experience appear in the autobiographical writings of emigrant women themselves, in many vivid visions of the psychological trauma of a woman stranded on the plains. Sarah Roberts's description of the loneliness she experienced during her time in Alberta (1906–1912), in *Alberta Homestead*, is typical: "I was left alone. How can I describe the terrible feeling of loneliness that then settled down upon me? Not a living thing in sight.

---

2. The reference is drawn from the title of R. V. Hine's discussion of community in the West: *Community on the Frontier: Separate but Not Alone*.

3. Belknap, "Keturah Penton Belknap," 137. For discussions about fears of running wild see Cayton and Onuf, *The MidWest and the Nation*, chapter 1; and Owram, *Promise of Eden*, 19 ff.

4. Faragher, *Women and Men on the Overland Trail*, 136–43. For other examples of the woes of the displaced woman represented see the examples in Ruth Moynihan, Susan Armitage, and Christiane Fischer Dichamp, *So Much to Be Done: Women Settlers on the Mining and Ranching Frontier*, especially the extract from Mrs. A. M. Green's *Sixteen Days on the Great American Desert; or the Trials and Tribulations of a Frontier Life* (Titusville, Pa.: Frank W. Truedell, 1887), 124–46; Fischer, *Let Them Speak for Themselves*, especially the extract from Virginia Wilcox Ivins, *Pen Pictures of Early Western Days* (Keokuk, Iowa, 1905), 75–82. Elizabeth Hampsten, in *Read This Only to Yourself*, quotes at length from the comparable (unpublished) narrative of Julia Carpenter, 187–208.

Not a sound broke the silence." It is also common to find the need for the company of other women to be registered not only in statements of their absence, but also in comment on the absence of sympathetic companions. There are often issues of class hostility in the latter case, but in evidence too is the depiction of the comfortless competitiveness of a small community as described by Eunice Bullard Beecher in *From Dawn to Daylight,* which insists that the emigrant wife of the local minister "must head the Sewing Society and Maternal Association, and preside at the Female Prayer Meeting, be 'at home' to calls, at all hours of the day, of the most unmerciful length, from the very ones, perhaps, who will go away and wonder that Mrs. -'s floors were not cleaner, or her work out the way in better season, or '*did* you see that hole in Mr. -'s coat?' 'Yes and Carrie's dress wanted mending sadly, and Willie's hands and face were really *dirty.* How can Mrs. — *be so careless?*'"[5]

However, if representations of the absence of a social and communal context are common, much rarer are representations of communities realized in anything approaching the meticulous detail accorded to individual achievements in the domestic space. For all this emphasis on social needs and the miseries of isolation, in many Anglo emigrant texts the discussion of social networks operating outside the domestic space, whether it is affirmative or critical, tends to reflect a space understood through the tropes of travelogue rather than through a knowledge of the social workings of a specific place and its networks of inhabitants. Thus, in some manifestations, we have communities as built developments and as the focus of boosterism, and in others we have the "characters," the linguistic idioms, the exotic customs, the prejudicial judgements—of "local color" in the sense that Fetterley and

5. Sarah Roberts, *Alberta Homestead: Chronicle of a Pioneer Family,* 41; Bullard Beecher, *From Dawn to Daylight,* 60. My reading of Roberts's memoir differs from that of Helen Buss, who, in *Mapping Our Selves: Canadian Women's Autobiography in English,* argues that Roberts learns to love the landscape (53–60). Here Buss works within and contributes to a tradition of portraying pioneer women as finding an affinity with the landscape paralleled in such American texts as Vera Norwood and Janice Monk, eds., *The Desert Is No Lady: Southwestern Landscapes in Women's Writing and Art* (New Haven, Conn.: Yale University Press, 1987). For a detailed discussion of women and landscape in the West, see Vera Norwood, "Women's Place: Continuity and Change in Response to Western Landscapes," in *Western Women: Their Land, Their Lives,* edited by Lillian Schlissel, Vicki L. Ruiz, and Janice Monk (Albuquerque: University of New Mexico Press, 1988).

Pryse describe (and dismiss) it, as generated by a self-positioning outside the life of the community.[6]

Scenes such as the following from Frances Stewart's *Our Forest Home*, a narrative of emigrant life in Upper Canada in the 1820s, trace a seamless process of growth of community:

> It is extremely interesting to observe all the operations, and I go there at four o'clock every fine evening, accompanied by some of the children, take my knitting and sit watching all they are doing until they separate after sunset . . . The bank is very high at this part of the river, and I generally take my seat on a log just above where they are at work, and have a full view of all that goes on. It is very pretty as well as interesting, and I feel quite sorry if rains or anything happens to prevent me from coming.[7]

Such passages seem to mark and approve the bustle of the expanding community of which the emigrant will become part. Yet, at the same time, they locate the writer at a distance from the settlement sufficient to leave the description uncluttered by the detail—or even the precise appearance—of an actual place.

Even passages as bland as Frances Stewart's are scarcely de rigeur even in narratives written to promote emigration or particular regions to women. Eliza Farnham's portrait of Tremont, Illinois, in *Life in Prairie Land*, exemplifies the degree to which a narrative explicitly promoting the western United States might desist from even a summarizing description of the life of a particular settlement exemplified by Stewart. Farnham devotes a single chapter to Tremont (out of more than fifty) and populates it with a series of quasi-literary village types: the gossip, the greedy pastor, "our Galen," and so on. Yet a community of some substance and complexity apparently existed. A. D. Jones, who visited Tremont while Farnham lived there, also starts his promotional comment, in *Illinois and the West*, with the anodyne "neat" and "pleasant." But he adds a number of observations that make some claim to specific knowledge of the settlement: three-quarters of the population are from New England, there is a temperance movement,

---

6. Fetterley and Pryse, *American Women Regionalists*, xi–xii.
7. Frances Stewart, *Our Forest Home: Being Extracts from the Correspondence of the late Frances Stewart*, 82–83.

an Episcopalian church is established there. Tremont, he claims, is exceptional for its "high moral tone of feeling, temperance, good order, public spirit and real intelligence." Nothing of this specificity appears in Farnham's text.[8]

On the contrary, Eliza Farnham, having defined the community as a predictable matrix of social types, also sets the social space of the community within a landscape that seems to have a largely symbolic significance: sometimes for the construction of the nation, as when the American West is lauded as "a strong and generous parent, whose arms are spread to extend protection, happiness, and life to throngs that seek them from other and less friendly climes"; sometimes in terms of pastoral, the "blossoming wilderness [of] . . . delicious odors . . . and unequaled beauty"; sometimes as the "wild, vast desolation" of a doom-laden plain. Against these shifting contexts, Tremont's community is always evidently a less interesting subject.[9]

Similar comments might be applied to Caroline Kirkland's method in *A New Home, Who'll Follow?* which transforms the ill-fated Pinckney, Michigan, into "Montacute," a name that evokes aristocratic privilege—even pastoral fantasy—rather than the circumstances of a backwoods community.[10] But the community of Kirkland's *A New Home* is a much more elaborate construction than Farnham's or Stewart's, and it is one that has attracted critics engaged in tracing a female, communitarian ethic within women's writing of the local from the mid-nineteenth century.[11] In the case of Kirkland, some of this atten-

---

8. Farnham, *Life in Prairie Land*, 104; A. D. Jones, *Illinois and the West*, 2–3. Farnham mentions Tremont's organization briefly (93), the development of the town in terms of claiming of land, politics, and religious heterogeneity in (98–99); this latter is extended into the descriptions of such types as "Deacon Cantwyne" and "Our Galen" (101–8), and the portrait of the intemperance of the owner of the grocery ("groggery would be the truer name"), 113–16.

9. Farnham, *Life in Prairie Land*, xxxiii, 111, 176. For the fullest discussion of Farnham's time in Illinois between 1835 and 1839, see Madeleine Stern's introduction to her edition of *Life in Prairie Land*, especially xi–xxv.

10. The development—or otherwise—of Pinckney and the Kirklands' investment in it is described in Frank Clever Bald, *Michigan in Four Centuries*, 172–73. Montacute is, in fact, the name of a distinguished though not particularly prominent Elizabethan mansion in the county of Somerset. I do not know if Kirkland knew of the house, but I suspect that she chose the name to evoke the aristocratic splendor of the country retreat and the glamor of the landscape that surrounded such great houses.

11. In addition to Sandra Zagarell, "America as Community in Three Antebellum Village Sketches," and Introduction to Kirkland, *A New Home*, see also

tion is focused on arguments about her commitment to depicting a community in development, some on the assimilation of the emigrant within it. The assumption, however, in either case is that *A New Home* is concerned with the mimetic representation of the social world of the Michigan backwoods, especially in its informal interactions.

I want, in this chapter, to use Kirkland's text to argue that the communities constructed and the spaces mapped by Kirkland's and other emigrant women's texts suggest a conception of neighborhood that is as often hostile as it is receptive to the community of the backwoods in general. *A New Home* does not, in my view, embrace the democratic, communitarian forms that it is argued to celebrate, nor is it unusual, among emigrant narratives, in its rejection of them. At the same time, however, I want to consider the community and the neighborhood that Kirkland's text does construct: a community of readers, a society shaped, and to some degree limited by, the activity of gossip, specifically gossip related to the domestic, but not, in any sense, a "new" kind of community.

For Sandra Zagarell, a highly influential critic of Kirkland's *A New Home*, this narrative represents an important and dynamic strand in writing about the community: one that is concerned to portray the local realistically, but that also purposefully proposes a model of openness in social relations. Far from rehearsing the "frontier" model of "separate but not alone," here is a representation of the local that gives the small community great significance as an "important site of an ongoing debate about the composition and character of America" and that engages in "[disputes] about the place of difference and conformity." If, Zagarell argues, many fictions of small-town life fantasize a scene of unchanging, sealed, and essentially American space, indulging a nativist impulse within their portraits, there are nevertheless some nineteenth-century women writers—of whom Kirkland is one—who choose to represent villages that are "heterogeneous and fairly open." Focusing on the "micro-dynamics of village life," writers such as Kirkland draw out the different ideologies, languages, and characteristics of the inhabitants, creating a "polyphony" that refuses to hierarchize the various attributes of the townspeople.[12]

Georgi-Findlay, *The Frontiers of Women's Writing*, 27–37; Leverenz, *Manhood and the American Renaissance;* and Merish, "'The Hand of Refined Taste.'"

12. Zagarell, "America as Community," 143, 145, 146, 147. Interestingly, a comparable argument is made by John Thurston in the specific context of a

According to Zagarell, Kirkland's Montacute not only represents an alternative to the usual understanding of the backwoods community as the scene of rampant individualism and prejudice but also rehearses a model of feminine collaboration and intimacy and extends it into a precisely described historical circumstance. The text shows a developing impulse, on the part of the narrator, toward drawing everyone within the backwoods community into her narrative. In that gradual process of inclusion we read the narrator's (and in Zagarell's reading, the narrator, "Mrs. Clavers," may be distinctly separated from the author) transformation from snobbish outsider to community member.[13]

Zagarell, in reading Kirkland against the work of other female "regionalist" writers—or, to use her term, writers of community—in the mid- and late nineteenth century, chooses to set aside any comparison that might be made between Kirkland and other middle-class emigrants who produced texts expressing despair at the lack of civilization: the similarities between Kirkland and Mrs. Trollope, Susanna Moodie, or indeed between Kirkland and anti-emigrationist writers are not addressed. And yet Mrs. Jennings, Kirkland's portrait of her "help," might stand as a perfect example of the portrayal of the wildly raffish "native" of the backwoods, a *locus classicus* of such literature: "The good lady's habits required strong green tea at least three times a day; and between these three times she drank the remains of the tea from the spout of the tea-pot, saying 'it tasted better so.' 'If she had n't it,' she said, 'she had the 'sterics so that she was n't able to do a chore.'"[14]

I would argue that Mrs. Jennings is an object of mirth to be shared between writer and audience, and that it is this sharing of experience (of poor "help," social inferiors, and rural uncouthness) around which the representation of the Michigan community of the text is constructed. Kirkland's pseudonym, "clavers," is an old word for gossip; Zagarell reads it as a critical term. I would propose that we think of it in the light of Patricia Meyer Spacks's argument in *Gossip*: as the talk between

---

discussion on narratives of emigration and travel in Upper Canada in "Ideologies of I: The Ideological Function of Life-Writing in Upper Canada," 25–28.

13. For me, one of the weaknesses in Zagarell's argument here lies in the evidence of Kirkland's replication, in *Forest Life*, the sequel to *A New Home*, of the same narrative persona, though this time with Kirkland's name advertised. *Forest Life* is at least as vituperative in its discussion of Pinckney as *A New Home*.

14. Kirkland, *A New Home*, 51.

intimates that revels in the enclosed (though not necessarily exclusive) circle in which that talk is circulated. It seems to me that the activity of gossip here identifies the community to which Kirkland perceives herself truly to belong: a community of readers who can share the jokes generated by the contrast between their own social sophistication and its absence in what is continually represented as an uncivilized space: a community "at home" in geographical terms and in terms of their appreciation of the subject matter.[15]

Kirkland was hardly unusual in writing rural life to the taste of an urban audience. But her insistence that her fellow settlers can only be the object of rueful mirth marks her as departing from norms within the writing of region that, while also written for a largely urban audience, were nonetheless highly attentive to the rural community. Within that tradition, we find portraits that are very different from that of "Mrs. Jennings." Mary Wilkins Freeman, for example, writing in the last decades of the nineteenth century, prompts the reader to share a common sense of alienation *with* rather than *from* her characters; she makes every nuance of each rural figure redolent of a life led on the geographical and social margins. Elsie in "Cinnamon Roses," for example, has a complex history that is reflective of a communal history expressed in shared everyday objects: "Elsie's chamber commanded a good view of her old home, which was a little farther down on the opposite side of the street. She could see the yard full of cinnamon roses, and the blue front door, which stood out bravely. That blue door was due to her; she had painted it herself. Silas had some blue paint after painting his farm and she had begged it." This thick texture of detail and representation of context, and the response it seems to seek to evoke in the reader, are not part of Kirkland's effect in describing fellow emigrants, unsurprisingly so given the newness and transient population of a community such as Pinckney.[16]

It is true that, as Zagarell argues, the joke of many episodes rebounds on Kirkland (or "Mrs. Clavers") for her dogged and exhausting pursuit of incongruously genteel habits in Montacute. Yet Kirkland's joke on

---

15. For another argument that uses gossip to characterize the emigrant writing of Susanna Moodie see Misao Dean, *Practising Femininity: Domestic Realism and the Performance of Gender in Early Canadian Fiction*, 39. Dean's argument is that this mode works to emphasize the domesticity and feminine identity of the writer.

16. Mary Wilkins Freeman, "Cinnamon Roses," 257.

her fellow settlers is by no means as flattering to them as the joking at her own expense is to her; nor is it as generous in its resolution. For example, in a chapter that begins with the celebration of the writer's own pleasure and expertise in gardening, but which goes on to point out the paucity of her neighbors' knowledge of flowers (despite the profusion of blooms in Michigan), Kirkland addresses her (eastern) readers thus: "The practical conclusion I wish to draw from all this wandering talk is, that it is well worth while to make [a] garden in Michigan. I hope that my reader will not be disposed to reply in that terse and forceful style which is cultivated in Montacute, and which has more than once been employed in answer to my enthusiastic lectures on this subject. 'Taters grow in the field and taters is good enough for me.'"[17]

For Zagarell, the joke here for Kirkland and the reader is as much on the narrator's "enthusiastic lectures" as upon the Montacutians' impatience. She reads the passage as "exposing the bias in Clavers's snobbish browbeating of her neighbors for their taste in flora": "Although she cannot see the implication of the 'taters' remark, its placement at the end of the chapter gives those neighbors the last word." I would argue, in contrast, that while Kirkland may present her own values as amusingly at odds with Michigan culture, even superfluous in certain circumstances, I do not find her making these values the object of her satire here or elsewhere in the text. It is the *distance* between the two value systems that is the joke in, for example, the passage in the same chapter where the inhabitants of Montacute refuse to appreciate her imported flowers: "A neighbor after looking approvingly at a glass of splendid tulips, of which I was vainglorious beyond all justification, asked me if I got 'them blossoms out of these here woods.' Another coolly broke off a spike of my finest hyacinths and after putting it to his undiscriminating nose, threw it on the ground with a 'pah!' as contemptuous as Hamlet's." The reader is not, I think, prompted to take that accusation of "vaingloriousness" about tulips as sharply self-critical. Can the narrator's pride be so reprehensible, after all, when it is directed at something so plainly without fault and so attractive as a tulip? And is her interlocutors' ignorance of the local flora as attractive a foible? Although the neighbor who breaks off the hyacinth

---

17. Kirkland, *A New Home*, 82; Zagarell, "America as Community," 155.

only to throw it on the ground is styled a country Hamlet, the point here surely rests on a bathetic contrast between Hamlet's psychological turmoil and this man's boorish behavior; between Hamlet's fine moral discriminations and this man's "undiscriminating" pragmatism. The neighbor's "last word" is something close to spite.[18]

A New Home, then, seems to me to be a narrative relatively unconcerned with the participation, much less the incorporation, of the narrator in the community she describes beyond the exigencies of practicality; Kirkland merely argues that it is important not to act snobbishly toward neighbors if one wants their help in such times of crisis as may be anticipated in backwoods Michigan: "If I treat Mrs Timson with neglect to-day can I with any face borrow her broom to-morrow? And what would become of me, if in revenge for my declining her invitation to tea this afternoon, she should decline coming to do my washing on Monday?"[19]

Historical writing about women's response to western communities in the United States tends to propose a class variable that seems to match Kirkland's outlook: middle-class women, it is argued, were unwilling to interpret the society they encountered as a community at all. Cayton and Onuf, for example, have argued that middle-class emigrants to the Midwest tended to regard "frontier" communities as chaotic and to reject the systems to regulate business and social activity that they found there.[20] Increasingly, where middle-class women have been involved in community work, their participation has been interpreted as incorporating a refusal to engage with the complex and heterogeneous society of the backwoods settlement.

At the same time, Kirkland's thin description of Pinckney seems to me to evoke a West in the form of a struggling backwoods settlement with uncertain goals. Perhaps the exotic name of "Montacute" plays on the town's actual position as the wobbly confection of eastern speculation; a speculation on which the Kirklands themselves had taken a financial chance. Significantly, the object of Kirkland's most specific discussion of Michigan is the dishonesty of land agents and speculators at the expense of settlers. The deception practiced by agents talking up

18. Zagarell, "America as Community," 155; Kirkland, *A New Home*, 79–80.
19. Ibid., 65.
20. Cayton and Onuf, *The MidWest and the Nation*, 52.

nonexistent settlements was a commonplace figure in the literature of emigration. While the mention of land speculators and their trickery was de rigeur in the work of most writers hostile to emigration, the mention of the "monster speculation" appeared in even the most flattering promotional material as well; if part of the purpose of the anti-emigration tract was to reveal the mendacity of speculators and agents, that of the emigrant's guide was to cast aside promotional rhetoric and show the "true picture." Promotion had actually created Pinckney, and the hostile reaction in Pinckney to the publication of Kirkland's text—itself a venture on the profit to be made from what she claimed to be "a veracious history of actual occurrences, an unvarnished transcript of real characters, and an impartial record of everyday speech"—may derive, one suspects, from a sense amongst Kirkland's neighbors that *A New Home* was yet another speculative venture, this time one making money at the expense of a community fruitlessly struggling to survive.[21]

But before we link texts such as *A New Home* to the expression of bourgeois preoccupations such as those described by Cayton and Onuf, we may also reflect on the expressions of dislike and separation to be found in the writing of female emigrants with less privileged social positions than the writer. It is not difficult, after all, to find writers with backgrounds—and experiences of emigration—different from Kirkland's insisting on the community as a "nowhere" and pouring scorn upon fellow settlers. The description of Richfield, Illinois, by Sara Stebbins to her mother, in a letter written in 1839, bears a kind of comparison with Kirkland's portrait of Pinckney. Kirkland tends to describe the forests of Michigan as if they were a man-made object: "We lacked not carpets, for there was the velvet sward, embroidered with blossoms, whose gemmy tints can never be equaled in Brussels or in Persia, nor canopy, for an emerald dome was over us, full of trembling light, and festooned and tasseled with the starry eglantine, the pride of our Western woods." Stebbins, apparently a less sophisticated and probably a less privileged settler than Kirkland, also described her forest surroundings as constructed and static: "this *wooden* world with nothing new or interesting but the same thing day after day."[22]

21. Kirkland, *A New Home*, 3.
22. Ibid., 149; Stebbins, "Frontier Life: Loneliness and Hope," 54.

The community for which Sarah Stebbins yearns is "at home" in Massachusetts, and, like Kirkland, she understands the society to which she has come as uncivilized and venal: "All I can do is to walk about and think of Friends and home. How different there situation from mine. They have meetings Friends neighbors books papers. Here we have non for the present inhabitants cannot be called civilized beings. They want no society nether are they fit for any . . . I did think we should have some of our eastern people here but I have about given up that any will ever come to Ill." As in Kirkland, the most striking aspect of society besides its wildness lies in the lack of scruple in businessmen: in Stebbins the behavior of merchants who "put on prices without any mercy." While Stebbins affirms, in a confirmation of the ideal of western self-sufficiency, that "a man that has a farm under cultivation and will cultivate his land can live independent of those merchants," this observation brings another in its wake:

> People are not obliged to live as they do here on hog and hominy. They can have all the luxuries if they ha[ve] a mind to. Evry kind of sauce or grain will grow. If they will only cultivete it the land will produse abundence of all kind of crops whatever . . . I wish som Eastern men with families would come in here for we knead them here as much as they do missionaris in India. . . . Let it becom setled and the people live here like human beings. . . . Women know nothing a bout cooking and lasy. If they have poltry eggs or butter it is for sale. They make no use of there milk untill it is soure. You cannot call this living.

This is at least comparable to Kirkland's discussions of the "class of settlers" "whose condition has always been inexplicable to me. They seem to work hard, to dress wretchedly, and to live in the most uncomfortable style in all respects, apparently denying themselves and their families every thing beyond the necessaries of life." Like Kirkland, Stebbins describes herself as occupying a domestic and social context grotesquely distant from that of her original home: "Mother do just ask the girls to comin som evening and take a game at wist. A basket of Apples and A mug of cider along with them would be acceptible. Come to the front dore fore oure back door is a blanket wich in the daytim serves as wind[o]w."[23]

23. Stebbins, "Frontier Life," 54–56; Kirkland, *A New Home*, 149, 107.

It hardly needs saying that Sarah Stebbins's letter is a completely different kind of utterance than that of Kirkland; indeed this is really my point.[24] For all its differences, it shares the particular emphases of emigration discourse with the work of other writers (such as Kitturah Belknap and Rebecca Burlend) who were working women of sufficient means to emigrate: the particular emphasis on material detail, on future hopes for progress and the mechanisms to achieve it, the discussion of others' decision to come, the experience of homesickness and the sacrifice of family for future prospects. It also shares with them and with the work of writers such as Kirkland the sense of community described by R. V. Hine as follows: "The frontier community existed for the individual not the other way round. A community was no more than the collection of its parts, with little or any right to suppress the human will." Don Harrison Doyle, writing about Illinois, evokes the specific problems inherent in creating a community compatible with ideals of individualism and egalitarianism, given a characteristic population of "uprooted newcomers" and the predictable "clash of unfamiliar cultures." Both descriptions seem to echo the verdict of these emigrant writers on the social world of the backwoods: that it is a space both foreign to the writer and easily summarized.[25]

I do not, then, read Kirkland's portrait of "Montacute" as Zagarell does: as expressive of a collaborative ethic nor of an assimilatory impulse. Rather, I would argue that *A New Home* creates a different type of social space and, in citing Mary Russell Mitford's *Our Village*, written between 1824 and 1832, as a source for her work, Kirkland advertises the grounds on which her portrait of a neighborhood may be understood: "It will of course, be observed that Miss Mitford's charming sketches of village life must have suggested the form of my rude attempt."[26]

Critics such as Kolodny and Josephine Donovan, who portray Kirkland as a writer striving for verisimilitude in her portrait of Montacute,

---

24. Discussion of letters as autobiographical utterances is also relatively rare, but Margaretta Jolly's "'Dear Laughing Motorbyke': Gender and Genre in Women's Letters from the Second World War," and Patricia Meyer Spacks, *Gossip*, 65–91, both set letters within a discussion of conventional autobiography.

25. Hine, *Community on the Frontier*, 26; Don Harrison Doyle, *The Social Order of a Frontier Community: Jacksonville Illinois, 1825–1870*, 3.

26. Kirkland, *A New Home*, 2.

play down her debt to Mitford. Kolodny argues that "from the outset . . . Kirkland's intentions differed somewhat from Mitford's" because "where Mitford sought merely to entertain, Kirkland sought also to enlighten." Donovan writes that "Kirkland carried the village sketch tradition far beyond its *genteel origins* [my italics] and paved the way for a genuine women's realism." For Gebhard, who links Kirkland with the satire of a writer such as Fielding, Mitford's work is too class-bound, too concerned with "forms and manners" to be anything but "hopelessly out of place in the American backwoods." Zagarell, though she sees writers such as Mitford more positively as involved in an "empirical, almost ethnographic, approach to character," argues, in her introduction to *A New Home,* that while Kirkland describes a dynamic of community development, writers such as Mitford by contrast "tend to be celebratory" of a space and group represented as fixed. In short, Mitford is not seen as an especially influential source, but rather as the inventor of a certain kind of village and a certain type of sketch: a genteel, quiescent, entertaining kind of canvas somewhat at odds with Kirkland's western subject.[27]

Yet the comparison with Mitford can be more fruitful than these critics have allowed. Through the association with Mitford, Kirkland and indeed other emigrant writers identify the emigrant community as a space that can be written in a high cultural form and with some seriousness. Although, from the start of *Our Village,* Mitford is deprecatory about the "little world" open to her as a well-born woman, she is nonetheless insistent on placing her work as part of a high literary tradition: "Nothing is so delightful as to sit down in a country village in one of Miss Austen's delicious novels . . . or ramble with Mr White . . . or to sail with Robinson Crusoe . . . or to be shipwrecked with Ferdinand." Kirkland's narrative, with its thick texture of high literary reference—Bacon, Shakespeare, Le Rochefoucauld—makes the

27. Kolodny, *The Land Before Her,* 156; Josephine Donovan, *New England Local Color Literature: A Women's Tradition,* 36; Gebhard, "Comic Displacement," 170; Zagarell, "America as Community," 146; Zagarell, Introduction to *A New Home,* xxviii. Mitford herself is rarely praised by literary historians. See the discussions in, for example, Veneta Colby, *Yesterday's Women: Domestic Realism in the English Novel;* P. D. Edwards, *Idyllic Realism from Mary Russell Mitford to Thomas Hardy;* W. J. Keith, *The Rural Tradition.* A more affirmative comment on the relationship between Mitford and western women writers may be found in Sandra Parker's *Home Material: Ohio's Nineteenth-Century Regional Women's Fiction.*

same claim for inclusion in the realms of high culture. Neither writer appears to aspire to be first and foremost a writer of region addressing the metropolitan center, but rather they seem to image themselves as writers participating in the cultural life of the center, albeit from a distance. Mitford describes the aspired-for position with aplomb: "The very happiest position that a woman of great talent can occupy in our high civilization, is that of living as a beloved and distinguished member of the best literary society . . . abstaining from the wider field of authorship, even while she throws out here and there such choice and chosen bits as prove that nothing but disinclination to enter the arena debars her from winning the prize." There was some justification in this in Mitford's case, for, from her home in Berkshire, she managed a career in literary circles with great shrewdness. Kirkland may be said to have used her sophisticated and erudite *A New Home* as a springboard to a literary career. Certainly, after seven years in Michigan, Caroline Kirkland returned to New York, where she and her husband continued to teach as they had before emigrating, and where she herself became a distinguished editor and a significant and well-connected figure in New York literary and intellectual life.[28]

Kirkland, in imitating Mitford, was neither too ambitious in her self-representation in literary terms, nor open to accusations of taking herself too seriously. Mitford, as a writer well respected within high cultural New England circles, was plainly a worthy model for an aspirant writer. The Mitfordian writer could claim, furthermore, a commanding knowledge of a particular space. At the same time, the sketch—provisional, unfinished, spontaneous, informal—was peculiarly suited to the description, for urban readers, of emigration to the West as a rural adventure to be savored for its literary potential (as opposed to the speculative venture that it actually was).[29]

---

28. See John Regan, *The Emigrant's Guide to the Western States of America or Backwoods and Prairies*, 60. Frances Trollope also works with the convention of the lady's rural walk to and from the "delicious" rural (or, more accurately, suburban) retreat in, for example, chapter 10 of *Domestic Manners of the Americans*. Mary Russell Mitford, *Our Village: Sketches of Rural Character and Scenery*, 1–2. Mitford defines her position thus in *Recollections of a Literary Life*, vol. 1, 249; see also John L. Idol, Jr., "Mary Russell Mitford: Champion of American Literature," to get a sense of Mitford's literary status.

29. The sketch is not a widely discussed or theorized form. For discussions that read the sketch as marginal and open-ended, see Elizabeth Ammons's introduc-

Mitford's type of mobile narrator constructed a shared experience with readers, allowing them, as Lawrence Buell suggests, to enjoy vicariously the "little world" of "our village" from their drawing rooms, or to think of their own walks as similar experiences. It was the written expression of the experience of neighborhood, of individuals moving through everyday routines, that Pierre Mayol describes as "the reciprocal habituation resulting from being neighbors, the processes of recognition—of identification—that are created thanks to proximity, to concrete co-existence in the same . . . territory."[30]

Recognition and identification, however, do not constitute a communitarian outlook. The reader is constantly made aware of what is not available to visual confirmation by the way in which the narrator's activity of observation is disrupted as the walk goes on. Drawn back to her domestic work, she hurries past, she hurries home, she breaks off to continue later. This narrative strategy is often understood as the sign of a writer determined to preserve the cloying effect of her portrait of rural bliss by not "looking" too closely. Much quoted is the moment in "Violeting" where Mitford writes of rushing past the workhouse:

> All about it is solid, substantial, useful—but so dreary! so cold! so dark! There are children in the court and yet all is silent. I always hurry past that place as if it were a prison. Restraint, sickness, age, extreme poverty, misery which I have no power to remove or alleviate—these are the ideas, the feelings, which the sight of these walls excites . . . There may be worse places than a parish workhouse—and yet I hurry past it. The feeling, the prejudice, will not be controlled.[31]

---

tion to Rose Terry Cooke, *How Celia Changed Her Mind and Selected Stories* (New Brunswick, N.J.: Rutgers University Press, 1986) and Carole Gerson and Kathy Mezei, *The Prose of Life: Sketches from Victorian Canada* (Downsview, Ontario: ECW Press, 1981); Zagarell, "America as Community," 252–53, provides an interesting literary context; see also Lawrence Buell, "The Village as Icon" in *New England Literary Culture* (New York: Cambridge University Press, 1986), 304–18, for another frame. To these constructions of the sketch we might add the Romantic idealization, in general, of the spontaneous and informal art form.

30. Mary Russell Mitford, *Our Village*, 1; Lawrence Buell, *The Environmental Imagination: Thoreau, Nature Writing and the Formation of American Culture*, 45; Pierre Mayol, "The Neighborhood," 9.

31. For discussions of Mitford's failure to represent the rural economy of her day, see Colby, *Yesterday's Women*, 233–34; Edwards, *Idyllic Realism*, 2–3; Keith, *The Rural Tradition*, 92 ff. Mitford, *Our Village*, 25.

There is no question that Mitford erased the controversies of social policy from *Our Village*, though she did not fail to represent its results, as is sometimes suggested: in "Violeting" she refers, immediately after the workhouse passage, to the miserable conditions of the "stooping" bean setters on piecework and the decay of an old Elizabethan house "under a careless landlord and a ruined tenant."[32] The atmosphere of the workhouse passage is surely, in any case, powerfully disquieting. It draws the reader's attention, as do many passages in *Our Village*, to the tension between what we see as we walk past and what "we" readers, it is implied, know is happening inside. Along with the expansive passages introducing the reassuringly familiar cast of talkers, gossips, and lovelorn young people, there are many moments in *Our Village* where figures whom we are asked to understand as representing actual people are described as trapped in miserable circumstances that are not—cannot be—fully delineated within the text. And if these figures are conspicuously revealed only in moments, this suggests all the more disturbingly the misery that eludes our gaze. Thus the commanding view that we expect from the traveler and "flaneuse" becomes, in Mitford, the gaze that also continually advertises what is not seen (in women's lives in particular) and what it pains us to imagine.

This strategy of momentary and partial revelations is much in evidence in *A New Home;* Kirkland's subtitle is, after all, *Glimpses of Western Life*. As in Mitford's grimly humorous tale of the Westons, she "glimpses" domestic cruelty, and then closes the image of it down. In the following passage, for example, we learn of Mr. Cathcart's cruelty; we guess at its brutal exercise, and we are left with its insubstantial but haunting presence in the talk of villagers:

> There are certain glances and tones which betray to the most careless observer that there *are* points of difference, behind the scenes at least; and little birds have whispered that after Mrs. Cathcart had spent the morning in transplanting flowers . . . Mr. Cathcart had been seen to come out and destroy all that she had been doing; ploughing up the neat flower-beds with his knife, tearing down the vines, and covering the turf sofas with gravel. And the same little birds have added, that when Mr. Cathcart, sated with mischief, turned to go into the house again, he found the front door

32. Mitford, *Our Village*, 25–26.

fastened, and then the back-door fastened; and after striding about for some time till his bald head was well-nigh fried, he was fain to crawl in at the little latticed window, and then—but further these deponents say not.

As Jane Marcus has argued, the gaze of the flaneuse, while it may simply replicate the appropriative gaze of the male flaneur, does, in some sense, make a claim on the woman's part to "look" and, in Rachel Bowlby's words, to have "nothing at all to fear (much less desire), on the streets or on the page." This raises questions (discussed by Jane Marcus) as to how far the narration of this look has at its heart the desire to open another disturbing world up to our gaze, a desire operating beyond the impulse to claim and inhabit a literary space for a female experience of equal status to that of men.[33]

Kirkland and Mitford do claim a literary space and a knowledge of a social world. They appeal, too, to a knowledge of women's lives shared with female readers; this is how, to use Mayol's words, they "[take] possession of the neighborhood." But having done so, they in a sense pass on without exploring this more problematic territory. These are, we may argue, the boundaries and the limitations of gossip—of Caroline Kirkland's "clavers"—a mode of interaction that, as Spacks points out, identifies a territory for the people who partake in it, but that also draws upon a mutual agreement *not* to draw the interlocutor into an explicit discussion of those issues which are most problematic.[34]

Yet if gossip draws back from explicit revelation, it is nonetheless very penetrating in its gathering of detail. The experience of domestic unhappiness or even cruelty may remain unexplored, but the spaces of the home are viewed in a minute detail that awaits interpretation. What we have in Kirkland's text is a process of engaging the reader in observation of the recesses of others' interiors, but not from the dominating position of one who "reads" those spaces in order to draw conclusions about the interior life of the inhabitants. In the following passage, we are shown a domestic interior where a profusion of different kinds of object appear within a space marked by clashing and receding

33. Ibid., 96–97; Kirkland, *A New Home*, 142; Marcus, "Registering Objections"; Rachel Bowlby, "Walking, Women and Writing: Virginia Woolf as Flaneuse," 33.
34. Mayol, "The Neighborhood," 9; Spacks, *Gossip*, 5.

surfaces. This is a space full of the traces of the "outside" domesticated and, equally, of the complex history and movements of a bourgeois family at mid-century:

> There was a harp in the recess, and the white-washed log-walls were hung with a variety of cabinet pictures. A tasteful drapery of French chintz partly concealed another recess, closely filled with books; a fowling piece hung over the chimney, and before a large old-fashioned looking-glass stood a French pier table, on which were piled fossil-specimens, mosses, vases of flowers, books, pictures and music . . . But there was more than all this. The bare floor was marked in every direction with that detestable yellow dye which mars everything in this country, although a great box filled with sand stood near the hearth, melancholy and fruitless provision against this filthy visitation.[35]

This kind of description conveys a fascination with the elaborate spaces of an interior, freighted as such spaces are with evocation of complex lives and different worlds. At one level, we have every nook and cranny opened up to the curious and accumulative gaze of the "gossip," at another we see the domestic space stretching, without boundaries into and beyond the neighborhood.

It is this way of eliding the boundaries between the domestic and the local and regional, the national and international (rather than a focus on the local) that, in my view, forms a link between Kirkland and the tradition of women's writing that critics have described as regionalist. One of the most striking moments in the defining text of regionalist writing, Sarah Orne Jewett's *Country of the Pointed Firs,* occurs as the visitor-narrator looks around the walls of the "little old-fashioned best room, with its few good bits of furniture and pictures of national interest" in Mrs. Blackett's house on Green Island:

> The green paper curtains were stamped with conventional landscapes of a foreign order,—castles on inaccessible crags, and lovely lakes with steep wooded shores; underfoot the treasured carpet was covered thick with home made rugs. There were empty glass lamps and crystallized bouquets of grass and some fine shells on the narrow mantelpiece.

35. Kirkland, *A New Home,* 74–75.

Ammons argues that such passages are part of Jewett's impulse to "[celebrate] houses as secular shrines." But surely what is striking about the objects in Mrs. Blackett's parlor is not that they are contained and decontextualized in order to intensify their symbolic meaning, but rather that the reader can scarcely imagine the worlds they reference nor indeed know what they mean for Mrs. Blackett, if indeed they "mean" anything at all in terms of their owner's own life experience.[36]

Kirkland's ramshackle Michigan home is represented in less elaborate terms, but seems to me to reach toward the same kind of enigmatic effect, referencing different times and other spaces: "Its clay-filled sticks, instead of a chimney-piece—the half-consumed wooden crane, which had, more than once, let our dinner fall—the Rocky Mountain hearth, and the reflector, baking biscuits for tea . . . the floor, with its gaping cracks, wide enough to admit a massasauga from below, and its inequalities, which might trip any but a sylph . . ." This passage (which describes the appearance of her home as it is observed by a visitor, while she is ill with ague) is preceded by an epigram from Spenser's *The Faerie Queene*, which complicates further our sense of the range of spatial reference generated by the home by drawing it—albeit ironically—into the ahistorical and heavily symbolic world of mythology:

> The house's form within was rude and strong,
> Like a huge cave hewn out of rocky clift;
> From whose rough vault the ragged breaches hung: -
> And over them Arachne high did lift
> Her cunning web, and spread her subtle net,
> Enwrapped in foul smoke, and clouds more black than jet.[37]

Meanwhile, the emphasis on the "matrifocal, pre-industrial, rustic" aspects of the life of a rural community that Elizabeth Ammons sees as at the celebratory feminist heart of regionalist writing has little attraction for Kirkland. If anything, the sewing society in *A New Home* represents what Kirkland claims to like least about Michigan: the covert politicking and the fighting over territory. Kirkland's asides, the humor, the focus on the interactions between small groups of highly in-

---

36. Sarah Orne Jewett, *The Country of the Pointed Firs*, 40; Elizabeth Ammons, "Material Culture, Empire and Jewett's *Country of the Pointed Firs*," 89.
37. Kirkland, *A New Home*, 63.

dividualized characters, and the outrageous portrait of the chief gossip, Mrs. Campasne Nippers, produce a scene of social battle, chaos, and "brusquerie"; perhaps a critique of Michigan competition or perhaps a pleasant piece of gossip by a disengaged "Mrs. Clavers" for circulation amongst readers who will recognize the writing of a type of village life.[38]

Her quotation from Spenser may link the writer to Arachne, but Kirkland firmly eschews the link between the feminine art of sewing and women's creativity. Kirkland's Mrs. Skinner, the president of the Montacute Beneficent Society, is quietly industrious in her work, but she is also styled in wry terms that scarcely elevate either needlework as art, or, more generally, the ties that bind women: Mrs. Skinner is simply "a pattern woman in all that makes woman indispensable, viz cookery and sewing." As Elaine Hedges argues: "For large numbers of women entering authorship in the nineteenth century, sewing—as material reality and also as a powerful symbolic marker of their cultural condition and their restricted domestic role—functioned both as a literal and psychological deterrent to ambition and achievement." One suspects that Kirkland would have held just such a view; certainly such a view seems to organize her sewing society scene.[39]

Kirkland was not unique in approaching community in this mode, nor in positioning herself as engaged in writing the backwoods for an urban audience. Eliza Farnham and Susanna Moodie, for example, both used the representation of visits and walks and outings to adopt the pose and the diction of a literary woman, or to open up the domestic worlds of fellow settlers for their readers. They used the Mitfordian strategy of evoking the life of the community through examining fragments of recalled or reported experiences, glimpses of elusive interior worlds. This was not a formula for representing backwoods communities in very specific or systematic ways. Indeed, it was not unusual for emigrant writers to be repelled by the social and economic life of their new community. However, not all Wests were plotted in the same way by emigrant autobiographers. In the next chapter, I want to move on to consider the variable of region.

---

38. Ammons, "Material Culture," 89; Kirkland, *A New Home*, 138.
39. Kirkland, *A New Home*, 134; Elaine Hedges, "The Needle or the Pen: The Literary Rediscovery of Women's Textile Work," 340.

6

Plotting the Golden West

Autobiographers of the Mining West

A KEY PREMISE of this study has been that emigrant women's writing has been much preoccupied with the meanings of home, the work undertaken in that space, and behavior of women within it. This is attributable, in part, to the importance of home within discourses of migration generally, and, in part, to the particular significance accorded to housekeeping within Anglo-American discourse during the early and mid-nineteenth century. I have argued that, in the context of representations of emigration, models of domesticity have been examined and assessed within the writing of emigration by women, and I have used a series of midwestern emigrant writings to explore this ground. At the same time, I have wanted to suggest that it is not only the work of homemaking that is explored in these texts' description of everyday domestic life, but also the work of emigration and settlement itself. The question I want to address in this chapter is the extent to which women's writing of emigration, as it addresses issues of home, work, and community, is susceptible to regional difference, and I have chosen to pursue this question through a consideration of the writing by Anglo emigrant women of the U.S. mining West.[1]

---

1. I am reusing the title of Stephen Fender's study of the rhetoric of the California Trail, *Plotting the Golden West: American Literature and the Rhetoric of the California Trail.* Fender's study is largely concerned with how people "at various levels of sophistication" wrote the Gold Rush (14). In this chapter, I am attempting to reconsider the plot starting from female emigrants' constructions of the "Golden West."

The interest of the region for the purposes of this discussion lies in the way in which the mining West has been represented as a space not only defined through conflicting gender relations but also antithetical or at least very hostile to domesticity as it is interpreted as a conservative and inflexible ideological position. The figure of the Anglo housewife remains an important site of discussions about gender, domesticity, and the domestic space, but the idea of an opposition between the domestic (female) and the public (masculine) life of the Gold Rush West takes center stage.

That opposition is scarcely peculiar to the scene of the mining camp. Narratives of, for example, army life in the West repeatedly endorse the view that it is "no life for a lady," that this is indeed an experience in which domestic happiness is severely compromised by the sacrifice of comforts and refinement. Accounts abound of months spent keeping house in a tent and delivering babies there, of the difficulty of performing menial tasks, and the grueling process of traveling from fort to fort.[2] In western fictions too, such as Bret Harte's "Luck of Roaring Camp," published in 1868, or Constance Fenimore Woolson's 1875 "The Lady of Little Fishing," the plots turn on the troubling presence even of a woman of ambiguous moral status within the male domain of the West.

Narratives of the Gold Rush West and understandings of the social shape of the society generated by that migration have always had a demographic exceptionalism at their core: young men dominated this migrant population. Richard White quotes the distorted population of 1850 California as 93 percent men, of whom 90 percent were between the ages of twenty and forty. Moreover, the Gold Rush has always been understood as an epic adventure of a profoundly masculine cast, "drenched" as Ralph Mann expresses it, in a "literary romance" of quest and vast riches to which men are understood to be particularly attracted. It is argued that the Gold Rush was, at some level, specifically and explicitly about the escape from women and the attempt—probably hopeless—to create a different (undomesticated) space. Mann

---

2. Two characteristic examples of army narratives are Martha Summerhayes's *Recollections of the Army Life of a New England Woman* (Salem, Mass.: Salem Press, 1911) and Mrs. Orsemus Boyd's *Cavalry Life in Tent and Field* (New York: J Selwin Tait, 1894).

writes of "a legitimate, temporary escape from elders and from feminized respectability," Stephen Fender of a "disguised holiday from . . . families . . . [and] any reminder of domestic tedium."[3]

The vague but powerful terms that Kevin Starr uses to frame the migration—"something primal and immemorial [was] going on"—remind us how this emigrant experience—perhaps above all others—has had a special and particular mythological resonance. Starr, with his "Homeric world of journeys, shipwreck, labor, treasure, killing, and chieftainship," follows the tradition of Harte and Twain in reading the Gold Rush as a narrative of masculinity tested and proved in a space where the human relations appear in stark simplicity. The single-minded commitment to an adventure that eschews the reassurances of the emotional and physical comfort of a social existence centered on the home has, of course, always had a dark underside: a poignant and desperate masculine experience of anomie. Nor was the great male adventure without an agenda in psycho-sexual terms. The traditional parallel between the Forty-Niners and the Argonauts recalls the avenging presence of betrayed and neglected relationships—Medea's betrayal of her father for Jason and then her murder of her children by Jason—and the alienation experienced within the heroic male quest.[4]

The extraordinary demographics of the Gold Rush and the mythology of primal adventure play against an understanding of Gold Rush California as itself an ephemeral space characterized by the thinnest surface of socialization. The existence of home and family becomes obscure or is forgotten, and a space formed by fantasy and speculation takes over. Fender writes of the phenomenon as follows: "California was so insubstantial really; founded on the illusory hopes (for the majority who went anyway) of finding a fortune in the mines; growing too fast for its roots; shallowly civilized, like the gambling houses . . . made of barns lined with French wallpaper."[5]

---

3. Richard White, *"It's Your Misfortune and None of My Own": A New History of the American West*, 303; Ralph Mann, *After the Gold Rush: Society in Grass Valley and Nevada City 1849–1870*, 1; Fender, *Plotting the Golden West*, 92–95. See also Christiane Fischer, "Women's California in the Early 1850s," for a discussion of demographics focused on women.
4. Kevin Starr, *Americans and the California Dream, 1850–1915*, 50–51.
5. Fender, *Plotting the Golden West*, 127.

This constantly dissolving context was emphasized from the start. As Eliza Farnham put it in *California, In-Doors and Out* (using another popular mythological parallel between the miners and the all-male band of lotus-eaters of the *Odyssey*, or, more probably, of Tennyson's poem), the very activity of searching for treasure drew the Forty-Niners into an alternative magical world: "Our lotos is the gold which has to be obtained by laborious diligence or hazardous scheming; but once tasted, like the fabled leaf, it causes forgetfulness of old ties, purpose, motives, restraints, with this essential difference, which also, is almost a fatal one, that while it buries old brotherhoods it does not create new ones."[6]

Thus, the romance of the Gold Rush has continually been plotted in opposition to the spaces and the processes of the everyday and the domestic, and against their supposed predictability. When R. V. Hine writes that, in the mining West, "the psychic needs of men were attainable outside of the community," we are given to understand that this community is concerned with these needs that are not "primal" but rather with control and routine. And indeed, even in a Gold Rush society imagined as controlled by the ruthless relations of capitalism rather than as developing to cater for the ambitions of individuals—a society, as White puts it, "where the search for wealth overwhelmed everything from labor to love, reducing them both to commodities"— the world of domestic relations remains irrelevant and largely invisible.[7]

In this context of cultural and historical tradition, the irrelevance of the values associated with women is as confidently averred as the absence of women in demographic terms. Starr, for example, chooses Sarah Royce's recollections to exemplify a feminine conformism and quiescent Christian ethic in contrast to the pagan atavism of the Argonauts. Royce, it would seem, has no means of understanding "primary experience," for she chooses to organize her experience in religious terms: she reads the Bible for two hours every day and refuses to travel on Sundays. Fender, for whom the response of women has much more interest in terms of accessing the gap between mythology and historical circumstance—"the women were not afraid to name things as they

---

6. Eliza W. Farnham, *California, In-doors and Out*, 251.
7. Hine, *Community on the American Frontier*, 26; White, *"It's Your Misfortune,"* 304.

were"—describes in detail women's indifference to the journey that framed, even defined, the great adventure of the Forty-Niners. Even the landscape, it seems, fails to inspire women, according to Anne F. Hyde:

> Women saw the West very differently from men, particularly in the nineteenth century. In general they saw much less economic opportunity and exciting adventure. As they looked at the great expanses stretching West and at the mountains looming overhead, they saw danger and real limits to stable agriculture and family existence . . . Although men mocked them for being frightened, these women held perceptions far more accurate than the optimistic ones of their brave husbands. In fact many women may have held the advantage in looking at the West because ambition and Manifest Destiny did not color their perceptions so strongly.[8]

The issue seems often to be that the Anglo housewife, typically a middle-class figure, will only respond to the new context by importing into it the conventional patterns of response and behavior that she has internalized. This is not an unfamiliar expectation: indeed, as we saw in chapter 1, the representation of some women as locked into stultifying convention has long defined the behavior of the "true" pioneer woman. Here, in the writing of the Gold Rush West, the abandonment of routine behavior and the wildly expansive expectations on the part of men—an extreme of "frontier" behavior—are matched by an extreme of conformist female behavior. The western women's history of the last twenty years has found little to add, beyond incorporating women into the fantasy formerly construed as exclusively male. Christiane Fischer, for example, who has edited and coedited some of the most interesting western mining narratives by women, agrees that those who went to California were robbed of aspiration by convention: " . . . for they had never been told to look for adventure, excitement and freedom, the essential things in life for many of them were sentimental relations with other people and cultural, social and religious activities."[9]

---

8. Starr, *Americans and the California Dream*, 51, 144. Fender's discussion in *Plotting the Golden West* is more complicated than this suggests. He surveys a range of female writers (85–96) before going on to read the letters of Mary Jane Mesquier as articulating the same paradigm of transformation as men (97–103). Anne F. Hyde, "Cultural Filters: The Significance of Perception," 183–84.

9. Fischer, *Let Them Speak for Themselves*, 13.

Where pioneer womanhood has been recovered in this Far West context, it has not been through a "healthy and useful domesticity" and immersion in the land, but through as enthusiastic an embrace of the marketplace and rejection of the domestic as that which characterizes representations of male Forty-Niners: "Contrary to nineteenth-century notions about feminine helplessness and passivity, pioneer women took decisive action to manage their own lives and maintain their hopes. The narratives in this book show that they were often the breadwinners and wage earners who provided crucial capital for male accomplishment."[10]

Thus, in the context of the writing of the Gold Rush, the ideological worlds of nineteenth-century Anglo women are insistently diminished. They are collapsed into models of domesticity generated by the scholarship of the 1970s: in Richard White's study, he refers merely to "the cult of true womanhood, or, more briefly, domesticity" and "the Victorian moral order" where "'true' women who were pure and pious made the home a haven from the world."[11]

The iconic female figure of the Gold Rush West is not, of course, the housewife at all, but the prostitute. As the farmer's wife is seen to share the life of the farm with her husband, so the prostitute is felt to occupy an economic position comparable to the miners' insecurity and social precariousness. Like the adventurous miner, the prostitute's raffishness has a gloss heightened by the sense of her transient glamour. Like the miner's brief freedom, that glamour is doomed to be sidelined when things return to a depressing normality (at the hands, in part, of community-building "respectable" women).

For some critics, the predicament of the prostitute is essentially typical of the situation of mining-camp women in general. Where the prostitute is read as a female individualist, the self-made woman in full flight from convention, the "respectable" woman represents the passive economic situation that the prostitute attempts to overcome. Or the figure of the prostitute is framed as epitomizing, in the most exaggerated form, the common female problem of finding economic support; she is seen as exemplifying the general position of women in a violently patriarchal scene.[12] It is not within the reach of this study

10. Moynihan, Armitage, and Fischer Dichamp, *So Much to Be Done*, xvii.
11. White, *"It's Your Misfortune,"* 308, 304.
12. For example, see Paula Petrik's "capitalists with rooms" in *No Step Backward: Women and Family on the Rocky Mountain Frontier, Helena Montana, 1865–*

to discuss the figure of the prostitute, but rather to point out that the fascination for and characterization of this figure invariably works to diminish the housewife further: to show her as more conventional, more oppressed.

Thus, it comes as something of a surprise to find that Gold Rush autobiographical writing produced by women is far from obscure in the field of historical study of the mining West: the pious Sarah Royce, the ladylike Mary Hallock Foote, the doughty and high-spirited Mollie Sanford, even the boisterous "Dame Shirley," are familiar figures in the discussion of the mining communities generated by the rush for wealth. Their representations of mining-camp communities have had a status as "evidence" about the life of the mining camp in a way that women's autobiographies of the midwestern farming community have not. Is it that their presumed lack of direct involvement with the "real" work of the mining camp acts as a guarantee of their objectivity? Certainly, in some of the following examples the writers assume a disengaged distance from their subject by reason of their class—Foote, in particular, presses home her status as a gentlewoman. "Dame Shirley" uses the device of comedy, and Sarah Royce the tropes of spiritual autobiography, to demonstrate their distance from a scene where greed and squalor reign supreme.

There may, however, be another explanation for the relative popularity of these narratives in the context of the mainstream of writing about the mining West. For all that the mining West has long been represented as creating, above all, an extreme of opposition between male and female worlds, in these narratives of life in the mining camp, that division is largely erased. The domestic space not only is not separate but also is not strongly "interior" either. Those constructions of domestic spaces that exclude the "outside" most determinedly—the elaborate sanctuaries, the emotionally charged spaces heavy with symbolism, the sacred shrines where the dead are memorialized, or indeed the agoraphobic spaces of self-denial—are almost invisible in

---

1900, 25–58, and Marion S. Goldman's discussion in *Gold Diggers and Silver Miners: Prostitution and Social Life on the Comstock Lode,* of the prostitutes' business as "a miniature of the city's economic world" (25). Anne M. Butler's discussion of the "corrosive, degrading experiences" of prostitutes (62), in *Daughters of Joy, Sisters of Misery: Prostitutes in the American West, 1865–1890,* is framed by a consideration of the predicament of young women seeking employment in the West.

emigrant women's narratives of life in western mining camps.[13] The domestic spaces in the autobiographical narratives to which we most frequently refer, in fact, recreate the domestic space as part of the familiar raffish and improvisatory world of mining-camp society. Luzena Wilson's narrative, *Luzena Stanley Wilson 49er*, for example, continually pictures the home in a process of re-formation. From the account of her journey West, where she describes the sloughing off of "burdensome luxuries" such as "pots and kettles," to her assertions about the peculiar quality of housekeeping in California, another domesticity emerges: "Housekeeping was not difficult then, no fussing with servants or housecleaning, no windows to wash or carpets to take up. I swept away the dirt with a broom of willow switches, and the drawing room where I received my company was 'all out doors'. When the dust grew inconvenient under foot, we moved the cook stove and table around the other side of the tree and began over again." Both here and in her description of her work feeding miners, Wilson describes the experience of a self-sufficiency and pragmatic action that we associate with emigrant discourse, while also focusing on the representation of a domestic experience that is not only *not* secluded, but actually largely free of personal association. It is made available to miners willing to pay for food and lodging in a gesture that is far from the concept of hospitality that draws outsiders into a private domestic space. Instead, her narrative is largely concerned with relating the ways in which her domestic skills become the main source of income for her family. Thus, in chapter 6 she describes her arrival in Nevada City and her new home: "We were not rich enough to indulge in the luxury of a canvas home; so a few pine boughs and branches of the undergrowth were cut and thrown into a rude shelter

---

13. I am thinking here of the range of readings of the nineteenth-century domestic space that foreground its complexity in psychological terms, for example, Kenneth Ames, *Death in the Dining Room and Other Tales of Victorian Culture* (Philadelphia: Temple University Press, 1992); Jean-Christophe Agnew's "A House of Fiction: Domestic Interiors and the Commodity Aesthetic" in Simon Bronner, ed., *Consuming Visions: Accumulation and Display of Goods in America, 1880–1920*, 133–56; Karen Sanchez Eppler's "Disrupted Genealogies," Nineteenth-Century American Women Writers in the Twenty-First Century Conference at Hartford, Conn., May 1996; Gillian Brown's "empire of agarophobia" in *Domestic Individualism: Imagining Self in Nineteenth-Century America*, 174–76.

for the present." On the same day she sets up a "hotel" for twenty miners.[14]

Luzena Wilson, narrating her experience thirty years after the event, seems to be engaged in matching her domestic experience with the familiar cast of economic life in the mining camps: informal, entrepreneurial, and subject to extremes of success and failure. At some level this impulse may be attributable to the circumstances in which it was written, for her narrative was dictated to a convalescent daughter (who wrote down her words "as nearly as I could") with ambitions, one suspects, for a public life. But the representation of the home primarily as an improvised space appears elsewhere as well. In a diary written during the Colorado strikes in 1861, Mollie Sanford describes her much less positive response to the prospect of cooking for the men of the camp as follows: "My heart sinks when I see there are 18 or 20, and no conveniences at all. There is a rough log cabin, neither chinked nor daubed, as they call it, no floor, and only a hole cut for a door and a window . . . I have to cook out of doors by a fire, but have mustered my small cook stove into service but that will only hold one loaf of bread, or one pie at a time . . . I fear I shall sink under this burden. It is not as my fancy painted it."[15]

This disappointment is not associated with her situation as a woman. Sanford's disappointed "fancy" matches the discouragement of the "men folks" who fail to make their fortunes, and her account of home-making is, if anything, more reflective than Wilson's of the airy hopes on which both her bid for her own "little cabin" and her husband's restless speculations rest. Meanwhile, the detail of Sanford's description also stresses the way in which her surroundings have been improvised out of nondomestic objects—the wagon cover on the ground, the barrel as a rocker: an intensity of aspiration rather than the weight of symbolic meaning. This imaging of home is not specific to the accounts of literate women broadly of the working class (such as Wilson and Sanford) who might have expected, at least in the first instance, to work for others beyond their family and to do so through domestic work. Sarah Royce, a more highly educated and prosperous woman of the middle class, also writes of the parlor "that was my pride" in terms

14. Luzena Stanley Wilson, *Luzena Stanley Wilson 49er,* 2, 46, 27.
15. Ibid., 1; Sanford, *Mollie,* 137.

that emphasize the play of imagination involved: it contains: "two or three plush-covered seats, which Mary and I called 'ottomans.' Their frames were rough boxes, which I had stuffed and covered myself." Her home is "a banquet hall, a cathedral"; her "establishment" is "quite aristocratic."[16]

What we have here, then, is a form of description of the domestic space that diminishes the sense of the home as a space of unchanging symbolic meaning for those living within it, and which increases the reader's sense of how quickly and arbitrarily the writer may attain a change of domestic circumstances. Thus Sanford, the young wife occupying the ground between working-class and bourgeois life styles, seems less concerned with the process of finding the ideal home, but rather depicts herself experimenting, in her home decoration, with the possibilities of upward mobility:

> I took some brick dust that I had been provided with for scouring purposes, and mixing with linseed oil, stained it so that it looks like light cherry. I have an oiled wagon cover on my ground floor, white curtains to my window of three panes of glass, my cook stove, and some stools. Have made a rocker out of a barrel, and covered and cushioned it. We have a large fireplace, and pile the pine logs on and really I feel as if I am in a palace now . . . I read a great deal, and am doing up some necessary sewing.[17]

Not only is the relationship between the home and other spaces (hotel, palace, cathedral) opened up in these narratives but also the inside and outside, far from being in opposition to one another, appear indistinctly differentiated, if not chaotically confused. The *Letters* of "Dame Shirley," published between 1851 and 1852, indeed seem to turn upside down the oppositional relations between the public chaos of a masculine world and a private feminine intimacy that Ida Rae Egli attributes to the text. Writers such as Dame Shirley fictionalized California Gold Rush vignettes from lynchings to quiet, slice-of-life moments between mothers and children, offering varied literary images of the West from uniquely female points of view. It is rather the office of her

---

16. Sanford, *Mollie*, 148, 150; Sarah Royce, *A Frontier Lady: Recollections of the Gold Rush and Early California*, 129–30, 132.
17. Sanford, *Mollie*, 150.

husband that becomes the "thing sacred and set apart for an almost admiring worship," where her husband's partner "literally 'lived, moved, and had his being,' his bed and his board." Dame Shirley meanwhile represents herself occupying a series of "rag and cardboard" homes, within which the activities of the camp and saloon can be heard (and imagined) at all hours. The penetrability of her homes is their most salient feature: "Enter my dear; you are perfectly welcome; besides, we could not keep you out if we would, as there is not even a latch on the canvas door, though we really intend in a day or two to have a hook put on to it."[18]

Even where the focus of these narratives is upon an activity that could decisively validate the sealing off of the middle-class Anglo housewife in the home—scenes of the nurture of small children, for example—the spaces of the home are not represented as in tension with the outside. Sarah Royce's scenes of happy child-rearing, for example, produce the expected idyll of the companionate family:

> When I had once more spread my carpeting and arranged my furniture, I sat down with my little melodeon and made the woods and the pretty little hills ring with some of my favorite songs: while the two older children, delighted with their new surroundings decked a play-house with acorns and wild flowers; and baby, in the large square box I had carpeted and lined for her, alternately peeped over its sides at them and me, or pulled herself up by her little fingers.[19]

Royce's passage imagines the home as a pastoral space within a larger pastoral landscape. The box, meanwhile, "carpeted and lined," is a home within a home. The boundaries of the home, like those of the family, are displaced, magnified, and miniaturized. As Stephanie Coontz argues, families are "a tool for channeling people into the prevailing structure of obligations and rights, then attaching the tasks and

---

18. Ida Rae Egli, "Early Western Literary Women," 82; "Dame Shirley," *The Shirley Letters: From the California Mines 1851–1852,* 31, 49, 57. The nature of the text of Dame Shirley has been a matter of some discussion. For opposing views of its narrative strategy see Fender, *Plotting the Golden West,* 106–7, 112–14, 117–18; Carl Wheat, Introduction, *The Shirley Letters* (New York: Knopf, 1965); and Blake Allmendinger, *Ten Most Wanted: The New Western Literature* (New York: Routledge, 1998), 73–77.

19. Royce, *A Frontier Lady,* 132–33.

rewards associated with that structure to a definition of self"; Coontz quotes Rayna Rapp's view that they are always in the process of "decomposing and recomposing" themselves "in continuous interaction with larger domains." This is very much the model of relations between domestic and "larger domains" that Royce's passage addresses.[20]

Thus these writers represent home in the mining West as matching the unconventional "outside" of the mining camp; indeed they suggest that the implications of such a context for the formation and life of the interior can scarcely be resisted. But the quality of imaginative play and the sense of parody that these writers lend to their descriptions of housekeeping are not extended to their representations of the "outside." Indeed, their depiction of mining society touches conventional points of reference: the societal chaos brought about by laissez-faire commercialism. In *California In-doors and Out*, for example, Eliza Farnham's comments on the "problems" of a society based on mining are so standard as to replicate the assumptions of those who described eastern cities as literally maddened by social change:

> The incessant strain upon the mental powers; the constant torture of the affections, either through the absence of their objects, or, what is far keener, their unworthy conduct when present; the disappointment of hopes; the prostration of plans, conceived and partially executed, with infinite labor; the absence of response and those restoring influences of home and society, which elsewhere soothe the irritability and mitigate the weariness of the commercial and speculating life; all these influences one foresees, must inevitably result in the frequent dethronement of reason.[21]

Farnham's commentary may repeat the diagnosis by social critics of the eastern urban context, but she does not, in *California, In-doors and Out,* position the female observer in the same kind of relation to this social turmoil and despair. Whereas in the critique of urban chaos the

---

20. Stephanie Coontz, *The Social Origins of Private Life: A History of American Families 1600–1900,* 13. Rayna Rapp, Ellen Ross, and Renate Bridenthal, "Examining Feminist History," *Feminist Studies* 5 (1979): 233.

21. Farnham, *California, In-doors and Out,* 367–68. The passage is highly reminiscent of the discussions conducted in the East about social psychology and rapid change; see the discussion in David Rothman, *The Discovery of the Asylum: Social Order and the New Republic,* rev. ed. (Boston: Little Brown, 1971), 113–19.

horrified observations of women are framed by movements into specific districts of degradation (supposed or actual), or by the descent into the "lairs" of the poor, here, in mining narratives, the activities marked as most shockingly dissident are placed in a closer spatial relationship to the middle-class domestic space in which the writer is situated. And they are not, as we might expect, articulated as threatening to the female observer.

This is interesting, especially in the light of Paula Petrik's research, which suggests that middle-class homes were, if not in the thick of the mining communities, certainly not in a separated district. Though the possibility of encountering a "fallen" woman is said to have exercised the minds of middle-class women in mining communities—the example of Sarah Royce's rejection of social contact with a woman beyond the pale of bourgeois marriage is well known—the "inside story" produced in other narratives seems to strive to make explicit the writer's involvement in and full knowledge of the life of the camp.[22]

The trope of an unseen lynching, for example, appears in a number of women's mining camp narratives over a considerable period. A much-quoted example appears much later in Mary Hallock Foote's unpublished autobiography, which she wrote in the 1920s. Here she observes the community of Leadville in the 1870s:

> One evening, in the face of one of those great silencing sunsets, as we watched it from our cabin porch—down in the town where light pricked through the twilight, this man and a holdup thief whom the town was equally tired of were at that moment being lynched by hanging in front of the prison door. A. knew it as he stood there beside me, but he did not speak of it till years after. He saw no reason why a woman who had no business down there should break into that life which twilight covered, or question what was going on in those houses whose lights from our distance looked not unworthy neighbors of the stars.

This passage is an interesting one. Foote knew a great deal about the legal and illegal activities of the mining camp, as she demonstrates in her fiction. Nonetheless, in the context of her autobiographical writing, she begins by attributing to herself a refined lack of firsthand knowledge

22. The incident is described in Royce, *A Frontier Lady,* 113.

of violence, and to her husband a chivalrous silence. Indeed, as she suggests at various points in her narrative, her homes are sited in such a way as to emphasize a separation—and exclusion—from the corrupt practices of a mining camp: "Wiser friends could have told us we were rash, making over a house not our own, perching aloof in an attitude of indifference to society. We were in the camp but not of it."[23]

Yet the sunset passage sets up a complex "attitude of indifference." That she and her husband have any chance of adopting a lofty position is a mere castle in the air, for Foote does, in the text, "see" the lynching that her husband seeks to protect her from. Though her husband does not speak of it and does not admit the possibility of conversation on the topic—their admiration of the sunset is "silencing"—still, in this episode, Foote does raise questions about the supposed gap between her knowledge and her husband's assumption that this is a knowledge that she does not—should not—have. The sense that this gap exists *only* as a convention (social or literary) and that this is precisely Foote's point is sharpened when one discovers that the incident the passage "recalls" was invented.[24]

The "not seeing" of lynchings dealt out in mining camps also appears in Dame Shirley's letters. In one example, enclosed in her cabin, she hears but cannot see the lynching mob at work:

> On the following morning I was awakened very early by a tremendous "aye"—so deep and mighty that it almost seemed to shake the cabin with its thrilling emphasis. I sprang up and ran to the window, but could *see* nothing, of course—as our house stands behind the Humboldt; but I could easily understand from the confused murmur of many voices, and the rapidly succeeding "ayes" and "noes," that a large crowd had collected in front of the latter.[25]

This is followed by a lengthy description of the proceedings, which, again, only serves to dissolve the sense that the writer cannot, as a middle-class woman, participate in the episode at any level. Indeed, as with Foote, her imagined separation coexists in the text with a detailed

---

23. Mary Hallock Foote, *A Victorian Gentlewoman in the Far West: The Reminiscences of Mary Hallock Foote*, 175–76, 125.
24. See the editor's footnote in ibid., 177.
25. "Dame Shirley," *The Shirley Letters*, 74.

knowledge and a clear claim for the realism of her portrait of the mining West.

Thus far, then, we have a group of well-known mining narratives written by Anglo emigrant women that generate a discussion which has, on the one hand, little overlap with conventions of thinking about the relations between women, domesticity, and the social scene of the mining camp, but which, on the other, shows a quite particular construction of women's participation in the familiar scenes of the mining West. The domesticity that is imagined here has little in common with the ideal which is celebrated, explored, or critiqued in narratives written in the backwoods or elsewhere. It is not a domestic scene of well-defined tasks briskly executed, nor of the satisfactions of seclusion. The extraordinary scene in *California, In-doors and Out* where Eliza Farnham performs the imaginative feat of turning her home inside out, so that the crowded, chaotic spaces of her Californian home become "outside" and inside can be transformed to a "fairy scene," is difficult to imagine in the narratives of domestic life with which the previous chapters have been concerned. Nor does the context of the mining camp apparently constitute the traumatic wrench into a new life that is attributed to the backwoods of, say, Rebecca Burlend or Harriet Noble; there is no sacrifice here nor any of the alienation of Moodie's "prison-house" in the woods.[26]

By focusing upon the narratives that Anglo women shaped for publication or, at least, for specific audiences, then, we can delineate an Anglo women's discourse of the mining West that participates very directly in contemporary constructions of the region. They are narratives that are organized around the imagination of a world turned inside-out and which produce a regionalized domestic space. Can we make the same observations, however, if we choose to look at a narrative that did not involve itself in a public or historical discourse of the Gold Rush West?

Moynihan, Armitage, and Fischer Dichamp imply that there is a powerful variable between "filtered reminiscences" and the writing of day-to-day experiences of mining-camp life in their gloss on the journal written between 1858 and 1864 by Carrie Williams, a young wife and mother living in a Sierra mining town with her husband, son, and

26. Farnham, *California In-doors and Out,* 46–48; Moodie, *Roughing It,* 515.

parents-in-law: "The diarist's exact descriptions of household tasks . . . combined with her own feelings, make this manuscript unusually appealing and historically valuable. Its portrayal of intense domesticity exemplifies the immediacy of a diary narrative in comparison with more filtered reminiscences." Certainly, we might argue that Williams's representation of child-rearing (an important subject within her journal) conveys a sense sharper than Royce's "filtered" memory of the continuous transformations in the formation of the family. Here, we seem to be reading a narrative of a mining-camp life of transience, uncertain value systems, and tensions between the sexes (a story that the divorce figures for mid-century California corroborate) in a particularly vivid form:

> This morning Wallace whipped Walla for laying down and screaming when some books were taken away from him. I felt so bad about it that I cried too, but he deserved it, I suppose. I know though that Wallace will feel bad all day when he thinks about it.
>
> Walla was extremely troublesome all day . . . I was so aggravated that I slapped him a little, at which he screamed lustily. His grandma came running in, pitying him up, and wanted to take him from me, but I, being as stubborn as he was, would not give him up, so she give me a down right talking to about my cruelty, as she called it.

There was nothing unusual about the expression of concerns relating to the disciplining of children during this period, but the representation of the dynamics of an emigrant family seems to reflect the exaggerated social tensions within the stripped-down society of the Gold Rush. And it is this kind of social scene that Williams's domestic description addresses and interprets.[27]

This is a diary structured around the record of a narrow range of domestic activity. Two housework activities appear over and over again—mopping the floors and sewing—while others are scarcely mentioned.

---

27. Moynihan, Armitage, and Fischer Dichamp, *So Much to Be Done,* 59; Carrie Williams, "No Persuits in Common Between Us Any More," 80–81, 84–85. For a discussion of marriage and divorce in Gold Rush California, see Richard de Castillo Griswold's study, *The Family and Divorce in California, 1850–1890: Victorian Illusions and Everyday Realities* (Albany: State University of New York Press, 1982). See Brodhead, *Cultures of Letters,* 18–23, for a discussion of the complexities of mid-nineteenth-century advice given on the punishment of children.

And while in other narratives discussed in this study domestic description has seemed to advertise the grounds of its significance in terms of class and race, here we strain to get beyond Moynihan, Armitage, and Fischer Dichamp's "appealing and historically valuable."

Eliza Farnham in *Life in Prairie Land* uses the figure of washing the floor to express the complex relations between ideals of domestic work hierarchized in terms of class and ethnicity, and the experience of the "frontier." Kirkland's blistered hands, meanwhile, locate housework within a carefully modulated narrative strand dealing with self-sacrifice. Williams's record of her mopping cannot be understood against either of these contexts. The following are the statements on the subject that appear within ten of the first twenty-three entries (of which three are Sundays, nonmopping days):

> 20nd Thursday Walla's grandma mopped the kitchen and dining room today . . .
>
> 3d Friday Walla's grandma mopped as usual today . . .
>
> 4th Saturday Walla's grandma mopped the dining room and kitch . . .
>
> Monday the 6th Walla's grandma mopped the dining [room] today . . .
>
> Tuesday the 7th I rinsed and put out my washing and mopped the kitchen.
>
> Friday the 10th Walla's grandma mopped . . .
>
> Monday the 13th I mopped the dining room and kitchen before I got dinner . . .
>
> Tuesday the 14th I mopped the dining and kitchen and got dinner . . .
>
> Saturday 18th I cleaned out my room and part of the hall. Walla['s] grandma cleaned dining and kitchen.[28]

Represented here is the informality of the arrangement between the two women, a ritual that seems to operate without recourse to expressed routine, or to hierarchy in terms of age. It is the repetition of routine that is not explicitly organized. The writing of this mopping is not, apparently, the celebration of the results of hard work, for Williams begins her diary with a comment on the Protestant work ethic that puts some distance between her own and her mother-in-law's rather

28. Williams, "No Persuits," 62–68.

more morally committed approach to work: "Work work work work till you die is her mottoe both in precept and example. Hers is a persevering nature through difficulties . . . She will have her reward, if not in this world in the next, is one of the hopes she cherishes."[29] Instead, Williams's writing focuses on the performance of work in the day, and on the occasions when her mother-in-law has undertaken a particular task that causes a shifting in those duties to be picked up by her daughter-in-law. It is the repetitive, untechnologized, informally organized open-ended endeavor that we might associate with the context of a western region defined by the routinized but unregulated and unpredictable work of mining. Devoid of the kinds of emotional satisfaction that mark the discussion of housework elsewhere in this period, this housework, we might argue, comes closer to the work that dominated the community: the focused drudgery of mining.

Certainly, the home is not a space for the ritualistic, traditionalist world of food preparation that we have seen in rural narratives. Food does not signify the nurturing context of the home in Williams's diary. Joseph R. Conlin's study of food in the Far West provides an evocative context for this, associating the development of mass production of tinned food with the populating of California during the Gold Rush. Food in Far West mining communities operated in much the same way as minerals and metals: it was subject to rushes and extreme fluctuations in the market, and it became the focus of a "hankering for fine food": "Prices of every edible from wheaten flour and salt pork to oranges and canned caviar did not start at high prices and only eventually decline to merely high levels. From the beginning they swung wildly from absurdly high to (for the merchants) disheartengly low."[30]

At the same time, the pleasure of eating discussed in Williams's diary tends to be located in the attraction to new, mass-produced products. Wallace's presents to Carrie Williams are often of packaged food: "Wallace brought me a beautiful little box with a glass in the top. It was filled with delicious prunes." And, by contrast, the baking of bread, the most commonly mentioned work of food preparation in the diary—and, as we have seen, an activity full of meaning in other narratives—is de-

29. Ibid., 60.
30. Joseph R. Conlin, *Bacon, Beans and Galantines: Food and Foodways on the Western Mining Frontier,* 16, 111, 95.

scribed by Williams as the pursuit of an ideal of predictable, standardized production.

> Friday 11th . . . I also got breakfast this morn, had a little too much salaratus in my bread.
> Monday Valentine's Day . . . I had too much salaratus in my bread
> March Tuesday 1st . . . I had good bread yesterday and extra good this morning . . . [31]

If mopping and cooking bread are differently encoded in Williams's diary, Williams's record of sewing has different nuances again. The following is a characteristic passage of description: "My sewing today consisted in finishing a couple of night gowns for Walla and the hemming of a three-breasted purple calico apron for your humble servant . . . Walla's grandma finished Mary a black silk spencer today trimmed with green fringe. Now she is working on the shirt of a foullard silk for her."[32]

The activity of sewing in general is one associated with the creation and knitting together of a social fabric, in both symbolic and actual terms, and here, certainly, we find Williams and her mother-in-law engaged in an activity directed toward servicing the family in an extended form and toward the appearances of its members in special public rituals. Here the sewing involves the binding together of a community of women, not only in what is clearly a carefully planned sharing out of work within the household, but also in the interactions with Miss Gibson, the seamstress, with whom Williams's mother-in-law gossips.

Yet the structures of work described here follow the ruthless patterns of other forms of work in the mining community. This activity, unlike mopping, allows the demarcation of an informal but nonetheless rigid hierarchy within the domestic space. Williams herself is often engaged in the relative drudgery of sewing Walla's aprons, recording the

---

31. Williams, "No Persuits," 92, 70, 91. There is an interesting parallel to this baking discussion in the diary of Rachel Haskell, reprinted in Fischer, *Let Them Speak for Themselves*, 58–72. See for example the "raised biscuit" in Haskell (69), the "cunning little tarts" (61) and the setting of doughnuts (63), all of which seem to address an ideal of standardization.

32. Williams, "No Persuits," 60.

quantity of work completed, and keeping house, while the more difficult sewing is done by her mother-in-law. The latter does the "fancy" work, aided by Miss Gibson, who moves in and out of the household according to requirement: sometimes she is deemed indispensable for the performance of a difficult or lengthy task, sometimes crushingly superfluous. That the status of family members is registered against the ambiguous position of the seamstress is evident even without recourse to the research of historians such as Marion Goldman, who describes the tenuous hold on respectability experienced by such women workers in the mining West.[33]

As with food preparation, the sewing in this text links Williams's desires with the world of mass production and domestic consumption of goods. Recent arguments about women and magazines in the nineteenth century are justified, I think, in refusing the "teleological account of fashion as if it were an unfolding cultural map," and to adding the improvisatory nature of fashion and the opportunities it offers for the construction of different selves to our sense of what following fashion means. Certainly, Williams seems much concerned with the aspect of trimming and retrimming garments with materials that she has bought rather than with the more complex business of making up the garment itself. She and her companions pick up their decorative braids and their cloth from itinerant salesmen, but the patterns they make derive from national magazines. Margaret Beetham has looked at the way in which the development of paper patterns at the midcentury "defined a femininity that the reader did not yet possess and which therefore was to be desired." Certainly, the description of the continual and unceasing effort of Williams and her mother-in-law, and the record of each finished item, suggest such dictates and desires.[34]

Williams's diary, then, provides a "rich lode," as Suzanne Bunkers and Cynthia Huff put it, for the modern scholar to mine.[35] It is suggestive of the relationships between the domestic and other contexts:

---

33. Goldman, *Gold Diggers and Silver Miners*, 25.

34. Jennifer Craik, *The Face of Fashion: Cultural Studies in Fashion*, x; Margaret Beetham, *A Magazine of Her Own? Domesticity and Desire in the Woman's Magazine, 1800–1914*, 79. There are continual references to trimming and retrimming of garments in Williams's diary. See "No Persuits," 60, 62, 70, 73, 74, 75, 76, 77, 78, 88, 92, 95, 97, 99, 100, 106, 107.

35. Suzanne Bunkers and Cynthia Huff, *Inscribing the Daily: Critical Essays on Women's Diaries*, 1.

on the one hand, it depicts a domestic space shaped by the harsh life and precarious structures of the mining camp; on the other, it reflects that sense of the mining West as a stripped-down version of capitalist relations. And certainly, beside Williams's account, the writing of the mining community produced by Royce, Sanford, and so on appears a distant exoticized Fairy Land.

We cannot "mine" Williams's text, however, without addressing the question of what kind of text this is. Generally, texts such as Williams's are regarded simply as a record of oppression. Elaine Hedges writes of "litanies of . . . entries, month after month, year after year, a monotony of repetition and routine"; Motz of the lists of tasks performed as no more than an "alibi" for the hard work performed that day.[36]

What such readings of housework records tend to play down, however, is the work that may be performed by writing a diary. As Elizabeth Grosz puts it, "a text is not the repository of knowledges or the site for the storage of information" but a "form of action." In Williams's case, where no self-publicity is planned and where the writer is the person whose views appear to have little influence within the household and, apparently, none outside it, we need to consider what kind of action is undertaken here.[37]

The sociologists Stanley Cohen and Laurie Taylor have suggested, in *Escape Attempts,* that we all "become strangely disturbed by the predictability of the journey, the accuracy of the map, the knowledge that today's route will be much like yesterday's." As they argue, we may distinguish predictable activity from activity that defines our real selves, "viewing inessential elements of our life as unreflective chains of behaviour," while concentrating upon "self-expression in the remaining areas." When we look at Williams's journal, are we looking at the unreflective record of "unreflective chains of behaviour" in a diary bought for her by her husband; another chore, in fact? Or is diary writing the activity by which she seeks to define herself, a "remaining area" of "self-expression"? Is this what Cohen and Taylor would call a "reinvestment in routine," where domestic tasks are reinvented as special and loaded with interest as opposed to being simply "inevitable

---

36. Elaine Hedges, "The Nineteenth-Century Diarist and Her Quilts," 294; Marilyn Ferris Motz, "The Private Alibi: Literacy and Community in the Diaries of Two Nineteenth-Century American Women," 202.
37. Grosz, *Space, Time and Perversion,* 125–26.

repetitions"? Plainly, these are questions that we cannot answer, but they should perhaps discourage the reading of texts such as Williams's as litanies of repetition.[38]

We may tentatively create a mining-camp autobiography of seen and unseen, of improvisation, of fluid structures, a subgenre of emigrant autobiographical writing that resists the mythology of Anglo housewives at odds with the mining West. Though the meaning and function of those texts closest to the everyday remains elusive, Williams's text seems vividly to evoke a close grain of mining-camp domestic life both unstable and knotted within the practices of capitalism.

All these texts seem, strikingly, to have caught the attention of readers. The unambiguous texts of Sanford, Royce, and "Dame Shirley" remain in print, Foote is much cited, and even Williams's opaque text has been recovered and printed in a successful anthology of women's writing of the Far West: a better record than that achieved by some of the narratives discussed in earlier chapters, and these latter are scarcely obscure. At some level, these texts produce an experience recognizable as descriptive of one of the great myths of western expansion. Theirs is indeed the chaotic, churning mining West of convention. What of the narratives that remain obscure? Are there texts that fail to produce a recognizable experience? The mass of published materials seems to suggest otherwise. In the next chapter, I want to look at an autobiographical text of domestic life that is apparently comparatively insignificant and consider why this may be so.

---

38. Stanley Cohen and Laurie Taylor, *Escape Attempts: The Theory and Practice of Resistance to Everyday Life*, 46, 49, 59, 67.

7

"To Recover Those Once Known but Now Forgotten"

Anne Langton's Journal and Memoir

*T*HIS STUDY BEGAN by reflecting on the recovery of the Anglo pioneer woman. In chapter 1, I discussed the construction of pioneer womanhood: the rejection of constraint, the embrace of active work and open spaces, the escape from a stifling domesticity. Some strands within the writing of the "female frontier" remain profoundly attracted to the frontier mythology of individual expansion, to the point where individual freedom for the white emigrant woman, or her love for the land, retain an absolute worth. And indeed, the rather compromising terms of colonial discovery and expansion are still used to frame scholarship in the field: we are still exploring "richer lodes" of women's writing, digging out buried treasures, exploring new areas. Helen Buss writes of having "found a veritable continent of published materials . . . the wealth of a new land." In a project always evidently engaged in the consideration of women's behavior, it has been possible, through the figure of the pioneer woman, to measure change in women's lives in the last 150 years. As Julia Hirsch has argued, we long to read our own lives as "the fulfilment of our ancestors' dreams"; the recovery of the pioneer woman has allowed us that sense of tradition and achievement.[1]

---

1. The quotation in the title is from Lorraine McMullen, ed., *Re(Dis)covering Our Foremothers: Nineteenth-Century Canadian Women Writers*, 1. "Richer lodes" are explored in Bunkers and Huff, *Inscribing the Daily*, 1; Helen Buss, "Canadian Women's Autobiography: Some Critical Directions," 154; Julia Hirsch, *Family Photographs*, 119.

Enthusiasm and rhetoric notwithstanding, this process has had particular limits. For all the exhaustive archival research, for all the editing and anthologizing of private diaries and fragments of autobiography alongside published work, for all the apparent impulse to celebrate in a democratic spirit the writing, however prosaic, of "ordinary" pioneer women, some narratives have not been included within the embrace of the project of recovery. Is this because some emigrant women's narratives are too poorly written, too bland or too featureless, too disengaged from their "frontier" surroundings to have caught the attention of editors and historians? Perhaps, but neither literary merit nor even fluency of expression have traditionally been important criteria in judging whether an emigrant text is suitable for reproduction or recovery; on the contrary, their roughness and routine detail have signaled authenticity of response. Even "the daily grind of oppressions, institutionalized and internalized . . . indelibly etched in memory" of which Rosy Martin writes, has been grist to the scholarly mill.[2]

In this chapter, I want to consider the writing of Anne Langton, which, though not utterly obscure, has occupied the margins of the discussion of pioneer women conducted in Canada. Certainly, it has yielded neither the hidden treasure of "frontier" individualism and expansion nor the opposing model of Victorian suppression. Clara Thomas has argued that Langton was a "willing, even eager emigrant" and describes her journals as full of the "constant ring of irrepressible good humour, adaptability and high hopes that make her unique in the literature of settlement," while Elizabeth Thompson mentions her as a "cheerful pragmatist."[3] Still, Langton has rarely attracted anything approaching sustained attention. What I want to suggest here is that Langton's texts and their relegation to the borderlands of the enquiry into pioneer womanhood may draw our attention to some of the blind spots of the project. What the history of Langton's autobiographical writings shows is the twisting processes through which a text is kept, reproduced, and recovered. It draws our attention to the participation of different interests in "recovering" the meaning of texts.

2. Rosy Martin, "Unwind the Ties that Bind," 213.
3. Clara Thomas, "Anne Langton," 195; Elizabeth Thompson, *The Pioneer Woman: A Character Type*, 39–40, 43–44.

Anne Langton's writing of her emigration took two forms. First, she wrote quarterly letters each consisting of a journal kept for a month. These journals have been by far the most visible of Langton's texts. They were sent to her sister-in-law in England during the first period of her life in Upper Canada (where she emigrated at the age of thirty-three) between 1837 and 1847. This was a period spent keeping house for her brother John (four years younger than herself), who lived in his own quarters close to the family home, while living and keeping house with her mother (who was in her seventies), "Aunt Currer" (her mother's sister), and (until his death in 1838) her father, Thomas.[4]

Second, Langton, writing in Toronto at the end of the 1870s, produced a record of her family's adventures that was privately published for family and friends in 1881 in Manchester as *The Story of Our Family*. This much more obscure text has three parts. The first gives an account of what was apparently a quite lavish family tour of Europe between 1815 and 1820, followed by a subsequent experience of life in straitened circumstances in and near Liverpool in the 1820s and 1830s. The second part deals with the period beginning in 1837 in Canada, and ends at the point of her brother's marriage (in 1845) and the death of her mother and aunt within six weeks of one another in 1846. This was the sequence of events that marked the end of Anne Langton's life of keeping house for her brother, mother, and aunt, and the beginning of a much less easily defined middle age spent moving between England and Canada, visiting friends and assisting in rearing John and Lydia Langton's children. This middle age is the subject of the third part of *The Story of Our Family*, and here the emphasis shifts away from the representation of her immediate experience to the recording of the achievements and movements of "our family" in the thirty years between her first return from Canada and the present time of the text.

One way in which we can try to explain Langton's marginal position in the field is by looking at how Langton herself and her work fail to fit

---

4. Secondary sources on Langton's life are scant, but see H. H. Langton's preface to *A Gentlewoman in Upper Canada;* Barbara Williams, "Anne Langton"; and for discussions of family fortunes, see W. A. Langton, *Early Days in Upper Canada: Letters of John Langton,* and G. H. Needler, *Otonabee Pioneers: The Story of the Stewarts, the Stricklands, the Traills and the Moodies.*

the pioneer ideal. They are often characterized by reference to her origins in the world of the English middle-class drawing-room. D. M. R. Bentley's brief mention of Langton's emigration, for example, begins with a suggestive image of the psychological fallout of being displaced from such a background: "For Langton, the distress of 'embarking on [her] awful voyage' to North America was compounded by the middle-class necessity of keeping up the appearance of being unmoved . . . It may even be that the melancholia evident at various points in Langton's later letters is traceable in part to the repression of her emotions on leaving England." Barbara Williams, the scholar writing with the greatest depth of knowledge on Langton, emphasizes the gentility of middle-class Anglo emigrants, writing of her as "educated to flourish as a tender exotic."[5] The extraordinary circumstances of Langton's education, an elongated and intellectually distinguished version of a grand tour, are used as a way to speculate on the implications of a potentially debilitating gap between an educated past and a frontier present, rather than as a context in which to understand the emigrant texts of an exceptionally well-educated woman.

The use, in addition, of Langton's portrait of herself as a ringletted and becapped early-nineteenth-century lady to illustrate all editions of her work emphasizes the reference to an order of literary endeavor familiar from, say, the literary and biographical portraits of Jane Austen of twenty years ago. In 1978, David Cecil framed Austen within the context of a "quiet sheltered life, strictly bound by convention," and underscored Austen's self-deprecating comments on the small span of her output: "that little bit of ivory (two inches wide)" on which Austen portrayed herself working "with so fine a brush as produces little effect after much labour." Langton was herself a miniaturist and she too writes that she "feel(s) inclined to confine my interest to the smallest possible compass." Hers also is a wit expended within a circle of economically and socially superfluous women and an experience of spinsterhood. And, at times, Langton does evoke a life engaged in warding off genteel tedium: "Generally if we [her aunt, mother, and herself] do go out for

---

5. D. R. M. Bentley, "'Breaking the Cake of Custom': The Atlantic Crossing as a Rubicon for Female Emigrants to Canada?" 97–98; Williams, "Anne Langton," 525; Barbara Williams, *Anne Langton: Pioneer Woman and Artist*, 2–3.

the sake of a walk [we] sally forth the three in a body. But there is an advantage in dividing our numbers, for when we meet again we have our little adventures to relate."[6]

Scenes of leisured walks, terms of genteel domesticity and "tender exotics" are not, as we have seen, generally regarded as consistent with pioneer womanhood. Familiarity with middle-class drawing rooms tends to be a signifier of a blinkered unsuitability for emigration. Thus, we may choose to argue that this is the reason for Langton's shadowy presence in the field. An equally compelling explanation, though, lies in the way that Langton understands emigration as a family event in which past and present remain irretrievably connected. In this sense, she never leaves home, never lights out to find a new life on the "frontier." Of course, most emigrants set out with family members, met other members at their destination, and wrote "home" to encourage those left behind to join their migrant relatives. Likewise, Langton wrote to and for her family, but her writing does not evoke scenes of intimacy and collaborative enterprise buttressing success in a new land. The narratives of family life that she produces speak rather to a complex and oppressive family network that, far from falling away on the "frontier," was reinvigorated in the colonial context.

This was a network in which, for all her education, Langton was scarcely granted the authority of the maker of a family record, much less the status of the autobiographer. Her work actually formed part of a family record organized and regulated by the family itself. Eventually, Langton's letter-journals were published by her relatives as part of an ambitious project of recording, over four generations, the progress of the Langton family in Canada. W. A. Langton, John Langton's son and Anne's nephew, editing the letters of his father in *Early Days in Upper Canada,* makes the point in his preface that this series of letters (written before the rest of the family followed John to Canada) were "carefully copied by [John's] father . . . and . . . bound in book form."[7] Anne Langton's letter-journals were edited by her niece and privately published in 1904 in Britain, eleven years after Anne's death, for family

---

6. David Cecil, *A Portrait of Jane Austen,* 9, 147; Anne Langton, *Langton Records,* 176, 73.
7. W. A. Langton, *Early Days,* v.

circulation as *Langton Records*. A generation later, in 1950, her great-nephew, Hugh Hornby Langton, re-edited them and published them for a general audience.

In *Langton Records*, it seems that the Langtons sought to produce and project, for themselves, a narrative of emigration in which ties that still bound parts of the family living apart from one another were made evident, and whereby the flight from Britain could be constructed as an exciting part of a whole family enterprise. Their emigration had, in fact, taken place in circumstances of desperate economic need originating in the poor business climate after the Napoleonic Wars. For all the prevailing critical tendency to position Langton as a lady of some status, a reading of Langton's memoir, *The Story of Our Family* (which has not been reprinted), makes it clear that the Langtons (with the exception of William, the son and brother who was sufficiently well off not to need to leave Britain) had long abandoned the social practices appropriate to their class by the time they rushed to Upper Canada (earlier than planned) to escape social and financial oblivion.

Ellen Philips, who edited *Langton Records*, interspersed the letter-journals with miscellaneous letters, insistently placing the writer of the journals within a male-dominated family and colonial enterprise. If the Langtons' social disgrace is understandably erased from *Langton Records*, it is perhaps more surprising to find the pains of Anne Langton's single womanhood so unflinchingly reproduced. Revealed here are the dimensions of the relationship of an unmarried sister to her brother, on whose decisions, appearances, and social activities she attends, and on whose unmarried status her vicarious access to a life of apparent status (through her role as his housekeeper) depends. So we read: "I think it very questionable whether it would not be for my happiness that he should continue to want his sister"; that "the time may come when I shall not be worth a straw to anybody. It will be a great change, and one which I cannot estimate the effect on me"; that "I am sure I ought not to wish John married unless a suitable person turned up."[8]

The family life Langton herself represents is one where her position is always peripheral. In *The Family Party at Blythe in 1840*, she has drawn herself hovering outside the charmed domestic circle of her

---

8. Langton, *Langton Records*, 74, 185, 189.

mother, aunt, and brother as, seated, they engage in reading, sewing, and conversation. This is not a modest self-effacement alone, but rather a subject position that is of a piece with the emphasis of the volume. Ellen Philips inserts a quotation from a letter from Langton's father, for example, on the subject of room allocation on the family's arrival at Sturgeon Lake in Upper Canada:

> All the rooms are very comfortable except Anne's.... Anne's room, a small one over the entrance, intended to be heated by a Franklin stove ... let in more smoke from the [dining-room] flue than it took away, and filled the other two bedrooms. We have been obliged to close the flue, and give up the bedroom, and reserve it as a store-room, which will be much wanted. In the meantime Anne has the travelling bed put up in our room, and dresses in Aunt Alice's. Another arrangement may be made by and by, but for the present this answers very well.[9]

Many of the scenes represented by Langton herself show family relations, as they affect the writer, turning on a continual complex practice of power and on the internalization of restriction. Again, interspersed letters show how Langton's mother's indisposition, for example, marks her power over the daughter who cannot move if her mother cannot. Equally, her mother's own good health seems to produce an insistence that Anne, by contrast, is too delicate to go out. And again, Langton describes her collusion in this sequestration. For example, in an episode where she comments wryly on the way in which a trip to the home of a neighboring family precipitates fears in her mother "as to what might be done without damage to her precious daughter," Langton suggests that the result of the trip may be, in a sense, damaging: "having had one 'out,'" she fears "getting restless." Her mother insists on her incapability, and Langton, recalling perhaps what Ellen Moers has described as "the equality of the nursery"—"the only heterosexual world that Victorian literary spinsters were ever freely and physically to explore"—embraces her infantilization: "I felt a little like a child with a treat in prospect, and thought it well worth staying at home for a long time to have a feeling so juvenile."[10]

9. Ibid., 43–44.
10. Ibid., 95–96; Ellen Moers, *Literary Women,* 105.

Anne Langton, *The Family Party at Blythe in 1840*. Frontispiece of *The Story of Our Family* (Manchester: Thomas Sowler, 1881.)

Quite plainly, then, *Langton Records* does not show emigration primarily as the discovery of a new space, or as an exploration of new identities. Rather, the description of her position by Langton herself, by those around her, and by the editors of her work continually remind the reader of the way in which the hierarchy of the family is maintained and indeed of the chasm of nonidentity existing outside its boundaries. It would seem that, at the same time, Ellen Philips was, in editing her aunt's work, participating in anxious debates, within British culture, about the "origins" of those populating Canada at the turn of the century. As A. Ross McCormack notes, this era was a point at which, as outward sailings from Britain increased, networks in Canada that "[grew] out of the nuclear family" were encouraged, in order to "maximize group advantage in Canada's heterogeneous society" (that is, to ward off the possibility that Canada "would become cosmopolitan rather than British").[11]

11. A. Ross McCormack, "Networks among British Immigrants and Accommodation to Canadian Society 1900–1914," 55, 164.

Anne Langton's situation was of particular interest in this context. It was considered the peculiar task of the unmarried (and, it was argued, economically superfluous) emigrant gentlewoman to disseminate "family values" in the colonies. It was presumed that such women, if unmarriageable even in male-dominated Canada, would teach or keep house according to British middle-class practice. If, as A. James Hammerton writes, "Notions of imperial destiny and class and racial superiority were grafted on to the traditional views of refined English motherhood to produce a concept of the Englishwoman as an invincible global civilizing agent," then the single gentlewoman was gratifyingly well positioned to perform the role of nurturing "civilization." Her superfluousness within the British economy and her own family meant that her emigration would cause minimal disruption to the family left behind. Hammerton quotes a contemporary apologist for the migration of single women arguing that unmarried women could "cease to think of themselves as exiles, but may realize that they have but migrated from one part of the family estate to another, and are still among their own people." In this comment, there is a clear understanding of the family—national or nuclear—as an organization with limitless potential for appropriating more space—more "estates"—by replicating itself through its less important members.[12]

If Anne Langton perhaps seemed to her niece the perfect pattern of a single gentlewoman, Langton herself had regarded her emigration in a similar light, as, twenty or so years earlier, she wrote her memoir, *The Story of Our Family*. From the start of the memoir, Langton draws our attention to the interdependence of family fortunes and imperial destiny in marking her account of leaving Britain as the day on which Queen Victoria, "mother" of the empire, was crowned. In what Annette Kuhn refers to as a "ceremonial moment" in family portraiture, Langton creates a portrait of family departure that subsumes the

---

12. A. James Hammerton, *Emigrant Gentlewomen, Genteel Poverty and Female Emigration*, 162, 163. Hammerton is citing J. R. Chitty, "The Young Old Maid as Emigrant," *The Imperial Colonist* 5 (August 1906): 116–18. For a detailed discussion of the assumptions of those involved in promoting Canada to unmarried women, see Susan Jackel, ed., *A Flannel Shirt and Liberty: British Emigrant Gentlewomen in the Canadian West 1880–1914*, and Beth Light and Joy Parr, eds., *Canadian Women on the Move, 1867–1920* includes a section on the assisted emigration of less privileged women, 62–68. See Hammerton also for British attitudes and policy.

individualities of those taking part to larger communities; to attachments that go beyond and even overshadow the personal lives of those pictured. Moments of great import, most particularly the death of her father, are specifically associated with the progress of empire: folding family history into imperial progress, Langton records the day of the demise of a father too old to enjoy "the pursuits of the young men" with which backwoods Canada was glamorized and promoted, as the occasion when she told him of the first steamer, signifier of the powerful trading economies of an empire-dominated world, traveling across to Canada, once again.[13]

Langton does not even authorize herself, as have other writers in this study, by drawing attention to her own active part in the process of colonization. Although we find references to her work teaching in *Langton Records,* in *Story of Our Family,* Langton actually erases her work as the teacher of local children at Blythe. Instead, the delineation of her domestic role defines the project of the family, and she is emphatic in representing her subservient usefulness in supporting their progress: "I have often found when we had company, that it was most convenient to do the room and lay the breakfast table over night, and I have sat up the night through and merely changed my dress before appearing to make breakfast." This, of course, is why her removal from the structure of the colonial family, on the marriage of her brother, reduces her, in her words, to "a very insignificant individual."[14]

The Story of Our Family remained obscure, but Langton's letter-journals enjoyed a revival in the latter half of the twentieth century. *A Gentlewoman in Upper Canada,* published in 1950, consisted of a re-editing of the letter-journals by her Canadian great-nephew, Hugh Hornby Langton. It appeared alongside a number of historical narratives of migrating families of "gentlefolk": G. H. Needler's *Otonabee Pioneers;* Florence Partridge's "The Stewarts and the Stricklands, the Moodies and the Traills"; Lloyd M. Scott's "The English Gentlefolk in the Backwoods of Canada." These and Hugh Hornby Langton's text not only promoted a narrative of Canadian racial origins resting on genteel British arriving in a "new land" but also insisted on refined

---

13. Annette Kuhn, *Family Secrets: Acts of Memory and Imagination,* 62; Langton, *The Story of Our Family,* 54, 74–75.
14. Anne Langton, *The Story of Our Family,* 92, 104.

qualities of Britishness planted, through pioneer *families,* in the open spaces of New World culture. Needler finishes his introduction in this kind of vein:

> I know of no other district in North America that was so fortunate in the character of its settlers as the upper Otonabee. Here we have in the Stewarts, the Stricklands, the Traills, the Moodies fortitude that endured most exacting hardships in rare union with high literary gifts. . . . This is not to say that their experience was exceptional. The foundation of Upper Canada was laid by numberless lives of similar but unchronicled heroism. Here the exception is that they who toiled could also tell their own story so charmingly.[15]

The model of Anglo occupation as a family affair seems to have not only sentimentalized colonial expansion but also worked to address some of the tensions around immigration in mid-twentieth-century Canada. Both ends of the decade in which Langton was first recovered were highly significant in the history of Canadian immigration policy, in the sense that eligibility for immigration was a matter of high-profile government deliberation; indeed, the early 1950s saw the creation of a quota system, and the early 1960s (when the book appeared in paperback) a new round of immigration regulation. The admission of a multiracial population (beyond the British, French, and Americans) was being approached, it seems, with some fear for the survival (at least in a dominant position) of the "peculiar customs, habits, modes of life, or methods of holding property" characterizing Anglo-dominated Canada.[16] The recovery of Anglo-Canadian pioneers as *the* ancestors of the nation delivered a narrative of Canadian origins (and families) to which some Canadians at least wished to assent.

Hugh Hornby Langton, recovering his great-aunt's journals, edited the text in order to sharpen its focus on the narration of emigration undertaken with firmness and familial unity of purpose. He opens *A Gentlewoman in Upper Canada* with letters written in 1834 between John Langton (who had emigrated ahead of the rest of the family in 1833) and his father that set out their understanding of the move,

---

15. Needler, *Otonabee Pioneers,* 5.
16. Freda Hawkins, *Canada and Immigration: Public Policy and Public Concern,* 99–100.

an understanding in which family was the defining political structure within the colony and empire. He quotes John Langton writing: "I should assign you each a separate office. My father of course would be my adviser and in my absence the *alter ego;* to you [his mother] should be exclusively left the duties of beautifying the house and garden, no sinecure on a new farm; Anne must be the Prime Minister in the Home department, and Aunt Alice, for, if you come, she must accompany you, shall reign paramount in the pigstye, poultry yard, etc., and shall be my Master of the Wardrobe."[17]

In order to produce a national story of Upper Canada, Hugh Hornby Langton adds passages from letters of other family members to address "omissions" in the record of national history; so, for example, Thomas Langton's bracingly nationalistic account of the MacKenzie rebellion is incorporated into the text. So uninterested, indeed, is this editor in the writer of the journals herself that in addition to excising passages which do not accord with the most positive construction of emigration (including most of the passages so far quoted here), he gives most of his Preface and Epilogue over to the achievements of John Langton in various public roles, prefacing—finally—his scanty remarks about the "gentlewoman" of the title with the remark, "As most of the letters in this volume are from Anne, it might be as well to give some account of her."[18]

The writing, editing, printing, and use, then, of Langton's autobiographical records have taken the form of an "instrument of the families' togetherness" in a context where the personal and the national are made one; they have signified a determination to perpetuate "familial myths." In our own time, we retain, as Jo Spence writes, a compelling desire to "[privilege] the nuclear family by naturalizing, romanticizing and idealizing family relations above all others," but our predilection has, perhaps, taken a different form. Our preference, at least in critical terms, has been to valorize the relations between mother and child. Helen Buss, in *Mapping Our Selves,* has used Anglo emigrant women's autobiographical texts to articulate a critical practice informed by the relations of birthing and nurture, a model that gives the autobiographer and the scholar who recovers her a mothering role:

---

17. H. H. Langton, *A Gentlewoman in Upper Canada,* 5–6.
18. Ibid., xiii.

the autobiographer is a foremother within the tradition of producing women's texts, the scholar nurtures the text attentively, while allowing that, as Buss puts it, the text "is not an extension of myself.... If I am to fully read it, I must recognize its separateness, its own life." The case of Langton reminds us not only of the yawning divide between the relationships to which Buss is attracted, and those suffered and stoically recorded by Langton, but also that the range of "frontier" family portraits we now choose to recover and reproduce is a narrow one.[19]

In the context of the imagined closeness between mother and daughter, Donna E. Smyth exhorts us to "[attempt] to decode" the writings of pioneers: "so much that is hidden within us, that is silent in us, still awaits discovery, uncovering." Some autobiographical writings do indeed seem, as Julia Hirsch writes of old photographs of people unknown to us, to offer "an intimacy without any formal introductions." This is plainly the case with texts such as Elinore Pruitt Stewart's, or Nannie Alderson's, or Mollie Sanford's. Other texts produce a more conflicted self: Kitturah Belknap's, or Christiana Tillson's. It is these that Buss and Smyth look to read "like a signed confession or an hour of psychoanalysis."[20]

Langton's texts have not received such treatment. Part of the reason has to do with the issues raised above: she fails to represent herself as a pioneer woman in the sense that we understand that term, and those who have edited her have produced a pioneer for whom we do not particularly care. There is, however, another way of explaining the way in which Langton's work has been relegated to what Annette Kuhn calls the "borderlands of memory." This has to do with her autobiographical method, and it is to this issue that I want now to turn.

Langton's texts thwart the impulses that Smyth describes and deflect intimate understanding. They not only fail to produce a picture "to which we can assent," to use Julia Hirsch's description of the photographs that we reject, but also fail to "[lay] bare" the intimacies of

19. Marianne Hirsch, *Family Frames: Photography, Narrative and Post-Memory*, 7; Jo Spence, *Putting Myself in the Picture: A Political, Personal and Photographic Autobiography*, 136; Buss, *Mapping Ourselves*, 26.
20. Donna E. Smyth, "'Thinking Back through Our Mothers': Tradition in Canadian Women's Writing," 18, 15; Hirsch, *Family Photographs*, 106.

the writer's inner life.[21] As readers we accept, as Timothy Dow Adams argues, that "to record the story of the self . . . [is] a virtually impossible task." But Langton actually makes a point of emphasizing the gap between her self and her production of writing from a position of subservience for the benefit of the extended family. This is not only a matter of suggesting that she is not telling what she is thinking: "I scribble away, dear Margaret, but I never tell you what I have been thinking about. That I leave you to imagine." She also continually insists on the public nature of text and its slippery and changeable quality. In *Story of Our Family* she writes: "In any verbal account I gave at home, according to the preconceived notions of those I was enlightening, I had to dwell sometimes on the one, sometimes on the other so much, that they might almost think, and I used to feel myself, as if I were telling two different stories." The comment with which she ends *Story of Our Family* specifically references fiction: "And may not these pages, which I have divided into three little volumes, fitly conclude, like a novel, with a wedding." Here she refers to the way in which her narrative is a "story" to please her listeners, whilst reminding her readers that the narrative of her experience has not in fact been organized around a wedding. And the marriage between her brother and Lydia Dunsford that looms at the center of her text (and which, apparently, she could neither bring herself to attend nor to describe) has not, as in the nineteenth-century novel, muted or resolved all problems but has rather resulted in a very problematic search for a continuation of a life of unobtrusive usefulness.[22]

To insist as she does that her narrative is written as a tale to please her readers is, of course, a standard preface to the writing of women of Langton's generation: coy, self-deprecating, safe. But Langton goes further than this, placing an almost uncomfortable emphasis on the performative aspects of her narrative: "I now take leave of my readers for the present; if they have derived an evening's amusement from the foregoing pages, and have finished with a little matter for thought and conversation then I am more than repaid, and shall have great pleasure appearing before them again at a future time." Here she seems not only

21. Kuhn, *Family Secrets*, 2; Hirsch, *Family Photographs*, 106.
22. Adams, *Telling Lies in Modern American Autobiography*, 170; Langton, *Langton Records*, 19; Langton, *Story of Our Family*, 104, 204.

to evoke the formality of a performance, but her movement between "front" and "back" stage.²³

Erving Goffman, in *The Presentation of Self in Everyday Life*, describes the quality of "dramatizing one's own work": "To the degree that a performance highlights the common official values of the society in which it occurs, we may look upon it . . . as a ceremony—as an expressive rejuvenation and reaffirmation of the moral values of the community." As Goffman points out, in such a performance, "the extent and character of the cooperation" between those "engaged in maintaining the stability of some definitions of the situation" is considerable, and it is only after the performance—backstage, as it were—that "the impression fostered by the performance is knowingly contradicted as a matter of course." Langton is not only prone to making that "knowing contradiction"—that admission that her writing *is* a performance—onstage, as it were, in her text; she also points out, in her account of getting ready to write her journal every three months, that she "has acted," as she puts it, "with the page in view that has to be written." Both the performance of the conventional "script," as it were, and the activity on which the performance of writing is based, are set up—confected—for her audience's pleasure.²⁴

The sense of the hollowness of the text's writing of experience is compounded by the way in which Langton does not always make it easy for the reader to see how her anecdotes of family life "performed" actually affirm the "moral values of the community." This is especially true of *Story of Our Family*. For example, there is the plainly apocryphal story of the emigrant pet, Fury:

> Aunt Alice was "Fury's" chief guardian, and she was generally fastened up in her room. Poor little thing! She did not live long after we got to our home, but survived the first winter and felt the cold very much, especially the frozen snow to her poor little feet. If she had gone out with anyone she would sometimes throw herself on her back and hold up her four paws, complaining bitterly, and once, when she was found on her back, not having the resolution to put down her feet and trot home.

23. Langton, *Langton Records*, 88.
24. Erving Goffman, *The Presentation of Self in Everyday Life*, 35, 105, 112.

Here we have the usual true story of emigration; the tale we expect to hear of the bad emigrant, the first winter, the complaining female. The story is miniaturized, for the amusement and reassurance of her readers: recollected as a detail evoking a larger scene and yet also reducing the meaning of that scene to the fate of a pet. It is the position of such anecdotes as this among other apparently unconnected "scenes" that leaves us always uncertain as to their meaning. We want, surely, to read a possible subtext of confinement, suffering, and death associated with unmarried Aunt Alice (also dead by the time of writing), Anne Langton's shadowy double; or perhaps the ponder the meaning of the story's outcome in terms of the exercise of "fury."

Buss writes of searching the emigrant text for "an undercurrent of forbidden discourse, a discourse of rebellious accusation and multiple breakings and misdeeds of men." But this becomes difficult to achieve when there is no continuously held position in Langton's texts, no overall narrative structure or consistent generic reference, nor any "characters" to form the kind of patterns that make "undercurrents" perceptible. No earlier narratives of the same events as those described in *Story of Our Family* allow us to find meaning in the gap between one version and another; on the contrary, the most dramatic scenes of *Story of Our Family*—the drowning, for example, of a young woman's fiancé within earshot, his "strange cries . . . attributed to wild animals"—are unmentioned in the journals. Instead, we have two texts made up of the traces of experience recovered and characterized by what Kuhn calls the "fragmentary, non-linear quality of moments recalled out of time."[25]

This concept of "moments recalled out of time" is a helpful one in the context of the attempt to read Langton's texts. When such apparently random images are called up without warning in our imagination, they seem to us particularly true, as with the so-called "flashbulb" memories described by Brown and Kulik: they have a "primary, 'live' quality . . . like a photograph that indiscriminately preserves a scene . . . when the flashbulb was fired." Such memories have a "full and fleshy" vividness that seems to defy the passing of time and our habit of understanding memories as, in Mark Freeman's words, no more than a "pale

---

25. Langton, *Story of Our Family*, 58–59, 90; Helen Buss, "Settling the Score with Myths of Settlement: Two Women Who Roughed It and Wrote It," 167; Kuhn, *Family Secrets*, 213.

and shadowy replica of experience." At the same time, their very vividness and comprehensiveness suggest a creative process of imagination rather than mere repetition.[26]

Langton's most powerful passages seem closer to "flashbulb memories" than autobiographical narrative. An extraordinary example appears in Langton's recalling of scenes, in both *The Story of Our Family* and the letter-journals, of herself butchering meat. Doubtless, many emigrant women put their hands to butchering the carcasses of dead animals (as opposed to preparing meat through preserving and cooking), but no other narratives I have read represent the writers with meat choppers in their hands, with recently slaughtered flesh around them, or as covered in blood. The only late Victorian scene remotely comparable to this occurs in Thomas Hardy's *Jude the Obscure* where the girls at Marygreen kneel washing pigs' offal and Arabella, one of their number, hurls a pig's "characteristic part" at the high-minded and virginal Jude. Arabella is described as "a complete and substantial human animal."[27] These, then, are "full and fleshy" memories indeed, and yet the reader struggles to grasp their meaning within the text. Here is Langton on the subject in *Story of Our Family:*

> About October the slaughtering of our beasts began. Oh! what a vision rises up before me of sheep, and quarters of beef and pigs, cutting up, boiling down, stewing and potting &c &c; and then to look in the larder, one felt as if one could never possibly get to the end of all that meat . . . A great deal of the cutting up used to devolve upon me. A man would have done it in half the time, but my mother was very particular in having the joints properly shaped, and it was not easy to get anyone else to take her directions.

On some levels, we see a predictable symbolism of power here. As Nick Fiddes has argued, "Meat provided the ideal expression by which the power of industry could be demonstrated . . . We do not esteem meat *in spite of* the domination of sentient beings. Rather . . . we (as a society) esteem meat so highly *because* of that power." The freedom to kill animals to eat in North America was also laden with class significance,

---

26. R. Brown and J. Kulik, "Flashbulb Memories," 74; Mark Freeman, *Rewriting the Self: History, Memory, Narrative*, 89–90.
27. Thomas Hardy, *Jude the Obscure*, 41.

of course: it was a potent symbol of greater democracy in the United States, and of the pleasures of colonial power in Canada. Certainly, the fabled superfluity of meat and game available prompted troubling fears of plenty without effort, but the process of dominating the land as represented by dead animals was not in question. Thus, at the end of the second part of *Story of Our Family,* John Langton's description of Canadian animals is incorporated into his sister's narrative, and Langton produces this vision of herself also involved in the disposition of power in a scene of plenty.[28]

Thus, it might be argued that Anne Langton's memory of herself engaged in converting nature (animals) to "cultural artefact" (meat) matches the "civilizing" project of the emigrant woman. This is the representation of a bloodless process of butchering that disguises the appropriation of land in energetic domestic industry, while also imaging the traditional duty of women to provide meat for the male: Alan Beardsmore and Teresa Keil write of the "crucial association in patriarchal societies between meat eating and male power" whereby the preparation of meat is part of "the demands men make upon women." Langton has to butcher the meat in a particular way, using a method to which a servant, apparently, cannot be trusted to adhere.[29]

And yet the association between the dead flesh of animals and women is surely also marked by a forest of "complicated taboos and restrictions." Is Langton, in this flashbulb memory, transgressively imitating the "male" activity of butchery, and, in doing so, claiming an equal role to that of her brother? Or is this a more troubling and ambivalent mimicry of the carnage involved in a (male-dominated) process of colonization?

There is no blood in the butchery passage from *Story of Our Family,* and thus a kind of conceptual purity is given to the moment. However, blood appears in a dramatic form in a similar passage in the journals, a passage that, unsurprisingly, was edited out of *A Gentlewoman in Upper Canada:* "This morning my mother and I cut up little porkling we had had killed yesterday, and we agreed, when on a small scale, it was more agreeable to operate ourselves than stand by and give directions.

---

28. Langton, *Story of Our Family,* 84; Nick Fiddes, *Meat: A Natural Symbol,* 227–28.
29. Fiddes, *Meat,* 91; Alan Beardsmore and Teresa Keil, *Sociology on the Menu: An Invitation to the Study of Food and Society,* 212.

Afterwards we were all buried in red moreen. I rather like a piece of work of this kind to be done in a hurry . . . one sets about it with energy, and it gets finished."[30]

Here, mother and daughter are represented reveling in their opportunity to butcher the piglet. The scene, with its reference to raw meat and dripping blood, seems to evoke something close to savagery. As Julia Kristeva writes, blood is "a vital element" that refers to women and their fertility, but which also indicates the impure, the animal, the murderous: "Blood, indicating the impure, takes on the 'animal' scene . . . and inherits the propensity for murder of which man must cleanse himself. But blood, as a vital element, also refers to women, fertility and the assurance of fecundation . . . [It is] a fascinating semantic crossroads, the propitious place for abjection where death and femininity, murder and procreation, cessation of life and vitality all come together."[31]

Here, for once, as Elizabeth Grosz puts it, the "author's corporeality—not the author's interiority, psyche, consciousness, concepts, or ideas—intrudes into the text," and not, as in *Life in Prairie Land,* in the form of wounded but nonetheless scrupulously cleansed hands. Rather, Langton makes a spectacle of herself covered—"buried"—in the stiff, blood-soaked moreen fabric. Carol Adams has described how, in butchery, the self is doubly annihilated in slaughter and dismemberment: the butcher must not only force himself to refuse the relationship between his body and that of the animal he kills, he must also absent himself psychologically from the horrifying process of dismemberment. Langton's strange memory of defilement, of familial collusion, of tragic ritual creates a scene in the text inassimilable into the story of family, emigration, and homemaking. What defiled or justified self is being recollected by Langton—erstwhile "tender exotic"—here? The complications of such a moment, of the memory and of the record of it seem, suddenly, to break out not only of Langton's family text, but even out of the familiar régime of images that we recover in emigrant women's writing.[32]

Which experience is such a passage about? As we interrogate such texts as these for their interpretation of the experience of emigration, we easily neglect to consider the text's present. The Langton who

30. Langton, *Langton Records,* 76.
31. Julia Kristeva, *The Powers of Horror: An Essay on Abjection,* 96.
32. Grosz, *Space, Time and Perversion,* 21; Carol Adams, *The Sexual Politics of Meat: A Feminist Vegetarian Critical Theory,* 53.

wrote *The Story of Our Family* was rejoining events of long ago: the humiliation of a scarcely genteel poverty fifty years earlier, her brother's sudden abandonment of her on his marriage ten years later. Of what present was she trying to make sense? The decision, in 1879, as she embarked on the writing of her memoir, that her trip in that year back to England (aged seventy-five) would be her last? The retirement of her brother after his often problematic career of "public service"?[33] In writing, did she take on the dutiful role (of the few available to her) of family portraitist whose own figure is never in the picture, or was she the creator of a story told in well-known family anecdotes? Or are her memories the work of someone on whom her family had depended but who now was merely peripheral to their sense of themselves?

How then can we set about answering the question with which this chapter began: why has Anne Langton, a writer whose texts are far from invisible, not been drawn into the discussion of pioneer women? Some explanation must lie with Langton's emphasis on her subservience, and our sense of her rigidly positioned in the circles of a familial system to which she was always a marginal and eventually expendable member. Langton, well educated as she was and capable though she must surely have been, cannot produce the familiar narrative of personal development, or perhaps refuses to do so.

What Langton achieves, however, is a body of autobiographical writing that should give us pause for thought. She produces her experience in a succession of troubling memories that scarcely cohere into a narrative. She advertises the absence of her "real" thoughts from texts that tell the "usual story." More than anything else, her texts draw to our attention the harmoniousness that the other writers in this study have produced, all that they have chosen not to write, and all that we evade in our work of recovery. In straining to support the expectations that we bring to these texts, in our attentive reading of their contradictions—in rereading Anne Langton—we should address the task, as Marianne Hirsch suggests, with the consciousness of all that their portraits cannot show and all that we cannot see in them.[34]

---

33. The cloud over the end of John Langton's career is described by Wendy Cameron in "John Langton," *Canadian Dictionary of National Biography*, vol. 12, 528.

34. Hirsch, *Family Frames,* 106.

Conclusion

Writing the Pioneer Woman

THE PIONEER WOMAN continues to make appearances within a range of cultural forms: in fiction, movies, TV series, popular histories, cook books. The signifiers that have long rendered her instantly recognizable attach to her still: her plain speaking, her plain garb, her capability, her readiness to embrace the unconventional. She remains indifferent to fashion, to the quadrille of Victorian courtship, to the strictures of a "civilized" world "back home." She is invariably independent-minded and often financially independent too. She withstands male cruelty and, if she is often married, she is at least not bound by its ties.

In her recent reincarnations in fictions such as Jane Smiley's 1998 novel, *The All-True Travels and Adventures of Lidie Newton*, or Maggie Greenwald's 1993 movie "The Ballad of Little Jo," we see the independent pioneer women finding freedom of action by going West. Lidie Newton escapes a world shaped by the instructions of Catherine Beecher's *Treatise on Domestic Economy, for the Use of Young Ladies at Home*—"I have to say that there was nothing in Miss Beecher about hunting game over the prairie"[1]—to participate in the campaign against the adoption of slavery in Kansas. Meanwhile, Josephine Monaghan escapes the stranglehold of social disgrace that falls on an unmarried mother in the East and the vulnerability of lone women in the West: she becomes "Little Jo," a cross-dressing single female homesteader.

---

1. Jane Smiley, *The All-True Travels and Adventures of Lidie Newton*, 102.

Though Lidie Newton experiences tragedy as a result of becoming embroiled in conflict and Little Jo is forced to live apart from society in order to defend her freedom, both find profound satisfaction in relationships that are, to some extent, unconventional. Lidie's gentle, otherworldly New England husband and Jo's "Tinman" Wong are feminized males who become dependent upon female partners while their womenfolk engage dynamically and rationally with landscape and events. Mr. Newton is quiet, thoughtful, and tentative in action. Tinman, long-haired and physically weak, survives only by remaining enclosed within the domestic space, cooking wonderful food for "Mr. Jo."

These heroines do not merely evade marital subservience; they are also women of democratic principle. Lidie Newton immerses herself in Kansas politics. Little Jo abhors the racism that allows the oppression of the Chinese and defies the corporate takeover of land by the ranching industry. As befits a tradition of womanhood that is wary of intellectual activity, they are not doctrinaire: their outlook originates from no stated source, but rather from a temperamental openness to difference and change that the western environment avowedly promotes and supports.

Our attraction to the pioneer woman's indifference to convention and her capacity for self-invention, meanwhile, continue to encourage us not only to search out, reread, and reprint those narratives of the nineteenth and early twentieth century that are compatible with our vision of this magnificent ancestor but also to strive to copy her nineteenth-century voice. In *These Is My Words: The Diary of Sarah Agnes Prine,* published in 1999, for example, Nancy Turner evokes the "true" pioneer in ungrammatical sentences and artless self-revelation: "Ernest and Albert is my big brothers, of which I got two youngern's, Harland and Clover. Had a baby sister who went with the angels before she was a year old, so my folks calls her Harriet Jane but on the inside I calls her my Angel Sister. I always thinks of her in my prayers and berried one of my dolls in her little grave so she could grow up and we'd play together."[2]

Sarah Agnes Prine develops in predictable directions as a pioneer. Her voice has the directness and energy of a woman growing in confidence as she tackles her western trials. But as we have seen, the nineteenth-century texts that are imitated and the pioneer women who

2. Nancy Turner, *These Is My Words: The Diary of Sarah Agnes Prine,* 1.

are rewritten actually appeared in far more diverse forms than their imitators suggest. It is not only that texts such as Susanna Moodie's *Roughing It in the Bush* are full of angry diatribes against emigration agents, the Irish, squatters, servants, and so on, or that Caroline Kirkland adopts tones of weary despair in describing the distance between herself and "civilization": "Those only whom fate and a wayward choice has removed from these advantages (of society, conversation and that collision of differing yet kindred minds) can describe the aspect which they wear when viewed from an almost hopeless distance; or the sense of alienation, of isolation, of loneliness which is apt to beset the heart or the imagination of the emigrant."[3] It is not only that, for all the celebration of escape from eastern domesticity that some texts offer, the writing of pioneer womanhood is characteristically engaged in examining debates about women and domesticity generated at the center. Nor that, drawing on so diverse a group of sources—colonial and emigration discourse, village portrait, the literature of housekeeping, the literature of sentiment—and so many generic modes—diary, spiritual autobiography, as well as emigrant narrative and sketch—they produce selves that are more difficult to summarize than we have assumed and continue to assert.

What gives these nineteenth-century texts their elusive, complex quality is the way in which so much attention is focused on the leaving, making, and keeping of homes. Certainly, they are narratives that bring home the meaning of the "cult" of domesticity, but they do not simply reveal the gap between domesticity and the life of the domestic space. In detailing the minutiae of their domestic lives, they draw our attention to the variousness and weight of the world of the interior, with all the significances (psychological, spatial, and political) that that word holds. The Lidie Newtons and the Sarah Agnes Prines of late-twentieth-century fiction avoid being drawn into that world. Indeed, the difficulties of their situation are often solved by sidelining the domestic.

This is not to say that the contemporary imagination of the pioneer woman is any less serious-minded in its content. Such texts produce an "outside" that is far more problematic than that which we find in many of the narratives discussed in this study. There is usually a feminist

---

3. Caroline Kirkland, *Forest Life*, 11.

agenda to their portraits of a West of the most unreconstructed masculinity: both *These Is My Words* and "The Ballad of Little Jo" rehearse the specter of rape with terrible vividness. More than this, they evoke scenes of inexplicable violence in comfortless, unfamiliar landscapes that are as relentlessly revisited as they were in, say, the westerns of the 1950s. For all their attraction to an ancestral past and their idealizing of figures of freedom, these fictions nonetheless produce a present in which life is always and inescapably contingent and protagonists battle on in the face of rapid change, even of catastrophe. The heroines maintain their equilibrium as subjects, but only through cleaving to those whom they love. When lovers are removed, we see them dispossessed in a menacing world. The unconventional life produces only a miniature, temporary victory.

Of course, the complex relationship between past and present, always difficult to grasp in historical texts, is as evident in the most unrestrainedly nostalgic contemporary narratives of the pioneer West as it was in Elinore Pruitt Stewart's *Letters of a Woman Homesteader*. Carl Hamilton, in a collection of Iowan memoirs called *Pure Nostalgia*, remarks as follows: "You probably read [the memoirs] for fun. But did they—perhaps unknowingly—arouse some misgivings about our present-day problems? . . . When we experience the complexity and confusion of our contemporary times we say 'Please let us go back'! and their recollections we can reach out and—figuratively speaking—touch a good bit of all of American history." At the same time, though, that impulse to do what Hamilton calls "a little stocktaking" exists alongside our knowledge that the past we long for has itself disappeared in that same flurry of change that disturbs us so much: these "snippets of pure nostalgia," "sugar-coated," give us pleasure but they scarcely represent even the traces of the lost world of the West.[4]

It is interesting that Hamilton coats his "pure nostalgia" for the harsh certainties of the "frontier" with sugar. While recent representations of pioneer womanhood have tended to assert the connection between freedom and "outside," the domesticity of the West nonetheless retains a presence in contemporary culture in cook books. Lon Walters's *The Old West Baking Book* suggests that here at least a nostalgia for the "healthy and useful domesticity" of the frontier remains

---

4. Carl Hamilton, ed., *Pure Nostalgia: Memoirs of Early Iowa*, 211–12.

undimmed: "Imagine," Walters suggests, "putting a cake together without fresh supplies, measuring spoons, or a dedicated work area; imagine baking that cake without a thermometer, steady heat, or a timer. . . . Unfortunately the creative blending and baking of the nineteenth century has given way to megamarket fluff and mass-packaged baked goods. . . . we have little appreciation for our early ancestors' efforts to make even basic foods interesting. Despite our capacity to bake in the world's most advanced and well-equipped home kitchens, we often do less than a pioneer did with just a campfire."[5] The simplicity of the past would give greater pleasure and inspire greater creativity. The old fantasy of an escape from an over-elaborate, stifling domesticity into an uncluttered, unpretentious, even instinctive domestic practice has, it would seem, survived intact.

Lon Walters's *The Old West Baking Book* is full of nineteenth-century photographs and commentary on how particular kinds of baking were performed. But of course its "true picture" obscures the wider truth that not all of those who migrated West were resistant to the fruits of technologized production—or could afford to be so. In any case, much of the West could not be farmed economically without modern technologies. And though, in the nineteenth century, writers certainly fantasized about effortless "natural" bakery, emigrant women writers gloried in their possession of newly developed and time-saving inventions, not least because they were marks of class and regional status. Christiana Tillson, for example, writes of her raising agent specifically in terms of its purity, that is, its separation from the dirt and drudgery of Illinois, and in terms of its unfamiliarity to her southern neighbors. When her neighbor asks to be lent some "purlass" for her baking, Tillson sneers at the woman's ignorance of the use of pearl ash: "'They say, too, you put a lot of nasty truck in your bread. It is what you keep in a bottle, purlass, I believe is the name, and they say it is full of dead flies, and bugs, and cricket legs.' I brought forth my little bottle of dissolved pearl ash, looking so clean and pure, and showed it to her, but it seemed hard to give up her old prejudice."[6]

Yet *The Old West Baking Book* illustrates how difficult it is—and has always been—to make the different aspects of the fantasy of pioneering

5. Lon Walters, *The Old West Baking Book*, 1.
6. Tillson, *Reminiscences*, 123.

fit together. The photographs, with their embroidered and lacy cloths and evocations of the laden table, seem to reflect nostalgia's characteristic return to the small objects and practices of the everyday, in the attempt to find a pleasurable release from the conditions of the present. But the book also insistently reaffirms something quite different: the frontier myth that it is always possible and desirable to make a "new beginning." It studiously avoids the representation of cooking taking place within the home. The nineteenth-century photographs in the text show men in transit (often with no sign of food in the picture), or, in two cases, Native American (Hopi and Taos) women cooking outside. Only two small line drawings show white female figures, without the context of surroundings, involved in the process of food preparation: one is peeling fruit and the other kneading bread.

The book asserts the ease of relearning the ideals of the past for present readers who have been, in some sense, dispossessed of it, and yet what it most powerfully suggests is the gap between frontier ideology and homely comfort, the discontinuities of migration. Alongside the warmly colored photographs of golden, sugary bakery lie—without any sense of contradiction—the nineteenth-century photographs of pioneers, their position unexplained, their situation devoid of context and their lives indecipherable: the pioneer woman's "new home" indeed.

Works Cited

Adams, Carol. *The Sexual Politics of Meat: A Feminist Vegetarian Critical Theory.* Cambridge: Polity Press, 1990.

Adams, Timothy Dow. *Telling Lies in Modern American Autobiography.* Chapel Hill: University of North Carolina Press, 1990.

Akenson, Donald H. "The Historiography of English Speaking Canada and the Concept of Diaspora." *Canadian Historical Review* 76, no. 3 (1995): 372–409.

Alcott, Louisa May. *Good Wives.* Boston: Roberts, 1869. Reprt., London: Penguin, 1978.

Alderson, Nannie T. *A Bride Goes West.* New York: Farrar and Rinehart, 1942. Reprt., Lincoln: University of Nebraska Press, 1969.

Allison, Susan. *A Pioneer Gentlewoman in British Columbia: The Recollections of Susan Allison.* Vancouver: University of British Columbia Press, 1976.

Ammons, Elizabeth. "Material Culture, Empire and Jewett's *Country of the Pointed Firs.*" In *New Essays on* The Country of the Pointed Firs, edited by June Howard. Cambridge: Cambridge University Press, 1994.

Anon. "The Orphan Sisters." In *Lowell Offering: A Repository of Original Articles,* vol. 1 (1841), 263–66.

Anon. "The Patchwork Quilt." In *Lowell Offering: A Repository of Original Articles,* vol. 5 (1845), 200–203.

Armitage, Susan, and Elizabeth Jameson. *The Women's West.* Norman: University of Oklahoma Press, 1987.

Atkeson, Mary Meek. *The Woman on the Farm.* New York: Century Press, 1924.

Bailey, Ebenezer. *The Young Lady's Class Book*. Boston: Gould, Kendall and Lincoln, 1845.
Bald, Frank Clever. *Michigan in Four Centuries*. New York: Harper, 1954.
Ballstadt, Carl. "Catharine Parr Traill." In *Canadian Writers and Their Works*. Vol. 1, *Fiction Series*, edited by Robert Lecker, Jack David, and Ellen Quigley. Downsville, Ontario: ECW Press, 1983.
―――. Editor's Introduction. In *Roughing It in the Bush*. Ottawa: Carleton University Press, 1988.
―――. "'The Embryo Blossom': Susanna Moodie's Letters to Her Husband in Relation to *Roughing It in the Bush*." In *Re(Dis)covering Our Foremothers: Nineteenth-Century Canadian Women Writers*. Ottawa: University of Ottawa Press, 1990.
Ballstadt, Carl, Elizabeth Hopkins, and Michael A. Peterman, eds. *Susanna Moodie: Letters of a Lifetime*. Toronto: University of Toronto Press, 1985.
Barber, Mary. *Breadwinning: Or the Ledger and the Lute, an Auto-Biography*. London: n.p., 1865.
Barthes, Roland. "Ornamental Cookery." In *Mythologies*, translated by Annette Lavers. London: Vintage, 1993.
Beardsmore, Alan, and Teresa Keil. *Sociology on the Menu: An Invitation to the Study of Food and Society*. London: Routledge, 1997.
Beecher, Catherine. *A Treatise on Domestic Economy*. Boston: Marsh, Capen, Lyon and Webb, 1841.
Beecher, Eunice Bullard. *From Dawn to Daylight; or the Simple Story of a Western Home*. New York: Derby and Jackson, 1859.
Beetham, Margaret. *A Magazine of Her Own? Domesticity and Desire in the Woman's Magazine, 1800–1914*. London: Routledge, 1996.
Belknap, Kitturah. "Farm Life on the Frontier." *Annals of Iowa* 3d ser. 44 (summer 1977): 31–51.
―――. "Keturah Penton Belknap." In *Women of the West*, edited by Cathy Luchetti and Carol Olwell. Berkeley, Calif.: Antelope Island Press, 1982.
Benn, Stanley I., and Gerald F. Gaus. *Public and Private in Social Life*. London: Croom Helm, 1983.
Bentley, D. R. M. "'Breaking the Cake of Custom': The Atlantic Crossing as a Rubicon for Female Emigrants to Canada?" In *Re(Dis)Covering Our Foremothers: Nineteenth-Century Cana-*

dian Women Writers, edited by Lorraine McMullen. Ottawa: University of Ottawa Press, 1990.

Bhabha, Homi K. Keynote Address, "Empire, Design and Identity." Conference at the Victoria and Albert Museum, June 21–22, 1997.

———. *The Location of Culture.* London: Routledge, 1994.

Birkbeck, Morris. *Letters from Illinois.* Philadelphia: M. Carey and Son, 1818.

Bloom, Lynn Z. "Utopia and Anti-Utopia in Twentieth-Century Women's Frontier Autobiographies." In *American Women's Autobiography: Fea[s]ts of Memory,* edited by Margo Culley. Madison: University of Wisconsin Press, 1991.

Boardman, Kathleen A. "Paper Trail: Diaries, Letters and Reminiscences of the Overland Journey West." In *Updating the Literary West,* edited by Thomas J. Lyons et al. Fort Worth: Texas Christian University Press, 1998.

Bowlby, Rachel. "Domestication." In *Feminism Beside Itself,* edited by Diane Elam and Robyn Wiegman. London: Routledge, 1995.

———. "Walking, Women and Writing: Virginia Woolf as Flaneuse." In *New Feminist Discourses,* edited by Isabel Armstrong. London: Routledge, 1992.

Boydston, Jeanne. *Home and Work: Housework, Wages and the Ideology of Labor in the Early Republic.* New York: Oxford University Press, 1990.

Boydston, Jeanne, Mary Kelley, and Anne Margolis. *The Limits of Sisterhood: The Beecher Sisters on Women's Rights and Women's Sphere.* Chapel Hill: University of North Carolina Press, 1988.

Brah, Avtar. *Cartographies of Diaspora: Contesting Identities.* London: Routledge, 1996.

Brodhead, Richard H. *Cultures of Letters: Scenes of Reading and Writing in Nineteenth-Century America.* Chicago: Chicago University Press, 1993.

Bronner, Simon, ed. *Consuming Visions: Accumulation and Display of Goods in America, 1880–1920.* New York: Norton, 1989.

Brown, Elsa Barkley. "Polyrhythms and Improvisation: Lessons for Women's History." *History Journal Workshop* 31–32 (1991): 85–90.

Brown, Gillian. *Domestic Individualism: Imagining Self in Nineteenth-Century America*. Berkeley: University of California Press, 1990.

Brown, R., and J. Gulik. "Flashbulb Memories." *Cognition* 5 (1977): 73–99.

Buell, Lawrence. *The Environmental Imagination: Thoreau, Nature Writing and the Formation of American Culture*. Cambridge, Mass.: Harvard University Press, 1995.

Bunkers, Suzanne. "What Do Women REALLY Mean? Thoughts on Women's Diaries and Lives." In *The Intimate Critique: Autobiographical Literary Criticism*, edited by Diane P. Freedman et al. Durham, N.C.: Duke University Press, 1993.

Bunkers, Suzanne, and Cynthia Huff, eds. *Inscribing the Daily: Critical Essays on Women's Diaries*. Amherst: University of Massachusetts Press, 1996.

Burlend, Rebecca. *A True Picture of Emigration*. London: G. Berger, 1848.

Buss, Helen. "Canadian Women's Autobiography: Some Critical Directions." In *A Mazing Space: Writing Canadian Women Writing*, edited by Shirley Neuman and Smaro Kamboureli. Edmonton: Longspoon-NeWest, 1988.

———. *Mapping Our Selves: Canadian Women's Autobiography in English*. Montreal: McGill-Queen's University Press, 1993.

———. "Settling the Score with Myths of Settlement: Two Women Who Roughed It and Wrote It." In *Great Dames*, edited by Elspeth Cameron and Janice Dickin. Toronto: University of Toronto Press, 1997.

Butler, Anne M. *Daughters of Joy, Sisters of Misery: Prostitutes in the American West, 1865–1890*. Urbana: University of Illinois Press, 1985.

———. Introduction. In *Covered Wagon Women: Diaries and Letters from the Western Trails, 1840–1849*, vol. 1, edited by Kenneth L. Holmes. Glendale, Calif.: A. H. Clark Co., 1983. Reprt., Lincoln: University of Nebraska Press, 1995.

Callan, Hilary. Introduction. In *The Incorporated Wife*, edited by Hilary Callan and Shirley Ardener. London: Croom Helm, 1984.

Callaway, Helen. *Gender, Culture and Empire*. London: Macmillan, 1987.

Cameron, Wendy. "John Langton." In *Canadian Dictionary of National Biography,* vol. 12. Toronto: University of Toronto Press, 1991.
Carsten, Janet, and Stephen Hugh-Jones. Introduction. In *About the House: Levi-Strauss and Beyond.* Cambridge: Cambridge University Press, 1995.
Cather, Willa. *O Pioneers!* Boston: Houghton Mifflin, 1913.
Cayton, Andrew R. L., and Peter S. Onuf. *The MidWest and the Nation: Rethinking the History of an American Region.* Bloomington: Indiana University Press, 1990.
Cecil, David. *A Portrait of Jane Austen.* London: Constable, 1978.
Child, Lydia Maria. *The American Frugal Housewife.* Boston: Carter, Hendee, 1833.
Chow, Rey. *Writing Diaspora: Tactics of Intervention in Contemporary Cultural Studies.* Bloomington: Indiana University Press, 1993.
Clark, Steve, ed. *Travel Writing and Empire: Postcolonial Theory in Transit.* London: Zed Books, 1999.
Cleaveland, Agnes Morley. *No Life for a Lady.* Boston: Houghton Mifflin, 1941.
Cobbett, William. *Emigrant's Guide in Ten Letters.* London: published by the author, 1829.
Cohen, Stanley, and Laurie Taylor. *Escape Attempts: The Theory and Practice of Resistance to Everyday Life.* 2d ed. London: Routledge, 1992.
Colby, Veneta. *Yesterday's Women: Domestic Realism in the English Novel.* Princeton, N.J.: Princeton University Press, 1974.
Comer, Krista. "Literature, Gender Studies and the New Western History." *Arizona Quarterly* 53, no. 2 (1997): 99–134.
Conlin, Joseph R. *Bacon, Beans and Galantines: Food and Foodways on the Western Mining Frontier.* Reno: University of Nevada Press, 1986.
Coontz, Stephanie. *The Social Origins of Private Life: A History of American Families 1600–1900.* London: Verso, 1988.
Corbett, Mary Jean. *Representing Femininity: Middle-Class Subjectivity in Victorian and Edwardian Women's Autobiography.* New York: Oxford University Press, 1992.
Craik, Jennifer. *The Face of Fashion: Cultural Studies in Fashion.* London: Routledge, 1994.

Csikszentmihalyi, Mihalyi, and Eugene Rochberg-Halton. *The Meaning of Things: Domestic Symbols and the Self.* Cambridge: Cambridge University Press, 1981.

Curtiss, Daniel S. *Western Portraiture and Emigrant's Guide: A Description of Wisconsin, Illinois and Iowa.* New York: J. H. Cotton, 1852.

"Dame Shirley" (pseud. Louisa A. K. S. Clappe). *The Shirley Letters: From the California Mines, 1851–1852.* New York: Knopf, 1949.

Davidoff, Leonore. "The Rationalization of Housework." In Sheila Allen and D. Barker, eds., *Dependence and Exploitation in Work and Marriage.* London: Longman, 1976.

Davidoff, Leonore, and Catherine Hall, *Family Fortunes: Men and Women of the English Middle Class, 1780–1850.* London: Hutchinson, 1987. Reprt., London: Routledge, 1992.

Davis, Gayle R. "Writing for Good Reason." *Women's Studies* 14 (1987): 5–14.

Dean, Misao. *Practising Femininity: Domestic Realism and the Performance of Gender in Early Canadian Fiction.* Toronto: University of Toronto Press, 1998.

De Certeau, Michel. *The Practice of Everyday Life.* Translated by Steven Rendall. Berkeley: University of California Press, 1984.

Deutsch, Sara. *No Separate Refuge: Culture, Class and Gender on the Anglo-Hispanic Frontier in the American South-West.* New York: Oxford University Press, 1987.

Dickerson, Vanessa D., ed. *Keeping the Victorian Home.* New York: Garland Publishing, 1995.

Dillard, Heath. "Women in Reconquest Castile." In *Women in Mediaeval Society*, edited by S. Mosher Stuard. Philadelphia: University of Pennsylvania Press, 1976.

Donovan, Josephine. *New England Local Color Literature: A Women's Tradition.* New York: Frederick Ungar, 1983.

Douglas, Mary. *Purity and Danger: An Analysis of Concepts of Pollution and Taboo.* London: Routledge and Kegan Paul, 1966.

Doyle, Don Harrison. *The Social Order of a Frontier Community: Jacksonville Illinois, 1825–1870.* Urbana: University of Illinois Press, 1978.

Driesbach, Janice T. "Portrait Painter to the Elite: William Smith Jewett." In *Art of the Gold Rush,* edited by Janice Driesbach et al. Berkeley: University of California Press, 1998.

Dunlop, William. *Statistical Sketches of Upper Canada for the Use of Emigrants by a Backwoodsman.* London: John Murray, 1832.

Edwards, P. D. *Idyllic Realism from Mary Russell Mitford to Thomas Hardy.* London: MacMillan, 1988.

Egli, Ida Rae. "Early Western Literary Women." In *Updating the Literary West,* edited by Thomas J. Lyons et al. Fort Worth: Texas Christian University Press, 1998.

———, ed. *No Rooms of Their Own: Women Writers of Early California.* Berkeley, Calif.: Heyday Books, 1992.

Ellet, Elizabeth. *Pioneer Women of the West.* New York: Scribner, 1852.

Ellis, Ann. *The Life of an Ordinary Woman.* Boston: Houghton Mifflin, 1929.

Epstein, Barbara. *The Politics of Domesticity.* Middletown, Conn: Wesleyan University Press, 1981.

Erickson, Charlotte. *Invisible Immigrants: The Adaptation of English and Scottish Immigrants in Nineteenth-Century America.* London: Weidenfeld and Nicholson, 1972.

"Ex-Settler." *Canada in the Years 1832, 1833 and 1834: Containing Important Information and Instructions to Persons Intending to Emigrate Thither in 1835.* Dublin: n.p., 1835.

Fairbanks, Carol. *Prairie Women: Images in American and Canadian Fiction.* New Haven, Conn.: Yale University Press, 1986.

Fairbanks, Carol, and Bergine Haakenson, eds. *Writings of Farm Women: An Anthology.* New York: Garland, 1990.

"Fanny Fern" (pseud. Sara Payson Willis). *Ruth Hall.* New York: Mason Brothers, 1855. Reprt., New York: Penguin Books, 1997.

Faragher, John. "History from the Inside-Out: Writing the History of Rural Women in America." *American Quarterly* 33 (1981): 537–57.

———. *Sugar Creek.* New Haven, Conn.: Yale University Press, 1986.

———. *Women and Men on the Overland Trail.* New Haven, Conn.: Yale University Press, 1979.

Farnham, Eliza W. *California, In-doors and Out.* New York: Dix, Edwards and Co., 1856.

———. *Life in Prairie Land*. New York, 1846. Reprt., Urbana: University of Illinois Press, 1988.

Farnsworth, Martha. *Plains Woman: The Diary of Martha Farnsworth, 1882–1922*. Edited by Marlene Springer and Haskell Springer. Bloomington: Indiana University Press, 1988.

Farrar, Eliza W. *The Young Lady's Friend*. New York: S. and W. Wood, 1845.

Fender, Stephen. *Plotting the Golden West: American Literature and the Rhetoric of the California Trail*. Cambridge: Cambridge University Press, 1981.

———. *Sea Changes: British Emigration and American Literature*. Cambridge: Cambridge University Press, 1992.

Fetterley, Judith, and Marjorie Pryse, eds. *American Women Regionalists, 1850–1910*. New York: Norton, 1992.

Fiddes, Nick. *Meat: A Natural Symbol*. New York: Routledge, 1991.

Fischer, Christiane. "Women's California in the Early 1850s." *South California Quarterly* 60, no. 3 (1978): 231–53.

———, ed. *Let Them Speak for Themselves: Women in the American West, 1849–1900*. Hamden, Conn.: Archon Books, 1977.

Flint, Timothy. *A Biographical Memoir of Daniel Boone*. Cincinnati: Guilford, 1833.

Follen, Eliza. *Sketches of Married Life*. London: n.p., 1839.

Foote, Mary Hallock. *A Victorian Gentlewoman in the Far West: The Reminiscences of Mary Hallock Foote*. Edited by Rodman W. Paul. San Marino, Calif.: Huntington Library, 1972.

Fordyce, Eileen. "Cookbooks of the 1800s." In *Dining in America, 1850–1900*, edited by Kathryn Grover. Amherst: University of Massachusetts Press, 1987.

Freeman, Mark. *Rewriting the Self: History, Memory, Narrative*. New York: Routledge, 1993.

Freeman, Mary Wilkins. "Cinnamon Roses." In *A Humble Romance and Other Stories*. Edinburgh: David Douglas, 1890.

Freeman, Sarah. *Mutton and Oysters: The Victorians and Their Food*. London: Victor Gollancz, 1989.

Furst, Lillian R., ed. *Disorderly Eaters: Texts in Self-Empowerment*. State College: Pennsylvania State University Press, 1992.

Gagnier, Regenia. *Subjectivities: A History of Self-Representation in Britain*. Oxford: Oxford University Press, 1991.

Gandhi, Leela. *Postcolonial Theory: A Critical Introduction.* Edinburgh: Edinburgh University Press, 1998.
Gannett, Cinthia. *Gender and the Journal: Diaries and Academic Discourse.* New York: State University of New York, 1992.
Garland, Hamlin. *Main-Travelled Roads.* Boston: Arena Publishing, 1891. Reprt., New York: Signet, 1962.
Gartrell, Beverley. "Colonial Wives: Villains or Victims?" In *The Incorporated Wife,* edited by Hilary Callan and Shirley Ardener. London: Croom Helm, 1984.
Gebhard, Caroline. "Comic Displacement: Caroline M. Kirkland's Satire on Frontier Democracy in *A New Home, Who'll Follow?*" In *Women, America and Movement: Narratives of Relocation,* edited by Susan L. Roberson. Columbia: University of Missouri Press, 1998.
George, Rosemary Marangoly. *The Politics of Home: Postcolonial Relocations and Twentieth-Century Fiction.* Cambridge: Cambridge University Press, 1996.
George, Suzanne. *The Adventures of a Woman Homesteader.* Lincoln: University of Nebraska Press, 1992.
Georgi-Findlay, Brigitte. *The Frontiers of Women's Writing: Women's Narratives and the Rhetoric of Expansion.* Tucson: University of Arizona Press, 1996.
Giard, Luce. "Doing-Cooking." In *The Practice of Everyday Life II: Living and Cooking,* edited by Michel De Certeau, Luce Giard, and Pierre Mayol. Translated by Timothy J. Tomasik. Minneapolis: University of Minnesota Press, 1998.
Gilman, Caroline (pseud. "Mrs. Clarissa Packard"). *The Recollections of a Housekeeper.* New York: Harper, 1834.
Gilmore, Leigh. *Autobiographics: A Feminist Theory of Women's Self-Representation.* Ithaca, N.Y.: Cornell University Press, 1994.
Glanz, Dawn. *How the West Was Won: American Art and the Settling of the Frontier.* Ann Arbor, Mich.: UMI Research Press, 1982.
Goffman, Erving. *The Presentation of Self in Everyday Life.* Garden City, N.Y.: Doubleday, 1959.
Goldman, Anne. "'I Yam What I Yam': Cooking, Culture and Colonialism." In *De/Colonizing the Subject: The Politics of Gender in Women's Autobiography,* edited by Sidonie Smith and Julia Watson. Minneapolis: University of Minnesota Press, 1992.

Goldman, Marion S. *Gold Diggers and Silver Miners: Prostitution and Social Life on the Comstock Lode.* Ann Arbor: University of Michigan Press, 1981.

Graves, A. J. *Girlhood and Womanhood or Sketches of My Schoolmates.* Boston: T. H. Carter, 1844.

Grey, Zane. *Riders of the Purple Sage.* New York: Harper, 1912.

Griswold, Robert. "Anglo Women and Domestic Ideology in the Late Nineteenth and Early Twentieth Century." In *Western Women: Their Land, Their Lives,* edited by Lillian Schlissel, Vicki L. Ruiz, and Janice Monk. Albuquerque: University of New Mexico Press, 1988.

Grosz, Elizabeth A. *Space, Time and Perversion: Essays in the Politics of Bodies.* New York: Routledge, 1995.

Hale, Sara Josepha. *Keeping House and Housekeeping: A Story of Domestic Life.* New York: Harper, 1845.

Hall, Stuart. "The Local and the Global: Globalization and Ethnicity." In *Culture, Globalization and the World-System,* edited by A. King. London: Macmillan, 1991.

Hallwas, John. Introduction. In *Life in Prairie Land.* Urbana: University of Illinois Press, 1988.

Halttunen, Karen. *Confidence Men and Painted Women: A Study in Middle-Class Culture in America, 1830–1870.* New Haven, Conn.: Yale University Press, 1982.

Hamilton, Carl, ed. *Pure Nostalgia: Memoirs of Early Iowa.* Ames: Iowa State University Press, 1979.

Hamilton, Elizabeth. *The Cottagers of Glenburnie: A Tale for the Inglenook.* Edinburgh: Ballantyne, 1808.

Hammerton, A. James. *Emigrant Gentlewomen, Genteel Poverty and Female Emigration.* London: Croom Helm, 1979.

Hampsten, Elizabeth. "Considering More than the Single Reader." In *Interpreting Women's Lives,* edited by Personal Narratives Group. Bloomington: Indiana University Press, 1989.

———. *Read This Only to Yourself: The Private Writings of Midwestern Women, 1880–1910.* Bloomington: Indiana University Press, 1982.

Haraway, Donna. *Simians, Cyborgs and Women.* London: Free Association, 1991.

Hardy, Thomas. *Jude the Obscure.* London, 1895. Reprt., London: MacMillan, 1965.
Harte, Bret. *The Luck of Roaring Camp and Other Sketches.* Boston: Fields, Osgood and Co., 1870.
Hawkins, Freda. *Canada and Immigration: Public Policy and Public Concern.* Montreal: McGill-Queen's University Press, 1972.
Hedges, Elaine. "The Needle or the Pen: The Literary Rediscovery of Women's Textile Work." In *Tradition and the Talents of Women,* edited by Florence Howe. Urbana: University of Illinois Press, 1991.
———. "The Nineteenth-Century Diarist and Her Quilts." *Feminist Studies* 8, no. 2 (summer 1982): 293–308.
Heldke, Lisa M. "Foodmaking as a Thoughtful Practice." In *Cooking, Eating, Thinking: Transformative Philosophies of Food,* edited by Deane W. Curtin and Lisa M. Heldke. Bloomington: Indiana University Press, 1992.
Higonnet, Margaret R. "New Cartographies." In *Reconfiguring Spheres: Feminist Explorations of Literary Space,* edited by Margaret R. Higonnet and Joan Templeton. Amherst: University of Massachusetts Press, 1994.
Hine, R. V. *Community on the American Frontier: Separate but Not Alone.* Norman: University of Oklahoma Press, 1980.
Hirsch, Julia. *Family Photographs.* New York: Oxford University Press, 1981.
Hirsch, Marianne. *Family Frames: Photography, Narrative and Post-Memory.* Cambridge, Mass.: Harvard University Press, 1997.
Hobsbawm, Eric. Introduction to "Exile: A Keynote Address." In *Home: A Place in the World,* edited by Arien Mack. New York: New York University Press, 1993.
Holmes, Kenneth L., ed. *Covered Wagon Women: Diaries and Letters from the Western Trails, 1840–1849,* vol. 1. Glendale, Calif.: A. H. Clark Co., 1983. Reprt., Lincoln: University of Nebraska Press, 1995.
Howard, June. "Sarah Orne Jewett and the Traffic in Words." In *New Essays on* Country of the Pointed Firs. Cambridge: Cambridge University Press, 1994.
Howison, John. *Sketches of Upper Canada, Domestic, Local and Characteristic.* Edinburgh: n.p., 1832.

Howitt, William, and Mary Howitt. "The Emigrant." In *The Desolation of Eyam, The Emigrant and Other Poems*. London: Wightman and Cramp, 1827.

Hyde, Anne F. "Cultural Filters: The Significance of Perception." In *A New Significance: Re-Envisaging the History of the American West*, edited by Clyde A. Milner II. New York: Oxford University Press, 1996.

Idol, John L., Jr. "Mary Russell Mitford: Champion of American Literature." *Studies in the American Renaissance* (1983): 313–34.

Jackel, Susan, ed. *A Flannel Shirt and Liberty: British Emigrant Gentlewomen in the Canadian West, 1867–1914*. Vancouver: University of British Columbia Press, 1982.

Jameson, Elizabeth, and Susan Armitage, eds. *Writing the Range: Race, Class and Culture in the Women's West*. Norman: University of Oklahoma Press, 1997.

Jeffrey, Julie Roy. *Frontier Women: The Trans-Mississippi West, 1840–1880*. New York: Hill and Wang, 1979.

Jensen, Katherine. "Commentary." In *Western Women: Their Land, Their Lives*, edited by Lillian Schlissel, Vicki L. Ruiz, and Janice Monk. Albuquerque: University of New Mexico Press, 1988.

Jewett, Sarah Orne. *The Country of the Pointed Firs*. Boston: Houghton, Mifflin, 1896. Reprt., New York: Norton, 1981.

Johnson, Lesley. "'As Housewives We Are Worms': Women, Modernity and the Home Question." In *Feminism and Cultural Studies*, edited by Morag Shiach. New York: Oxford University Press, 1999.

Johnson, Susan Lee. "'A Memory Sweet to Soldiers': The Significance of Gender." In *A New Significance: Re-Envisioning the History of the American West*, edited by Clyde A. Milner II. Oxford: Oxford University Press, 1996.

Jolly, Margaretta. "'Dear Laughing Motorbyke': Gender and Genre in Women's Letters from the Second World War." In *The Uses of Autobiography*, edited by Julia Swindells. London: Taylor and Francis, 1995.

Jones, A. D. *Illinois and the West*. Boston: Weeks, Jordan and Co., 1838.

Jones, Henrietta. *Sketches of Real Life*. Watertown, N.Y.: O. E. Hungerford, 1898.

Kaplan, Caren. "Resisting Autobiography: Outlaw Genres and Transnational Feminist Subjects." In *De-Colonizing the Subject: The Politics of Gender in Women's Autobiography*, edited by Sidonie Smith and Julia Watson. Minneapolis: University of Minnesota Press, 1992.

Kaplan, Deborah. "'Representing Two Cultures': Jane Austen's Letters." In *The Private Self*, edited by Shari Benstock. Chapel Hill: University of North Carolina Press, 1988.

Keetley, Dawn E. "Unsettling the Frontier: Gender and Racial Hegemony in Caroline Kirkland's *A New Home, Who'll Follow?*" *Legacy* 12, no. 1 (1995): 17–37.

Keith, W. J. *The Rural Tradition*. Toronto: University of Toronto Press, 1975.

Kessler-Harris, Alice. *A History of Wage-Earning Women in the United States*. New York: Oxford University Press, 1982.

Kirkland, Caroline. *Forest Life*. New York: C. S. Francis, 1842.

———. *A New Home, Who'll Follow?* New York: C. S. Francis, 1839. Reprt., New Brunswick, N.J.: Rutgers University Press, 1990.

Kline, Marcia. *Beyond the Land Itself: Views of Nature in Canada and the U.S.* Cambridge, Mass.: Harvard University Press, 1970.

Knight, Sarah Kemble. *The Journals of Madam Knight and Rev. Mr. Buckingham*. New York: Wilder and Campbell, 1825.

Kolodny, Annette. *The Land Before Her: Fantasy and Experience on the American Frontiers 1630–1860*. Chapel Hill: University of North Carolina Press, 1984.

Kranidis, Rita S., ed. *Imperial Objects: Essays on Victorian Women's Emigration and the Unauthorized Imperial Experience*. New York: Twayne, 1998.

Kristeva, Julia. *The Powers of Horror: An Essay on Abjection*. Translated by Leon S. Roudiez. New York: Columbia University Press, 1982.

Kuhn, Annette. *Family Secrets: Acts of Memory and Imagination*. London: Verso, 1995.

Lander, Dawn. "Eve among the Indians." In *The Authority of Experience: Essays in Feminist Criticism*, edited by Arlyn Diamond and Lee R. Edwards. Amherst: University of Massachusetts Press, 1977.

Langton, Anne. *Langton Records*. Edited by Ellen Philips. Edinburgh: R. and R. Clark, 1904.

———. *The Story of Our Family.* Manchester: Thomas Sowler, 1881.

Langton, Hugh Hornby, ed. *A Gentlewoman in Upper Canada.* Toronto: Clarke, Irwin and Co., 1950.

Langton, W. A. *Early Days in Upper Canada: Letters of John Langton.* Canada: MacMillan, 1926.

Lavie, Smadar, and Ted Swedenburg, eds. *Displacement, Diaspora and Geographies of Identity.* Durham, N.C.: Duke University Press, 1996.

Lensink, Judy Nolte, ed. *"A Secret to Be Burried": The Diary and Life of Emily Gillespie, 1858–1888.* Iowa City: University of Iowa Press, 1989.

Leonardi, Susan J. "Recipes for Reading: Summer Pasta, Lobster à la Riseholme and Key Lime Pie." *PMLA* 104, no. 3 (May 1989): 340–47.

Leverenz, David. *Manhood and the American Renaissance.* Ithaca, N.Y.: Cornell University Press, 1989.

Levi-Strauss, Claude. "The Culinary Triangle." *Partisan Review* 33 (1966): 586–95.

Lewis, Sarah. *Woman's Mission.* London, 1839.

Light, Beth, and Joy Parr, eds. *Canadian Women on the Move, 1867–1920.* Toronto: Hogtown Press, 1983.

Limerick, Patricia Nelson. *The Legacy of Conquest: The Unbroken Past of the American West.* New York: Norton, 1987.

Logan, Thad. "Decorating Domestic Space: Middle-Class Women and Victorian Interiors." In *Keeping the Victorian House,* edited by Vanessa Dickerson. New York: Garland Publishing, 1995.

Loudon, J. *The Lady's Country Companion; or How to Enjoy a Country Life Rationally.* London: Longman, 1845.

Luchetti, Cathy, and Carol Olwell, eds. *Women of the West.* Berkeley, Calif.: Antelope Island Press, 1982.

McClintock, Anne. *Imperial Leather: Race, Gender and Sexuality in the Imperial Contest.* New York: Routledge, 1995.

McCormack, A. Ross. "Networks among British Immigrants and Accomodation to Canadian Society 1900–1914." In *The Diaspora of the British.* University of London Institute of Commonwealth Studies Seminar Papers no. 31, 1982.

McCracken, Grant. *Culture and Consumption: New Approaches to the Symbolic Characteristics of Consumer Goods and Activities.* Bloomington: Indiana University Press, 1991.

McDonald, John. *Narrative of a Journey to Quebec and Journey from Thence to New Lanark and Upper Canada.* Edinburgh: n.p., 1823.

MacDonald, Norman. *Canada: Immigration and Colonization, 1841–1903.* Aberdeen: Aberdeen University Press, 1966.

McKnight, Jeanie. "American Dream, Nightmare Underside." In *Women, Women Writers and the West,* edited by L. L. Lee and Merrill Lewis. Troy, N.Y.: Whitston Publishing, 1980.

McMullen, Lorraine, ed. *Re(Dis)Covering Our Foremothers: Nineteenth-Century Canadian Women Writers.* Ottawa: University of Ottawa Press, 1990.

Mann, Ralph. *After the Gold Rush: Society in Grass Valley and Nevada City 1849–1870.* Stanford, Calif.: Stanford University Press, 1982.

Marcus, Jane. "'Invisible Mediocrity': The Private Selves of Public Women." In *The Private Self,* edited by Shari Benstock. Chapel Hill: University of North Carolina Press, 1988.

———. "Invisible Mending." In *Between Women: Biographers, Novelists, Teachers and Artists Write about Their Work,* edited by Carol Ascher et al. Boston: Beacon Press, 1984.

———. "Registering Objections: Grounding Feminist Alibis." In *Reconfigured Spheres: Feminist Explorations of the Literary Space,* edited by Margaret Higonnet and Joan Templeton. Amherst: University of Massachusetts Press, 1994.

Martin, Rosy. "Unwind the Ties that Bind." In *Family Snaps: The Meanings of Domestic Photography,* edited by Jo Spence and Patricia Holland. London: Virago, 1991.

Mayol, Pierre. "The Neighborhood." In *The Practice of Everyday Life II: Living and Cooking,* edited by Michel De Certeau, Luce Giard, and Pierre Mayol. Translated by Timothy J. Tomasik. Minneapolis: University of Minnesota Press, 1998.

Merish, Lori. "'The Hand of Refined Taste' in the Frontier Landscape: Caroline Kirkland's *A New Home, Who'll Follow?* and the Feminization of American Consumerism." *American Quarterly* 45, no. 4 (December 1993): 485–523.

Mertes, Cara. "There's No Place Like Home: Women and Domestic Labor." In *Dirt and Domesticity: Constructions of the Feminine,* edited by Jesus Fuenmajor et al. New York: Whitney Museum of American Art, 1992.

Miller, Nancy K. *Getting Personal: Feminist Occasions and Other Autobiographical Acts.* New York: Routledge, 1991.

Mills, Sara. *Discourses of Difference: An Analysis of Women's Travel Writing and Colonialism.* London: Routledge, 1991.

Mitford, Mary Russell. *Our Village: Sketches of Rural Character and Scenery.* London: Henry G. Bohn, 1848.

———. *Recollections of a Literary Life.* 2 vols. London: Richard Bentley, 1852.

Moers, Ellen. *Literary Women.* London: Women's Press, 1978.

Moffat, Aileen C. "Great Women, Separate Spheres and Diversity: Comments on Saskatchewan Women's Historiography." In *"Other" Voices: Historical Essays on Saskatchewan Women,* edited by David De Bron and Aileen C. Moffat. Regina: University of Regina Press, 1995.

Moodie, Susanna. *Flora Lindsay or Passages in an Eventful Life.* London: Richard Bentley, 1854.

———. *Roughing It in the Bush, or Life in Canada.* London: Richard Bentley, 1852. Reprt., edited by Carl Ballstadt, Ottawa: Carleton University Press, 1988.

Moore, Henrietta L. *Space, Time and Gender: An Anthropological Study of the Marakwet of Kenya.* Cambridge: Cambridge University Press, 1986.

Morrissey, Katherine. "Engendering the West." In *Under an Open Sky: Rethinking America's West,* edited by William Cronon, George Miles and Jay Gitlin. New York: Norton and Co., 1992.

Motz, Marilyn Ferris. "The Private Alibi: Literacy and Community in the Diaries of Two Nineteenth-Century American Women." In *Inscribing the Daily: Critical Essays on Women's Diaries,* edited by Suzanne Bunkers and Cynthia Huff. Amherst: University of Massachusetts Press, 1996.

Moynihan, Ruth B. Review of Brigitte Georgi-Findlay's *The Frontiers of Women's Writing. Western Historical Quarterly* 28, no. 2 (summer 1997): 236–37.

Moynihan, Ruth B., Susan Armitage, and Christiane Fischer Dichamp, eds. *So Much to Be Done: Women Settlers on the Mining and Ranching Frontier.* Lincoln: University of Nebraska Press, 1990.

Myres, Sandra L. *Westering Women and the Frontier Experience, 1800–1915.* Albuquerque: University of New Mexico Press, 1984.

Needler, G. H. *Otonabee Pioneers: The Story of the Stewarts, the Stricklands, the Traills and the Moodies.* Toronto: Burns and McEachern, 1953.

Newhall, John. *Sketches of Iowa or the Emigrant's Guide.* New York: J. H. Cotton, 1841.

Norton, Anne. *Alternative Americas: A Reading of Antebellum Political Culture.* Chicago: University of Chicago Press, 1986.

Nowlin, William. *The Bark-Covered House or Back in the Woods Again.* Chicago: R. R. Donnelley, 1937.

O'Leary, Elizabeth. *At Beck and Call: The Representation of Domestic Servants in Nineteenth-Century American Painting.* Washington, D.C.: Smithsonian Institute, 1996.

Owram, Douglas. *Promise of Eden: The Canadian Expansionist Movement and the Idea of the West.* Toronto: University of Toronto Press, 1980.

Palmer, Phyllis. *Domesticity and Dirt: Housewives and Domestic Servants in the U.S., 1920–1945.* Philadelphia: Temple University Press, 1989.

Parker, Sandra. *Home Material: Ohio's Nineteenth-Century Regional Women's Fiction.* Bowling Green, Ohio: Bowling Green State University Popular Press, 1998.

Partridge, Florence. "The Stewarts and the Stricklands, the Moodies and the Traills." *Ontario Library Review* 40 (August 1956): 179–81.

Pascoe, Peggy. *Relations of Rescue: The Search for Female Moral Authority in the American West 1874–1939.* New York: Oxford University Press, 1990.

Paxton, Nancy I. "Disembodied Subjects: English Women's Autobiography under the Raj." In *De/Colonizing the Subject: The Politics of Gender in Women's Autobiography,* edited by Sidonie Smith and Julia Watson. Minneapolis: University of Minnesota Press, 1992.

Peck, J. M. *A New Guide for Emigrants to the West.* Boston: Gould, Kendall and Lincoln, 1837.

Peterman, Michael. Editor's Introduction. In *The Backwoods of Canada.* Ottawa: Carleton University Press, 1997.

———. "*Roughing It in the Bush* as Autobiography." In *Reflections: Autobiography and Canadian Literature,* edited by K. P. Stich. Ottawa: University of Ottawa Press, 1988.

———. "Susanna Moodie." In *Canadian Writers and Their Works*. Vol. 1, *Fiction Series*, edited by Robert Lecker, Jack David, and Ellen Quigley. Downsville, Ontario: ECW Press, 1983.

Petrik, Paula. *No Step Backward: Women and Family on the Rocky Mountain Frontier, Helena Montana, 1865–1900*. Helena: Montana Historical Society, 1987.

Porteus, J. Douglas. "Home: The Territorial Core." *Geographical Review* 66 (1976): 383–90.

Pratt, Mary Louise. *Through Imperial Eyes: Travel Writing and Transculturation*. London: Routledge, 1992.

Pruitt Stewart, Elinore. *Letters of a Woman Homesteader*. Boston: Houghton Mifflin, 1914.

Rasmussen, Linda. *A Harvest Yet to Reap: A History of Prairie Women*. Toronto: Women's Press, 1976.

Regan, John. *The Emigrant's Guide to the Western States of America or Backwoods and Prairies*. Edinburgh: Oliver and Boyd, 1852.

Riley, Glenda. "Farm Life on the Frontier: The Diary of Kitturah Penton Belknap." *Annals of Iowa* 3d ser., 44 (summer 1977): 31–51.

———. *The Female Frontier: A Comparative View of Women on the Prairies and the Plains*. Lawrence: University of Kansas Press, 1988.

———. *Frontierswomen: The Iowa Experience*. Ames: Iowa State University Press, 1981.

Robbins, Bruce. *The Servant's Hand: English Fiction from Below*. Durham, N.C.: Duke University Press, 1993.

Roberson, Susan L. "'With the Wind Rocking the Wagon': Women's Narratives of the Way West." In *Women, America and Movement: Narratives of Relocation*. Columbia: University of Missouri Press, 1998.

Roberts, Sarah. *Alberta Homestead: Chronicle of a Pioneer Family*. Austin: University of Texas Press, 1971.

Royall, Anne. *Sketches of History, Life and Manners in the United States*. New Haven, Conn.: privately published, 1826.

Royce, Sarah. *A Frontier Lady: Recollections of the Gold Rush and Early California*. New Haven, Conn.: Yale University Press, 1932. Reprt., Lincoln: University of Nebraska Press, 1977.

Russell, Shannon. "Recycling the Poor and Fallen: Emigration Politics and the Narrative Resolutions of *Mary Barton* and *David Cop-*

perfield." In *Imperial Objects: Victorian Women's Emigration and the Unauthorized Imperial Experience*, edited by Rita S. Kranidis. New York: Twayne, 1998.

Sackett, Mary. "Journal 1841–2." Unpublished manuscript in the Newberry Library, Chicago.

Sanford, Mollie Dorsey. *Mollie: The Journal of Mollie Dorsey Sanford in Nebraska and Colorado Territories, 1857–1866*. Lincoln: University of Nebraska Press, 1976.

Savage, William. *Observations on Emigration to the United States of America Illustrated by Original Facts*. London: Sherwood, Neely and Jones, 1819.

Scharff, Virginia. "Else Surely We Shall All Hang Separately: The Politics of Western Women's History." *Pacific Historical Review* 61, no. 4 (November 1992): 535–55.

Schieder, Rupert. "Editor's Introduction." In *Canadian Crusoes: A Tale of the Rice Lake Plains*. Ottawa: Carleton University Press, 1986.

Schlissel, Lillian. "Frontier Families: Crisis in Ideology." In *The American Self: Myth, Ideology and Popular Culture*, edited by Sam Girgus. Albuquerque: University of New Mexico Press, 1981.

Schlissel, Lillian, Byrd Gibbens, and Elizabeth Hampsten, eds. *Far from Home: Families of the Westward Journey*. New York: Schocken Books, 1989.

Schlissel, Lillian, Vicki L. Ruiz, and Janice Monk. *Western Women: Their Land, Their Lives*. Albuquerque: University of New Mexico Press, 1988.

Schteir, Ann. *Cultivating Women, Cultivating Science: Flora's Daughters and Botany, 1760–1860*. Baltimore: Johns Hopkins Press, 1996.

Schwantes, Carlos A. "Wage Earners and Wealth Makers." In *The Oxford History of the American West*, edited by Clyde A. Milner II, Carol A. O'Connor, and Martha A. Sandweiss. Oxford: Oxford University Press, 1994.

Scott, Joan W. "The Evidence of Experience." *Critical Inquiry* 17 (summer 1991): 773–97.

Scott, Lloyd M. "The English Gentlefolk in the Backwoods of Canada." *Dalhousie Review* 39, no. 1 (spring 1959): 56–69.

Scrope, George Poulett. *Extracts of Letters from Poor Persons who Emigrated Last Year to Canada and the United States.* London: James Ridgeway, 1831.

Shapiro, Laura. *Perfection Salad: Women and Cooking at the Turn of the Century.* New York: Farrar, Strauss and Giroux, 1986.

Shepperson, Wilbur. *Emigration and Disenchantment: Portraits of Englishmen Repatriated from the United States.* Norman: University of Oklahoma Press, 1965.

———. *Promotion of British Emigration by Agents for American Lands, 1840–1860.* Reno: University of Nevada Press, 1954.

Shirreff, Patrick. *A Tour through North America.* Edinburgh: Oliver and Boyd, 1835.

Sigourney, Lydia. *The Western Home and Other Poems.* Philadelphia: Parry and McMillan, 1854.

———. *Zinzendorff, and Other Poems.* New York: Leavit, Lors and Co., 1837.

Silverman, Eliane L. *The Last Best West.* Rev. ed. Calgary: Fifth House, 1998.

Smiley, Jane. *The All-True Travels and Adventures of Lidie Newton.* New York: Alfred Knopf, 1998.

Smith, Sherry L. "Single Women Homesteaders: The Perplexing Case of Elinore Pruitt Stewart." *Western Historical Quarterly* 22 (May 1991): 163–83.

Smith, Sidonie. *A Poetics of Women's Autobiography.* Bloomington: Indiana University Press, 1987.

———. *Subjectivity, Identity, and the Body: Women's Autobiographical Practices in the Twentieth Century.* Bloomington: Indiana University Press, 1993.

Smith of Mountfield, Benjamin. *24 Letters from Labourers in America to Their Friends in England.* 2d ed. London: Edward Rainford, 1829.

Smyth, Donna E. "'Thinking Back through Our Mothers': Tradition in Canadaian Women's Writing." In *Re(Dis)Covering Our Foremothers: Nineteenth-Century Canadian Women Writers,* edited by Lorraine McMullen. Ottawa: University of Ottawa Press, 1990.

Spacks, Patricia. *Gossip.* Chicago: University of Chicago Press, 1985.

Spence, Jo. *Putting Myself in the Picture: A Political, Personal and Photographic Autobiography.* Seattle: Real Comet Press, 1988.

Spivak, Gayatri. "Three Women's Texts and a Critique of Imperialism." In *The Feminist Reader*, edited by Catherine Belsey and Jane Moore. Basingstoke, England: MacMillan, 1989.

Spurr, David. *The Rhetoric of Empire: Colonial Discourse in Journalism, Travel Writing and Imperial Administration*. Durham, N.C.: Duke University Press, 1993.

Starr, Kevin. *Americans and the California Dream, 1850–1915*. New York: Oxford University Press, 1973.

Stebbins, Sara. "Frontier Life: Loneliness and Hope." *Indiana Magazine of History* 6 (1965): 53–57.

Steel, Flora Anne, and Grace Gardiner. *The Complete Indian Housekeeper and Cook*. London: W. Heinemann, 1898.

Steele, Eliza R. *A Summer Journey in the West*. New York: J. S. Taylor, 1841.

Stern, Madeleine B. Introduction. In *Life in Prairie Land*. Nieuwkoop: B. de Graaf, 1972.

Stewart, Catherine. *New Homes in the West*. Nashville: Cameron and Fall, 1843.

Stewart, Frances. *Our Forest Home: Being Extracts from the Correspondence of the late Frances Stewart*. Toronto: Presbyterian Printing and Publishing, 1889.

Strasser, Susan. *Never Done: A History of American Housework*. New York: Pantheon Books, 1982.

Strickland, Samuel. *Twenty-Seven Years in Canada West*. London: Richard Bentley, 1853.

Strong-Boag, Veronica, and Anita Clair Fellman, eds. *Rethinking Canada: The Promise of Women's History*. 2d ed. Toronto: Copp Clark Pitman.

Suckow, Ruth. *Country People*. New York: Knopf, 1924.

Talbot, Edward Allen. *Five Years' Residence in Canada Including a Tour through Part of the United States of America in the Year 1823*. London: Longman, Hurst, Rees, Orme, Brown and Green, 1824.

Taylor, Mrs. Ann Martin. *Practical Hints to Young Females on the Duties of a Wife, a Mother, and a Mistress of a Family*. London: Taylor and Hennessy, 1815.

Tentler, Leslie. *Wage-Earning Women: Industrial Work and Family Life in the U.S., 1900–1930*. London: Oxford University Press, 1979.

Thomas, Clara. "Anne Langton." In *Dictionary of Literary Biography*, vol. 99. Detroit: Gale Research Inc., 1990.

Thompson, Elizabeth. *The Pioneer Woman: A Character Type*. Montreal: McGill-Queens University Press, 1991.

Thurston, John. "Ideologies of I: The Ideological Function of Life Writing in Upper Canada." *Wordsworth Circle* 25, no. 1 (winter 1994): 25–28.

———. *The Work of Words: The Writing of Susanna Strickland Moodie*. Montreal: McGill-Queen's, 1996.

Tillson, Christiana. *Reminiscences of Early Life in Illinois*. Amherst: privately printed, 1873.

Tocqueville, Alexis de. *Democracy in America*. Vol. 2. Paris, 1835. Translated by Francis Bowen. London: Everyman Library, 1994.

Traill, Catharine Parr. *The Backwoods of Canada: Being Letters from the Wife of an Emigrant Officer, Illustrative of the Domestic Economy of British America*. London: Charles Knight, 1836. Reprt., Toronto: McClelland and Stewart, 1989.

———. *Canadian Crusoes: A Tale of the Rice Lake Plains*. London: Arthur Hall, Virtue and Co., 1852.

———. *The Female Emigrant's Guide and Hints on Canadian Housekeeping*. Toronto: Maclear, 1854. Reprt., 2d ed. (1855). *The Canadian Settler's Guide*. Toronto: McClelland and Stewart, 1969.

———. "Forest Gleanings No. XIII: The Lodge in the Wilderness." *Anglo American Magazine* 3 (1853): 493–98.

———. *The Young Emigrants; or Pictures of Canada*. London: Harvey and Darton, 1826.

Trollope, Frances. *The Domestic Manners of the Americans*. London: Whittaker and Treacher, 1832. Reprt., London: Penguin Books, 1997.

Turner, Nancy. *These Is My Words: The Diary of Sarah Agnes Prine*. London: Hodder and Stoughton, 1999.

Underwood, Kathleen. *Town-Building on the Colorado Frontier*. Albuquerque: University of New Mexico Press, 1987.

Van Kirk, Sylvia. *Many Tender Ties: Women in Fur Trade Society, 1670–1870*. Norman: University of Oklahoma Press, 1980.

Wallach, Alan. "Thomas Cole and the Course of American Empire." In *Thomas Cole: Landscape into History*, edited by William Truettner and Alan Wallach. New Haven, Conn.: Yale University Press, 1994.

Walters, Lon. *The Old West Baking Book*. Flagstaff: Northland Publishing, 1996.

Walzer, M. "Political Action: The Problem of Dirty Hands." *Philosophy and Public Affairs* 2 (1973): 160–80.

Welter, Barbara. "The Cult of True Womanhood, 1820–1860." *American Quarterly* 18 (1966): 151–74.

White, Richard. *"It's Your Misfortune and None of My Own": A New History of the American West*. Norman: University of Oklahoma Press, 1991.

Williams, Barbara. "Anne Langton." *Dictionary of National Biography*, vol. 12. Toronto: University of Toronto Press, 1990, 523–27.

———. *Anne Langton: Pioneer Woman and Artist*. Peterborough, Ontario: Peterborough Historical Society, 1986.

Williams, Carrie. "No Persuits in Common Between Us Any More." In *So Much to Be Done: Women Settlers on the Mining and Ranching Frontier*, edited by Ruth B. Moynihan, Susan Armitage, and Christiane Fischer Dichamp. Lincoln: University of Nebraska Press, 1990.

Wilson, Luzena. *Luzena Stanley Wilson 49er*. Mills College, Calif.: Eucalyptus Press, 1937.

Woolson, Constance Fenimore. "The Lady of Little Fishing." *Castle Nowhere: Lake-Country Sketches*. Boston: J. R. Osgood, 1875.

Zagarell, Sandra A. "America as Community in Three Antebellum Village Sketches." In *The (Other) American Traditions*, edited by Joyce W. Warren. New Brunswick, N.J.: Rutgers University Press, 1993.

———. Introduction. In *A New Home, Who'll Follow? Glimpses of Western Life by Mrs. Mary Clavers, An Actual Settler*. New Brunswick, N.J.: Rutgers University Press, 1990.

Zeller, Suzanne. *Inventing Canada: Early Victorian Science and the Idea of a Transcendental Nation*. Toronto: University of Toronto Press, 1987.

Index

Adams, Carol, 185
Adams, Timothy Dow, 11, 180
Akenson, Donald H., 8, 13
Alberta Homestead (Roberts), 125–26, 126*n*5
Alcott, Louisa May, 106
Alderson, Mr., 21
Alderson, Nannie T., 21, 25, 179
All-True Travels and Adventures of Lidie Newton (Smiley), 187, 188
Allison, Susan, 21
America. *See* Canada; United States
Ammons, Elizabeth, 143
Anglo female emigrants. *See* Emigrant and pioneer women
Anglo-Saxonism, 37–38
Annals of Iowa, 54, 55
Anomie, 68–69, 72, 125–26, 147
Anthropology. *See* Social anthropology
Anti-emigration narratives, 69, 76*n1*
Argonauts, 147, 148
Armitage, Susan, 18, 33, 159–61
Army life, 146
Atkeson, Mary Meek, 38
Atlantic Monthly, 37
Austen, Jane, 170
Autobiography by women: and class difference, 50; deconstruction of, 34, 55; and diaries, 44–45, 61–62, 153–54, 159–66, 188–89; domestic space and domestic details in, 10–17, 47–48, 56–57; and gender issues, 44–45; "hyper-empiricism" of, 46–47, 47*n7*; and letters, 136*n24*, 154–55; Miller on reading of, 14–17; motherhood role of autobiographer, 178–79; movement as motivation for writing, 46–47; obstacles facing female autobiographer, 44; peripheral presence in, 9–10; scholarly approaches to, 44–49, 55; shifts in diction of, 64; spiritual autobiography, 67–68, 70, 148, 151, 189; Victorian women's autobiography, 9–10, 50, 68; writing, publication and circulation of, 14, 43, 46, 49–50, 54–55. *See also* Emigrant narratives; and specific women emigrants

Back-migration, 14, 69
Backwoods of Canada (Traill): biblical references in, 94; botanical description in, 81–83, 87; on child rearing, 93–94; on children's clothes, 93–94; critics on, 80–81; domesticity in, 79–100; on failure of pioneer women to do useful work, 28–29; and imperial self-justification, 79, 80–82; on impossibility of civilized life in Canada, 93; publication of, 79, 90, 90*n24*; reference to Dunlop in, 90; subtitle of, 83, 87; on withdrawal into domestic seclusion, 93–94
Bacon, Francis, 137
Bailey, Ebenezer, 94–95
Baking, 107–8, 119–22, 162–63, 163*n31*, 190–92
"Ballad of Little Jo," 187–88, 190
Ballstadt, Carl, 80–81, 81*n7*
Barber, Mary, 68
Bark-Covered Home (Nowlin), 60
Barthes, Roland, 89*n23*
Beardsmore, Alan, 184

Beecher, Catherine, 104, 187
Beecher, Eunice Bullard, 104, 126
Beetham, Margaret, 164
Belknap, Kitturah: birth and death dates of, 49; childhood of, 55–56; compared with Stebbins, 136; competitiveness of, 125; conflicted self in, 179; courtship and marriage of, 58–59; on death of child, 62, 63, 64; editing and printing of "Memorandum" in 1970s, 54–55, 54*n*21; health of, 64; homemaking and day-to-day work of, 26–27, 56–57; and revivalism, 63; shifts in diction in writing by, 64; and social activity, 125; working-class origins of, 50, 55
—work: "Memorandum," 49–51, 54–59, 54*n*21, 62–64
Bentley, D. M. R., 170
Bentley, Richard, 49
Bhabha, Homi, 3–4, 6
Birkbeck, Morris, 109
Blistered and marked hands, 113–15, 161
Bloom, Lynn Z., 38
Boardman, Kathleen A., 44
Boone, Daniel, 18
Borderlands, 7
Borrowing and lending, 95–100
Botanical description, 81–83, 87, 87*n*19. *See also* Gardening
Boundaries, 118–19, 122
Bowlby, Rachel, 3, 141
Boydston, Jeanne, 84*n*12, 113
Brah, Avtar, 3
Bread baking, 107–8, 119–22, 162–63
Breadwinning or the Ledger and the Lute (Barber), 68
Bride Goes West (Alderson), 21
Britain: and anti-emigration narratives, 69; circulation of texts between Canada and, 13; colonization of Canada by, 76, 79–82, 174, 176–77; domestic writers of, 94; emigrants' movement between new homes and, 14; Langton in, 169, 170; mobility in and emigration from, 88; and publication of emigrant narratives, 49, 51; social boundaries in, 100; unmarried women in, 175
British Columbia, 21
Brown, Elsa Barkley, 8
Brown, Gillian, 109

Brown, R., 182
Buell, Lawrence, 81–82*n*8, 139
Bunkers, Suzanne, 44–45, 164
Burlend, Rebecca, 53, 65, 114*n*20, 136, 159
Businessmen, 135
Buss, Helen, 126*n*5, 167, 178–79, 182
Butchery, 183–85
Butler, Anne M., 45–46, 151*n*12

Calamity Jane, 19
California, 24–25, 146–57, 159, 162. *See also* Mining West
California, In-Doors and Out (Farnham), 148, 156–57, 159
Callan, Hilary, 77*n*2, 78
Callaway, Helen, 77
Canada: autobiography and emigration literature from, 14*n*17, 21, 27, 28–29, 47–49, 51, 73, 76*n*1, 125–27; botanical description of, 81–83, 82*n*8, 87, 87*n*19; British colonization of, 76, 79–82, 174, 176–77; circulation of texts between Britain, United States, and, 13; civilization for, 82; class difference in, 90–93; Dunlop on, 90–92; frontier in, 14; immigration policy of, 177; Indians in, 79; pioneer work in, 57; promotion of, 82; Talbot on, 92*n*29; women's history scholars from, 18, 23*n*8. *See also Backwoods of Canada* (Traill); Langton, Anne; *Roughing It in the Bush* (Moodie)
Canadian Crusoes (Traill), 87
Capitalism, 15–16, 36–37, 148, 165
Carsten, Janet, 7
Cather, Willa, 36
Cayton, Andrew R. L., 92*n*30, 133, 134
Cecil, David, 170
Child, Lydia Maria, 84
Children: clothing of, 93–94; deaths of, 11, 35–36, 62; description of infant, 64; didactic tales for, 87; and emigration, 65; illness of, 63; in mining West, 155, 160; punishment of, 160
Chinese emigrant women, 32
Chow, Rey, 8
"Cinnamon Roses" (Freeman), 131
"Civilizing force" of women, 77
Clark, Steve, 46, 49
Class difference: Atkeson on, 38; in autobiography by women, 50; and borrowing, 95–99; in Canada, 90–93;

and community, 126, 133–35; and cookbooks, 89–90; and domestic squalor, 103–4; and domesticity generally, 111; Kirkland on, 96–97, 133–35; and mining West, 151; and sneering response of backwoods neighbor to Moodie, 108; Stebbins on, 135; and Tillson's refusal to eat, 118; Traill on, 90, 93, 95. *See also* Cult of domesticity
Clean versus dirty hands, 114, 120–22
Cleaning the floor, 112–14, 160, 161
Cleaveland, Agnes Morley, 20
Clements, William, 57
Clothing of children, 93–94
Cobbett, William, 69
Cohen, Stanley, 165–66
Colonial housekeeping, 6, 10, 77–79
Colonists versus emigrants, 77–79
Colorado, 153. *See also* Mining West
Comer, Krista, 10, 20–21
Community: and class difference, 126, 133–35; dislike of and separation from, in emigrant women's writing, 134–36; and domestic space, 31–32, 124–34, 143–44; in emigrant narratives, 16, 126–44; Farnham on, 127, 128, 144; and gossip, 130–31, 141–44; Hine on frontier community, 136; in Kirkland's *New Home*, 16, 128–34, 137, 143–44; and problems of individualism and egalitarianism, 136
Complete Indian Housekeeper and Cook (Steel and Gardiner), 89
Conlin, Joseph R., 162
Conversion experience, 62–63
Cookbooks and recipes, 87–90, 91, 190–92
Cooking. *See* Food
Coontz, Stephanie, 155–56
Corbett, Mary Jean, 9–10
Cottagers of Glenburnie (Hamilton), 103–4
Counter-discourse, 20–21, 25
Country of the Pointed Firs (Jewett), 142–43
Country People (Suckow), 29–30
Courtship. *See* Marriage
Covered Wagon Women (Holmes), 45–46
Csikszentmihalyi, Mihalyi, 99
Cult of domesticity, 15, 15*n*19, 32, 41, 77–79, 111–12, 120, 150, 189. *See also* Domesticity and domestic space
Cult of true womanhood, 150
Currer, Alice, 169, 178, 181–82

Dalhousie, Lady, 82*n*8
Dame Shirley, 151, 154–55, 158–59, 166
David Copperfield (Dickens), 106
Davis, Gayle R., 61–62
De Certeau, Michel, 123
Dean, Misao, 73*n*46, 131*n*15
Death imagery, 68
Death of infants and children, 11, 35–36, 62, 63–64
Deconstruction, 34, 55
Deutsch, Sara, 31–32
Diaries of emigrant women, 44–45, 61–62, 153–54, 159–66, 188–89
Diaspora, 3, 7, 8
Dickens, Charles, 63, 106
Dickerson, Vanessa D., 110
Domestic Manners of the Americans (Trollope), 48
Domestic plenty, images of, 57–58
Domesticity and domestic space: and army life in West, 146; boundaries within, 118–19; clean versus dirty hands, 114, 120–22; colonial context of, 6, 10, 77–79; and community in West, 31–32, 124–44; cult of domesticity, 15, 15*n*19, 32, 41, 77–79, 111–12, 120, 150, 189; and domestic angel, 110–11; in emigrant autobiographical narratives, 2–6, 47–48, 79–123; and emigrant home, 3–9, 93–94; and fantasy of effortless work, 109–10; Gold Rush versus, 146–50; and ideal of freeing work for pioneer women, 25–31, 38–41, 56–57; and imperialism, 79, 80–82, 100–103, 111; and industrial modes of work, 119; loss of homemaker's self-respect and domestic disaster, 106–8; mainstream domestic discourse versus texts about backwoods domesticity, 103–23; marked and blistered hands due to housework, 113–15, 161; metropolitan domestic space, 32; in mining West, 151–66; omission of women's agency from her own labor, 109; painting of, 120–22; public sphere versus domestic space, 5–6; sacrificial aspects of homemaking, 105–6, 161; as separate and independent from male activity, 31; and servants, 119–20, 122, 130–31; and social actors in the home, 112; in social anthropology, 7; unrealized fantasy of smooth-running home, 108–9; withdrawal into domestic

seclusion of backwoods, 93–95; in women's autobiography, 9–17. *See also* Home; Homemaking
Donovan, Josephine, 136, 137
Douglas, Mary, 122
Down, John, 58
Doyle, Don Harrison, 136
Drowning, 182
Dunlop, William, 90–92, 116

Early Days in Upper Canada (Langton), 171
Eating scenes, 115–19. *See also* Food
Economic migration, 14
Education of women, 40–41
Egli, Ida Rae, 24–25, 154
Ellet, Elizabeth, 18, 64
Ellis, Ann, 20
Emigrant and pioneer women: and borrowing, 95–100; character of, 56, 187; counter-discourse in writings by, 20–21, 25; cultural attention to, 19–20; definitions of, 1*n1*, 55; diaries of, 44–45, 61–62, 153–54, 159–66, 188–89; and dislike of and separation from community, 134–36; dissatisfactions of, 66; domestic incapability of untutored emigrant wife, 104–5; and domesticity, 10–17, 79–123; downward mobility of, 86–87; as exiles, 73–75, 175; and fear of wildness, 82; and "female frontier," 23–25; feminist stereotypes of, 22, 23*n8*, 189–90; fiction on, 36; food preparation and preservation by, 30, 38–39, 56–57, 84–85, 107–8, 109, 116–19, 153, 162–63; heroism of, 22–23; homes of and homemaking by, 2–9, 26–27, 76–77, 79–123; homesickness of, 134–36; ideal of freeing work for, 25–31, 38–41, 56–57; importance of, 1; loneliness and suffering of, 20, 23, 27, 29, 125–26; and loss of self-respect from domestic disasters, 107–8; marginal position of, 18–19, 80; marriage of, 11–12, 34, 35, 58–61, 86; in mining West, 145–66; objections to emigration by, 69–75; objects' significance to, 99–100; and "personal territorialism," 9; perversity of, in failing to do useful work, 27–29; position of, in West, 19–23; recent depictions of, 187–90; "territories" of, 124; threat to or loss of useful work for, 29–30; transmittal of societal values by, 76–77; as unmarried, 172–76; and unrealized fantasy of smooth-running home, 108–9; and withdrawal into domestic seclusion of backwoods, 93–95. *See also* Domesticity and domestic space; Emigrant narratives; Homemaking; and specific women writers

Emigrant narratives: anti-emigration narratives by back-migrants, 69, 76*n1*; botanical description in, 81–83, 87; and class difference, 50, 89–93, 95–99, 103–4, 108, 118, 126, 133–35; community in, 126–44; conclusion of, 64–65; critical moments and tests in, 62–64; day-to-day trials and hardships in, 66–69; and description of destination of emigrants, 76; diaries of emigrant women, 44–45, 61–62, 153–54, 159–66, 188–89; dislike of and separation from community in emigrant women's writing, 134–36; domestic disasters in, 107–8; domesticity and domestic details in, 47–48, 53, 56–57, 79–123, 161; eating scenes in, 115–19; and fantasy of effortless work, 109–10; "hyper-empiricism" in, 46–47; images of starvation and domestic plenty in, 57–58; list of, 51, 51–52*n15*; of mining West, 145–66; movement as motivation for writing, 46–47; pragmatism and day-to-day work in, 56–59; purpose of, 66; and questions on women's participation in pioneering, 45–46; rite of passage in, 52–53; self-invention in, 34–36; self-sufficiency in, 70–71, 135; shifts in diction of, 64; suitability criteria for reproduction and recovery of, 168; travel writing compared with, 48–49; unrealized fantasy of smooth-running home in, 108–9; on whole experience of emigration, 64–66; writing, publication and circulation of, 43, 49–50, 54–55. *See also* Autobiography by women; and specific emigrant writers

Emigrants: and borrowing, 95–100; civic and governmental responsibility of middle-class emigrants, 78–79; colonists versus, 77–79; definition of, 1*n1*; downward mobility of, 86–87; as exiles, 73–75, 175; government support for, 8; isolation and anomie of, 125–26; objects'

significance to, 99–100; paintings of, 3–5, 6, 70, 71, 72; poetry on, 60, 73–74. *See also* Emigrant and pioneer women; Emigrant narratives
Emigrant's Last Sight of Home (Redgrave), 70, 71
"Emily Howard" (Graves), 106, 107
England. *See* Britain
Epstein, Barbara, 63
Essentialist views of womanhood, 23–25
Evangelism, 63
Exile, 72–75, 175

Faerie Queene (Spenser), 143, 144
Fairbanks, Carol, 14*n17*, 20, 30, 55
Families, 155–56, 169–74, 178. *See also* Children; Marriage
Family Party at Blythe in 1840 (Langton), 172–74
Faragher, John, 23, 23*n8*, 77, 97, 111, 125
Farnham, Eliza: blistered and marked hands of, 113–15, 185; and bread baking, 119, 120; California home of, 159; and cleaning the floor, 112–14, 161, 185; on community, 127, 128, 144; and deaths of family members, 11; and domestic angel, 110–11; and domestic disasters, 107; domestic discourse of, 103–4, 107, 109–23; and domestic squalor, 103–4; and fantasy of effortless work, 109–10; and food preparation, 109, 119; Kolodny on, 10–12; marriage of, 11–12; as matron of Sing Sing, 12–13; on mining society, 156–57; and "room of one's own," 103–4, 119, 122–23; on Tremont, Ill., 127, 128*n8;* troubled early life of, in the East, 11; on West, 11–13, 128
—works: *California, In-Doors and Out*, 148, 156–57, 159; *Life in Prairie Land*, 10–13, 48, 103–4, 107, 109–15, 118, 119, 127, 128
Farnham, Thomas, 11–12
Farnsworth, Martha, 49–50
Farrar, Eliza, 98
Female emigrants. *See* Emigrant and pioneer women
Female Emigrant's Guide (Traill): borrowing in, 95–96, 98, 99; botanical description in, 81–83, 87; critics on, 80–81; domesticity in, 79–81; harvesting done by author in, 113–14; homemaking information and recipes in, 84–85, 87–90; and imperial self-justification, 79, 80–82; publication of, 79
Feminism, 22, 23*n8,* 189–90
Fender, Stephen, 46–48, 52–53, 60*n30*, 62–63, 145*n1,* 147–49, 149*n8*
Fern, Fanny, 95
Fetterley, Judith, 31*n20,* 126–27
Fiddes, Nick, 183
Fielding, Henry, 137
Fischer Dichamp, Christiane, 149, 159–61
Five Years' Residence in the Canadas (Talbot), 73, 92*n29*
Flashbulb memories, 182–83, 184
Flint, Timothy, 69
Floor cleaning, 112–14, 160, 161
Flora Lindsay (Moodie), 74
Follen, Eliza, 63, 106
Food: available food, 57–58; baking, 163*n31,* 190–92; bread baking, 107–8, 119–22, 162–63; breakfast meal, 117–18; butchering meat, 183–85; costs of, 53; disgusting food in the West, 115–19; eating scenes, 115–19; fruit cake, 88–89, 90; fruit substitute, 56–57; maple sugar, 84–85; meat preparation, 116–17; in mining West, 153, 162–63; packaged food, 162; painting of, 120–22; pickles, 116; preparation and preservation of, 30, 38–39, 56–57, 84–85, 87–90, 107–8, 109, 116–19, 153, 162–63; recipes for, 87–90, 91, 190–92; refusing to eat, 117–18
Foote, Mary Hallock, 151, 157–58, 166
Forest Life (Kirkland), 130*n13,* 189
Forty-Niners. *See* Mining West
Freeman, Mark, 182–83
Freeman, Mary Wilkins, 131
Freeman, Sarah, 89*n23*
From Dawn to Daylight or the Simple Story of a Western Home (E. B. Beecher), 104, 126
Frontier: and Canada, 14; definition of, 1*n1;* "female frontier," 23–25; and home, 3–5, 6; and ideal of freeing work for pioneer women, 25–31, 38–41, 56–57; masculinist frontier myth of West, 18, 20; and national identity, 13–14. *See also* Emigrant and pioneer women; Emigrant narratives; Emigrants; Mining West; West
Frugal Housewife (Child), 84
Fruit cake, 88–89, 90
Fruit substitute, 56–57

Furst, Lillian, 118

Gagnier, Regenia, 50
Gandhi, Leela, 75
Gannett, Cinthia, 46
Gardening, 82–83, 132. *See also* Botanical description
Gardiner, Grace, 89
Garland, Hamlin, 29, 29*n17*
Gartrell, Beverley, 77
Gaze, 140–42
Gebhard, Caroline, 61, 137
Gentlewoman in Upper Canada (Langton), 176–78, 184–85
George, Rosemary Marangoly, 6, 10, 78, 85
George, Suzanne, 34, 35
Georgi-Findlay, Brigitte, 20, 77*n2*
Giard, Luce, 118–19
Gibson, Miss, 163, 164
Gilman, Caroline, 106–7
Gilmore, Leigh, 43, 45
Girlhood and Womanhood (Graves), 106, 107, 109
Goffman, Erving, 181
Gold Rush West. *See* Mining West
Goldman, Anne, 88
Goldman, Marion S., 151*n12*, 164
Good Wives (Alcott), 106
Gossip, 130–31, 141–44, 163
Graves, Mrs., 106, 107, 109
Grayson, Andrew Jackson, 3–5, 6
Grayson, James, 53–54
Grayson, Mrs., 3–5, 6
Grayson family, 3–5, 6
Great Britain. *See* Britain
Greenwald, Maggie, 187
Grenfell, Charles, 90*n24*
Grey, Zane, 36
Griswold, Robert, 102
Grosz, Elizabeth, 27, 165, 185

Haakenson, Bergine, 30
Hale, Sara Josepha, 63, 93, 105–6, 107, 109
Hall, Lula, 41
Halton, Eugene Rochberg, 99
Hamilton, Carl, 190
Hamilton, Elizabeth, 103–4
Hammerton, A. James, 175
Hampsten, Elizabeth, 24*n9*, 31

Hands: blistered and marked hands from hard work, 113–15, 161, 185; clean versus dirty hands, 114, 120–22
Haraway, Donna, 45, 48
Hardy, Thomas, 183
Harte, Bret, 146, 147
Hedges, Elaine, 144, 165
Heldke, Lisa M., 122
Hine, R. V., 136, 148
Hirsch, Julia, 16, 167, 179–80
Hirsch, Marianne, 186
Hispanics, 8, 31
Hobsbawn, Eric, 49
Holmes, Kenneth L., 45–46, 54*n21*
Home: colonial context of, 6, 10, 77–79; details of interiors of, 141–43, 153–54; emigrant home, 3–9, 93–94, 108–9; of Grayson family, 3–5, 6; in mining West, 153–55; movement between old and new homes, 14; social actors in, 112; Victorian home, 102–3; withdrawal into domestic seclusion of backwoods, 93–95. *See also* Domesticity and domestic space; Homemaking
Homemaking: and clean versus dirty hands, 114, 120–22; cleaning the floor, 112–14, 160, 161; colonial context of, 6, 10, 77–79; domestic squalor versus, 103–4; dull routine of, 108; and fantasy of effortless work, 109–10; fiction on, 106; food preparation and preservation, 30, 38–39, 56–57, 84–85, 107–8, 109, 116–19, 153, 162–63; and ideal of freeing work for pioneer women, 25–31, 38–41, 56–57; loss of homemaker's self-respect from domestic disaster, 106–8; marked and blistered hands from, 113–15, 161; in mining West, 152–54, 160–64; omission of women's agency from her own labor, 109; painting of, 120–22; sacrificial aspects of, 105–6, 161; sewing, 143, 144, 154, 160, 163–64; symbolic meaning of, 77; and transmittal of societal values, 76–77; untutored emigrant wife and domestic incapability, 104–5; and values and processes of capitalist economy, 15–16; western and postcolonial historians on, 2–6. *See also* Domesticity and domestic space; Home
Homesickness, 134–36
Homesteading, 37

Housewifery. *See* Domesticity and domestic space; Homemaking
Howard, Emily, 106, 107
Huff, Cynthia, 164
Hugh-Jones, Stephen, 7
Hunt, Thomas, 53
Hyde, Anne F., 149

Illinois, 112, 115, 127–28, 128*n*8, 134–36
Illinois and the West (Jones), 127–28
Illness of children, 63
Imperialism, 79, 80–82, 100–103, 111, 175
"In-between," 4
Indians, 8, 79, 110–11, 117, 192
Infants. *See* Children
Iowa, 54–55, 58, 190

Jameson, Elizabeth, 18
Jason, 147
Jeffrey, Julie Roy, 22, 102
Jensen, Katherine, 5–6
Jewett, Sarah Orne, 142–43
Jewett, William Smith, 3–5, 6
Johnson, Susan Lee, 5–6, 18–19
Jolly, Margaretta, 136*n*24
Jones, A. D., 127–28
Jones, Henrietta, 20, 60–61
Journal of Madam Knight (Knight), 115
Jude the Obscure (Hardy), 183

Kansas, 25
Keeping House and Housekeeping (Hale), 63, 105–6, 107, 109
Keetley, Dawn, 110
Keil, Teresa, 184
Kessler-Harris, Alice, 39
Kilcup, Karen L., 31*n*20
Kirkland, Caroline: blistered hands of, 161; on borrowing, 96–97, 99–100; and class difference, 96–97, 133–35; and community, 16, 128–34, 137, 143–44; on domestic cruelty, 140–41; and domestic disasters, 107; on domestic interiors, 141–43; on dull routine of homemaking, 108; on forests, 134; and gardening, 132; and Indian woman, 110–11; on land agents and speculators, 133–34; literary references used by, 137–38; marriage and children of, 61, 78; and Mitford's *Our Village*, 13, 136–41; on Montacute, Mich., 128–34, 128*n*10, 136–37, 144; and Moodie's narrative, 13; Mrs. Jennings as servant of, 130–31; and New York literary and intellectual life, 138; relationship of, with neighbors, 132–33; and sewing society, 143, 144; weary despair of, at distance from civilization, 189
—works: *Forest Life,* 130*n*13, 189; *New Home, Who'll Follow?* 13, 48, 61, 108, 118, 128–38, 140–44
Kline, Marcia, 14*n*17
Knight, Charles, 90*n*24
Knight, Sarah Kemble, 115
Kolodny, Annette, 10–12, 20–21, 69, 102, 136–37
Kristeva, Julia, 185
Kuhn, Annette, 175–76, 179, 182
Kulik, J., 182

"Lady of Little Fishing" (Woolson), 146
Lady's Country Companion (Loudon), 116–17
Land agents and speculators, 133–34
Lander, Dawn, 23
Lane, Sedalia, 41
Langton, Anne: aunt of, 169, 178, 181–82; autobiographical method of, 179–86; in Britain, 169, 170; and brother John's marriage, 176, 180, 186; on butchering meat, 183–85; and deaths of family members, 169, 176; drawing by, 172–74; on drowning of woman's fiancé, 182; education of, 170, 186; emigration of, to Canada, 169, 171–73, 175–76; European tour by, 169, 170; family life of, 78, 169–74, 178, 186; and family pet, 181–82; and flashbulb memories, 182–83, 184; as inconsistent with pioneer ideal, 169–71, 179; letter-journals by, 169, 171–72, 176–78; marginal position of, as emigrant writer, 168–70, 179; as miniaturist, 170; mother of, 173; portrait of, 170; preservation and recovery of writing by, 16, 168; on role of frontier women, 27; room of, in family home, 173; subservient usefulness of, 176, 186; as teacher, 176; as unmarried, 172–76
—works: *Gentlewoman in Upper Canada,* 176–78, 184–85; *Langton Records,* 171–72, 174, 176; *Story of Our Family,* 169, 172, 175–76, 180–84, 186
Langton, Hugh Hornby, 176–78

Langton, John, 86, 169, 171, 172, 176, 177–78, 180, 184, 186
Langton, Lydia Dunsford, 169, 180
Langton, Thomas, 169, 176, 177–78
Langton, W. A., 171
Langton, William, 172
Langton Records (Langton), 171–72, 174, 176
Lavie, Smadar, 7
Le Rochefoucauld, 137
Leadville, 157–58
Leaving the Old Homestead (Wilkins), 70, 72
Lending and borrowing, 95–100
Lensink, Judy Nolte, 41
Leonardi, Susan, 88
Letters (Dame Shirley), 151, 154–55, 158–59, 166
Letters from Poor Persons Who Emigrated Last Year to Canada and the United States (Scrope), 47
Letters of a Woman Homesteader (Pruitt Stewart): and Anglo-Saxonism, 37–38; on death of baby, 35–36; on education of women, 40–41; and emigrant autobiographical narrative, 34–36, 190; and feminization of individualist ethic, 36–37; homemaking in, 26, 38–39; and homesteading, 37; and limits of self-expression, 15; marriage of Pruitt Stewart in, 35; mowing the lawn by Pruitt Stewart in, 37–38; on Other populations, 33, 33*n23*; pioneer woman and national debates about women, 15; publication of, in *Atlantic Monthly*, 37; scholarship on, 33–34; self-invention in, 34–36; as touchstone for arguments about western women, 43; utopianism of, 38; and women as special case, 20
Leverenz, David, 61
Levi-Strauss, Claude, 116, 117
Lewis, Sarah, 83*n11*
Life in Prairie Land (Farnham): bread baking in, 119, 120; cleaning the floor in, 112–15, 161, 185; community in, 127, 128, 144; domestic disasters in, 107; domestic discourse of, 103–4, 107, 109–23; domestic ideal in, 109–11; and domestic squalor, 103–4; fantasy of effortless work in, 109; Indian woman in, 110–11; Kolodny's interpretation of, 10–12; painful experiences in, 12; relationship between Farnham's circumstances and, 11–12; as travel writing, 48; on Tremont, Ill., 127, 128*n8*
Life of an Ordinary Woman (Ellis), 20
Limerick, Patricia, 27, 30
Local color, 126–27
"Lodge in the Wilderness" (Traill), 97
Loudon, Mrs., 116–17
Lowell Offering, 25–26, 113
Luchetti, Cathy, 54, 55
"Luck of Roaring Camp" (Harte), 146
Luzena Stanley Wilson 49er (Wilson), 152–53
Lynchings, 157–59

MacDonald, Norman, 92*n28*
Malick, Abigail, 30
Mann, Ralph, 146–47
Maple sugar, 84–85
Marcus, Jane, 47, 75, 104, 141
Marked and blistered hands, 113–15, 161
Marriage, 11–12, 34, 35, 58–61, 86
Martin, Rosy, 168
Mayol, Pierre, 139, 141
McClintock, Anne, 102–3
McCormack, A. Ross, 174
McKnight, Jeanie, 29*n17*
Meals. *See* Eating scenes; Food
Meat butchering, 183–85
Meat preparation, 116–17
Medea, 147
"Memorandum" (Belknap): childhood episodes in, 55–56; courtship and marriage in, 58–59; dates of writing of, 49; death of child in, 62, 63, 64; drawings added in later edition of, 55; as family record, 49, 55–56; homemaking and day-to-day work in, 26–27, 56–57; as narrative of emigration, 51, 56; opening of, 54; printing and editing of, 49–50, 49*n21*; retrospective entries in, 49; shifts in diction in, 64; and working-class origins of author, 50, 55
Merchants, 135
Merish, Lori, 96–97, 99
Mertes, Carla, 120
Mesquier, Mary Jane, 149*n8*
Mexicans, 8

Michigan, 64–65, 96–97, 128–34, 128*n10*, 136–37. *See also* New Home, Who'll Follow? (Kirkland)
Migration. *See* Emigrant and pioneer women
Miller, Nancy K., 9, 14, 16–17
Mills, Sara, 48
Mining West: and capitalism, 165; child-rearing in, 155, 160; and class difference, 151; Dame Shirley on, 151, 154–55, 158–59, 166; domesticity and domestic space in, 151–66; domesticity versus, 146–50; epic adventure of Gold Rush, 146–48; female emigrants' constructions of, 145–66; food preparation in, 153, 162–63; Foote on, 151, 157–58, 166; homemaking in, 152–54, 160–64; homes in, 153–55; lynchings in, 157–59; male world of, 146–48; mining society of, 156–57; and prostitutes, 150–51, 157; Royce on, 148, 151, 153–54, 155, 157, 160, 165, 166; Sanford on, 151, 153, 154, 165, 166; Carrie Williams on, 159–66; Luzena Wilson on, 152–53
Mitford, Mary Russell, 13, 136–41, 137*n27*, 144
Mock-heroic rhetoric, 113
Moers, Ellen, 173
Moffatt, Aileen, 23*n8*
Monk, Janice, 126*n5*
Montacute, Mich., 128–34, 128*n10*, 136–37, 144
Montana, 21
Moodie, Dunbar, 66, 70–71, 78–79
Moodie, Susanna: angry diatribes by, 189; birth and death dates of, 66; on community, 144; on day-to-day trials and hardships of emigrant life, 66–69; and domestic disasters, 107–8; on exiled womanhood, 74–75; and father's death, 66; and Kirkland's *New Home*, 13, 130; marriage of, 66; neighbor's sneer at housekeeping of, 108; self-sufficiency of, 70–71; spiritual struggle of, 67–68, 70; on undeserved sorrow and anomie, 68–69, 72, 159; and working in the fields, 114*n20*
—works: *Flora Lindsay*, 74; *Roughing It in the Bush*, 13, 49–51, 50*n13*, 66–72, 74–75, 107–8, 189
Moore, Henrietta, 112

Mopping the floor. *See* Cleaning the floor
Morrissey, Katherine, 19
Motherhood role, 178–79. *See also* Children
Motz, Marilyn Ferris, 165
Mowing, 40
Moynihan, Ruth B., 159–61
Myres, Sandra, 23–24, 23*n8*, 48, 102

Narrative of emigration. *See* Emigrant narratives
National identity, 13–14
Native Americans, 8, 79, 110–11, 117, 192
Nattali and Bond publishers, 90*n24*
Nebraska, 22
Needler, G. H., 176–77
Nevada City, 152–53
New Home, Who'll Follow? (Kirkland): borrowing in, 96–97, 99–100; Cathcart in, 140–41; class difference in, 96–97, 133–35; community in, 16, 128–34, 137, 143–44; domestic cruelty in, 140–41; domestic disasters in, 107; domestic interiors in, 141–43; forests in, 134; gardening in, 132; humor in, 130–33, 140, 143–44; Indian woman in, 110–11; land agents and speculators in, 133–34; literary references in, 137–38; marriage and children in, 61; as modeled on Mitford's *Our Village*, 13, 136–41; Montacute, Mich., in, 128–34, 128*n10*, 136–37, 144; Mrs. Jennings as servant in, 130–31; neighbors' relationship with author, 132–33; publication of, as speculative venture, 134; and pursuit of independence, 61; sewing society in, 143, 144; subtitle of, 140; as travel writing, 48; Westons in, 140
New Homes in the West (Stewart), 52*n16*
New York, 64, 138
No Life for a Lady (Cleaveland), 20
Noble, Harriet, 64–65, 159
North America. *See* Canada; United States
Norton, Anne, 117
Norwood, Vera, 126*n5*
Nowlin, William, 59–60

O Pioneers! (Cather), 36
Odyssey, 148
Ohio, 54, 55
Old West Baking Book (Walters), 190–92
Olwell, Carol, 54, 55
Onuf, Peter S., 92*n30*, 133, 134

Oregon, 54
Oregon Territory (Grenfell), 90*n24*
Others, 6, 33, 33*n23*, 38, 95, 118
Otonabee Pioneers (Needler), 176–77
Our Forest Home (Stewart), 127
Our Village (Mitford), 13, 136–41, 144
Owram, Douglas, 76*n1*

Paid work. *See* Work
Palmer, Phyllis, 120
Parker, Sarah, 137*n27*
Partridge, Florence, 176
Pascoe, Peggy, 32
"Patchwork Quilt," 113
Patriarchy, 77, 111, 184
Paxton, Nancy I., 114–15
Percival, Anne Marie, 82*n8*
Peripheral presence in women's autobiography, 9–10
Peterman, Michael, 67*n39*
Petrik, Paula, 150–51*n12*, 157
Pets, 181–82
Philips, Ellen, 172, 173, 174
Pickles, 116
Pinckney, Mich., 128, 128*n10*, 133, 134. *See also* Montacute, Mich.
Pioneer Gentlewoman in British Colombia (Allison), 21
Pioneer women. *See* Emigrant and pioneer women
Pioneer Women of the West (Ellet), 64–65
Porteus, J. Douglas, 3
Poultry raising, 61
Poverty, 68
Pragmatism in emigrant narratives, 56–59
Pratt, Mary Louise, 77, 81, 81–82*n8*, 100
Prisons, 12–13
Privacy, 104, 109. *See also* "Room of one's own"
Private sphere. *See* Domesticity and domestic space
Promised Land-The Grayson Family (Jewett), 3–5, 6
Prostitutes, 150–51, 157
Pruitt Stewart, Elinore: and Anglo-Saxonism, 37–38; dates of, 34; death of baby of, 35–36; education of, 40; on education of women, 40–41; and emigrant autobiographical narrative, 34–36; extended family of, 34; and feminization of individualist ethic, 36–37; homemaking by, 26, 38–39; and homesteading, 37; intimacy in writing of, 179; marriage of, 34, 35; and mowing the lawn, 40; on Other populations, 33, 33*n23*; scholarship on, 33–34; self-invention in writings by, 34–36; writing by generally, 36
—work: *Letters of a Woman Homesteader*, 15, 20, 33–41, 43, 190
Pryse, Marjorie, 31*n20*, 127
Public sphere: gendering of men's and women's paid work, 39; and women generally, 5–6, 9, 73*n46*
Pure Nostalgia (Hamilton), 190

Race and racial difference, 8
Rapp, Rayna, 156
Recipes. *See* Cookbooks and recipes; Food
Recollections of a Housekeeper (Gilman), 106–7
Redgrave, Richard, 70, 71
Regionalism, 16, 31, 31*n20*, 37–38, 124, 130, 142–43
Reminiscences of Early Life in Illinois (Tillson), 115, 117–18
Revivalism, 63
Richfield, Ill., 134–36
Riders of the Purple Sage (Grey), 36
Riley, Glenda, 23*n8*, 31, 54, 55
Rites of passage, 52–53, 59–60, 60*n30*
Roberson, Susan L., 124
Roberts, Sarah, 125–26, 126*n5*
"Room of one's own," 103–4, 119, 122–23
Roughing It in the Bush (Moodie): angry diatribes in, 189; bread baking in, 107–8; critics on, 67, 67*n39–40*; day-to-day trials and hardships in, 66–69; domestic disasters in, 107–8; on exiled womanhood, 74–75; and Kirkland's *New Home*, 13; neighbor's sneer at author's housekeeping in, 108; publication of, 49, 50*n13*; purpose of, 66; self-sufficiency of author of, 70–71; as spiritual autobiography, 67–68, 70; structure of text in, 66–67, 67*n39*; undeserved sorrow and anomie in, 68–69, 72; working in the fields in, 114*n20*
Royall, Anne, 115–16
Royce, Sarah, 148, 151, 153–55, 157, 160, 165, 166

Rural idyll, 95
Russell, Shannon, 73*n47*
Ruth Hall (Fern), 95

Sackett, Mary, 57
Sacrificial aspects of homemaking, 105–6, 161
Sanford, Mollie Dorsey, 22, 64, 151, 153, 154, 165, 166, 179
Schlissel, Lillian, 25, 27–28, 33
Schteir, Ann, 82–83
Scott, Joan, 45
Scrope, George Poulett, 47, 53, 57–58
Scrubbing the floor. *See* Cleaning the floor
Self-expression, 15
Self-invention, 34–36
Self-sufficiency, 70–71, 135
Servants, 119–20, 122, 130–31
Sewing, 143, 144, 154, 160, 163–64
Shake Hands? (Spencer), 120–22
Shakespeare, William, 137
Sheppard, Harriet, 82*n8*
Sheppard, William, 82*n8*
Shepperson, Wilbur, 51
Shirley Letters, 151, 154–55, 158–59, 166
Sigourney, Lydia, 60, 73–74
Silverman, Eliane, 26
Sing Sing, 12–13
Sketch, 138, 138–39*n29–30*
Sketches from Real Life (Jones), 20, 60–61
Sketches of History, Life and Manners in the United States (Royall), 115–16
Sketches of Married Life (Follen), 63, 106
Slavery, 8
Smiley, Jane, 187, 188
Smith, Benjamin, 54, 63
Smith, Sherry L., 34, 37
Smith, Sidonie, 9, 44, 46
Smyth, Donna E., 179
Snelgrove, William, 57–58
Social anthropology, 7
Social classes. *See* Class difference
Space. *See* Community; Domesticity and domestic space
Spacks, Patricia Meyer, 130–31, 136*n24*, 141
Spence, Jo, 178
Spencer, Lilly Martin, 120–22
Spenser, Edmund, 143, 144
Spiritual autobiography, 67–68, 70, 148, 151, 189

Spivak, Gayatri, 75
Spurr, David, 85, 118
Stanton, Elizabeth Cady, 9
Starr, Kevin, 147, 148
Statistical Studies of Upper Canada (Dunlop), 90–92
Stebbins, Sara, 134–36
Steel, Flora Anne, 89
Steele, Eliza R., 52*n16*
Stewart, Catherine, 52*n16*
Stewart, Clyde, 34, 35, 40
Stewart, Elinore Pruitt. *See* Pruitt Stewart, Elinore
Stewart, Frances, 127
"Stewarts and the Stricklands, the Moodies and the Traills" (Scott), 176
Story of Our Family (Langton), 169, 172, 175–76, 180–84, 186
Stowe, Harriet Beecher, 63
Strickland, Agnes, 86
Strickland, Samuel, 92–93
Strickland, Thomas, 66, 86
Suckow, Ruth, 29–30
Sugar Creek (Faragher), 97
Summer Journey in the West (Steele), 52*n16*
Sundberg, Sara, 23*n8*
Swedenburg, Ted, 7

Talbot, Edward, 73, 92*n29*
Taylor, Ann Martin, 94
Taylor, Laurie, 165–66
Temperance, 111, 127–28
Tennyson, Alfred Lord, 148
Tentler, Leslie, 39
These Is My Words: The Diary of Sarah Agnes Prine (Turner), 188–89, 190
Thomas, Clara, 168
Thompson, Elizabeth, 168
Thorpe, James, 63
Thurston, John, 48, 67*n39*, 129–30*n12*
Tillson, Christiana, 78, 115, 117–18, 179
Tocqueville, Alexis de, 20
Traill, Catharine Parr: biblical references by, 94; birth and death dates of, 79; on borrowing, 95–98, 99; botanical description by, 81–83, 82*n9*, 87, 87*n19*; children of, 87; children's stories written by, 87; and class difference, 90, 93, 95; class origins of, 86, 90; domesticity in works by, 79–101; economic insecurity and downward mobility of, 86–87,

93; on failure of pioneer women to do useful work, 28–29; family background of, 86; harvesting done by, 113–14; homemaking information and recipes by, 83–85, 87–90; and imperial self-justification, 79, 80–82; marriage of, 86; in Peterborough, 86–87; on rural simplicity, 94, 95; on withdrawal into domestic seclusion, 93–94
—works: *Backwoods of Canada*, 28–29, 79–87; *Canadian Crusoes*, 87; *Female Emigrant's Guide*, 79–82, 84–85, 87–90, 113–14; "Lodge in the Wilderness," 97; *Young Emigrants*, 86
Traill, Thomas, 86–87
Travel writing, 48–49, 52n16, 90, 115–16
Treasure, James, 47
Treatise on Domestic Economy (C. Beecher), 104–5, 187
Tremont, Ill., 127–28, 128n8
Trollope, Frances, 48, 130, 138n28
True Picture of Emigration (Burlend), 53, 65, 114n20
Turner, Nancy, 188
Twain, Mark, 147
Twenty Four Letters from Labourers in America (Thorpe), 63
Twenty-Seven Years in Canada (Strickland), 92–93

United States, 92, 92n30, 100, 184. *See also* Mining West; West; and specific states
Unmarried women, 172–76
Utopianism, 38

Van Kirk, Sylvia, 32
Victimhood, 72, 75
Victoria, Queen, 175
Victorian women: autobiography of, 9–10, 50, 68; and cult of true womanhood, 150; and domesticity, 102–3; and gardening, 82–83; and middle-class consumerism, 97
"Violeting" (Mitford), 139–40

Walters, Lon, 190–92
Watson, Elizabeth, 54
Wayne, John, 18
Welter, Barbara, 15n19, 32
West: army life in, 146; and "civilizing force" of women, 77; and community,

16, 31–32, 124–44; definition of, 1n1; domestic ideal in, 102; and economic activity of men, 19–20; fantasy of regeneration in, 11; Farnham on, 11–13, 128; fiction on, 146; general histories of, 19; masculinist frontier myth of, 18, 20; mining West, 145–66; pioneer women's position in, 19–22; regional difference in representation of, 16; women's gendered response to, 21, 22, 149. *See also* Emigrant and pioneer women; Frontier; Mining West
"Western Emigrant" (Sigourney), 73–74
"Western Home" (Sigourney), 60
White, Bernice, 26
White, Richard, 150
Whiteness, 8
Whitlock, Gillian, 51n14, 60n30
Wilkins, James F., 70, 72
Williams, Barbara, 170
Williams, Carrie, 159–66
Wilson, J. J., 24
Wilson, Luzena, 152–53
Woman on the Farm (Atkeson), 38
Woman's Mission (Lewis), 83n11
Women. *See* Autobiography by women; Domesticity and domestic space; Emigrant and pioneer women; Homemaking; Victorian women
Women of the West (Luchetti and Olwell), 54, 55
Women's education, 40–41
Women's prison, 12–13
Woolf, Virginia, 24
Woolson, Constance Fenimore, 146
Work: gendering of, 39–40, 57; ideal of freeing work for pioneer women, 25–31, 38–41, 56–57; men's and women's paid work, 39. *See also* Domesticity and domestic space; Homemaking
World War II, 25
Wyoming, 33–34

Young Emigrants (Traill), 86
Young Lady's Class Book (Bailey), 94–95

Zagarell, Sandra, 129–32, 130n13, 136, 137
Zeller, Suzanne, 82, 82n9